#4
11/21
signed

THE CRIMES, DETECTION AND DEATH OF JACK THE RIPPER

To Fred
With all good wishes
Martin Fido
10. 6. 90

For

Tom Cullen, Robin Odell, Donald McCormick, Dan Farson,
Donald Rumbelow, Stephen Knight and Richard Whittington-Egan
Who have added so much interest and information to the study
of the Whitechapel Murders over the last twenty-five years

And For

Harriet and Cheryl
Who saved at least some of their books from Forbes' conflagration.

THE CRIMES, DETECTION AND DEATH OF JACK THE RIPPER

Martin Fido

WEIDENFELD AND NICOLSON · LONDON

Published in Great Britain by
George Weidenfeld & Nicolson Limited
91 Clapham High Street
London SW4 7TA

This paperback edition published by
George Weidenfeld & Nicolson Limited 1989

ISBN 0 297 79566 X

Photoset by Deltatype Ltd, Ellesmere Port
Printed in Great Britain by
Guernsey Press Co. Ltd, C. I.

Contents

Preface

The centenary of the Whitechapel Murders in 1988 has produced a rash of books. These have stimulated the production of several previously unknown documents. And the surge of new information has carried the serious study of Jack the Ripper well away from the realms of armchair-detective theories and the Peter Rabbit Race Game to Find the Ripper. So-called 'Ripperologists' must now busy themselves with social history and the history of the police.

The feminists, who have objected to an apparent celebration of gross masculine sadism, may take heart from one major point that has been established. The radical press exploited the murders to draw attention to conditions in the East End and covert police involvement in anti-Irish politics. This influential press crusade, which stamped the memory of the murders on the national mind, also contributed to Mrs Besant's notable success in winning an East End seat on the first London County Council that year, following her instigation of the splendid match-girls' strike. Both Professor Bill Fishman and the BBC's *Timewatch* have drawn attention to these matters as important in our understanding of the legendary notoriety achieved by the squalid murderer.

Don Rumbelow, in revising and updating his *Complete Jack the Ripper*, has added to our knowledge of the victims; especially Elizabeth Stride. Bertil Falk made a a charmingly sympathetic TV programme for a Swedish audience detailing the sad career of this Swedish immigrant.

Melvin Harris has exploded most of the sillier so-called 'theories', though he regrettably blotted his work by introducing a new one of his own. Similarly, Martin Howells and Keith Skinner, after some first-rate research which debunked a lot of nonsense and brilliantly exposed the true nature of the supposed Australian evidence against M. J. Druitt which had eluded Dan Farson and Colin Wilson, unfortunately propounded an unnecessary and unhistorical enhancement of the case against Druitt. But after Harris', Howells' and Skinner's work, there is no further excuse for anyone giving a moment's credence to flights of fancy concerning Sir William Gull, the Duke of Clarence, the Freemasons, J. K. Stephen, the visions of R. J. Lees and the like. It is deplorable that, with a fanfare of alleged historical research, Thames Television should have broadcast a farrago of fiction making a totally unhistorical accusation against Gull, and cavalierly maligning other historical figures.

Robin Odell has continued his quiet, serious and useful work on the medical evidence supplied by the autopsies. Alexander Kelly has updated his invaluable bibliography. And Stéphane Bougoin has definitively covered the strange incursions of Jack the Ripper into art and fiction. He gives us the delightful fact that the very first film to feature the legendary murderer was the 1915 silent comedy, *Farmer Spudd and His Missus Go Up To Town*.

Paul Begg's splendid research trawl in all directions, aided in the latter stages by Keith Skinner's superlative collection of Ripper-related photocopies and transcripts, has established new data on almost every aspect of the murders, and provided more documented facts to the square inch than any other historian of the Whitechapel murders.

In the first edition of this book, I concluded that John Pizer was not really, as the police claimed, the original suspect, 'Leather Apron'; but that shadowy figure should be identified with the Polish Jew said by Assistant Commissioner Anderson to have been definitely identified as Jack the Ripper, and named by Sir Melville Macnaghten as 'Kosminski'. Keith Skinner's discovery of a letter from Philip Loftus to Lady Aberconway supports this conclusion. My conclusion that the actual Whitechapel Jew, Aaron Kozminski, was not Jack the Ripper, but had somehow had his name transferred to another inmate of Colney Hatch Asylum received considerable support, after I had published, from the emergence of the most important Ripper document since Dan Farson found Sir Melville Macnaghten's notes. The 'Swanson marginalia', in which Chief Inspector Swanson fleshed out Sir Robert Anderson's brief description of a poor Polish Jew, name the suspect as Kosminsky, yet provide an inaccurate description of him which in part applies uniquely to the other mental patient I had identified, 'David Cohen'. I remain convinced that 'David Cohen' was Jack the Ripper; almost certainly was Leather Apron; and very probably was the man who, under the name 'Nathan Kaminsky' was treated for syphilis in Whitechapel Workhouse Infirmary in March 1888. The ending of this book has been completely rewritten to include the new information, and to explain why it appeared so inconclusively in the first edition, where I had to insert new and vital evidence after the book was already in print.

The newly retrieved documents posted anonymously to Scotland Yard in November 1987, and released by the Yard in August 1988, contain two pieces of historical importance. The mortuary photograph of Elizabeth Stride shows that she was, as I had claimed, an extremely good-looking woman. And the detailed medical report on Marie Kelly shows that she was not pregnant, her uterus had not been taken away, and she had not been sodomized, thus eliminating claims used to bolster a handful of specious theories.

This revised and updated book carries all the corrections and additions made necessary by the torrent of new work and new discoveries. Research is continuing, with the aim of clarifying exactly why Scotland Yard's principal suspect was either named or described quite wrongly by a senior officer who had played a leading part in the enquiry.

I am indebted to Paul Begg, Stéphane Bougoin, Professor Luigi Cancrini, Ms Cohen, Dan Farson, Judith Fido, Mike Foale, Joe Gaute, David Goldberg, Mrs Anita Greene, Martin Howells, Nicki James, Mr B. Kaminsky, Mr D. Kaminsky, Mr H. Kaminsky, Mrs L. Kaminsky, Mr M. J. Kaye, Mrs Lynn Kemp, LBC Radio, Lesley Miranda, Mr and Mrs Bernard Moseley, Charles Nevin and the *Daily Telegraph*, Robin Odell, Jack O'Sullivan and *The Scotsman*, Mr Sidney Pizer, Bernard Porter, Don Rumbelow, Keith Skinner, David Streatfield, Jim Swanson, Bill Waddell of the Black Museum, Mr Norman Weissman, Richard Whittington-Egan, Paul Williams and Richard Sharp of the Metropolitan Police History Museum, Alan Wilkinson and Bradley Winterton.

For putting me in touch with several of the above, I am grateful to Cosgrove-Muerer Productions, Guided Walks of London, Mystfest 88, the Police History Society, and Yvonne Dwyer of that great meeting-place for Ripper historians, *The Ten Bells*, Spitalfields.

The following institutions and staff-members have kindly answered my queries, directed me to alternative sources, and checked records for me: Banstead Hospital (Ms Brenda Weedon), Cane Hill Hospital (Ms Whitley), Claybury Hospital (Ms H. Gurnhill and Mr Eric Pryor), Friern Hospital (Mr Tony Cook and Mr Colin Kirk), the Jewish Welfare Board (Mr Melvyn Carlowe), Maudsley Hospital (Ms Patricia Allderidge), Stone Hospital (Ms Sandra Brett and Ms Delia Jennings), Wellcome Institute for Medical History (Ms Julia

Sheppard), and, nameless voices on the telephone, the archivist at Scotland Yard and the desk sergeant at Bethnal Green Police Station. The Canadian High Commission kindly allowed me to search the Montreal Telephone Directory, and the Home Office gave me permission to see the closed file of Anderson's papers on his secret service work.

The kindness and help of the staffs of the following libraries was vital to the completion of the book: the British Library, the British Newspaper Library (Colindale), the Corporation of London Archives and Records Office, the Guildhall Library (especially the maps section), St Catherine's House Registry of Births, Marriages and Deaths, the Public Records Office (Kew and Chancery Lane), Tower Hamlets Local History Library, Hackney Records Office, the India Office Library, and, above all, for their patience and encouragement, the Greater London (formerly GLC) Archives and Record Office.

David Roberts and Martin Corteel of Weidenfeld and Nicolson have been endlessly patient with my demands for revisions, additions and alterations, and showed great faith in publishing the first edition with its difficult conclusion, at that time unsupported by the Swanson marginalia.

The *Oxford Times* kindly accused me of being 'incorrigibly nice' because I expressed gratitude and respect for Ripper writers whose work is sometimes inaccurate and whose conclusions I often find completely inadequate. The reason is that they did the spade-work: they established the shape of the case, leaving me the comparatively easy job of confirming or disproving their statements. Since then I have met most of the dedicatees, and, bracketing the names of Martin Howells, Keith Skinner and Paul Begg with theirs, I am happy to report that it would be hard to find a more charming, generous, helpful and friendly group of men than those who have studied Jack the Ripper.

M.F.
Heamoor/St Katherine by the Tower,
1987–9

The 'Victims' of Jack the Ripper

PRELUDE

'Fairy Fay'
Boxing night 1887
Whitechapel streets
(alleged nickname of mythical first Ripper victim)

Ada Wilson
28 March 1888
19 Maidman Street, Burdett Road, Mile End
(victim of attempted murder)

Emma Elizabeth Smith
3 April 1888
junction of Osborn Street and Brick Lane, Whitechapel
(frequently and wrongly ascribed by the press to the Ripper)

Martha Tabram or Turner
7 August 1888
George Building, George Yard, Whitechapel
(frequently and wrongly ascribed by the press to the Ripper)

JACK THE RIPPER'S FIVE VICTIMS

1 Mary Ann 'Polly' Nichols
     31 August 1888
     opposite Essex Wharf, Buck's Row, Whitechapel

2 Annie Chapman, alias 'Dark Annie' Siffey or Sievey
     8 September 1888
     29 Hanbury Street, Spitalfields

3 Elizabeth 'Long Liz' Stride
     30 September 1888
     Dutfield's Yard, Berner Street, Whitechapel
     (first on the night of the double murder)

4 Catherine Eddowes, alias Catherine Conway or Mary Anne Kelly
     30 September 1888

Mitre Square, City of London
(second on the night of the double murder)

5 *Marie Jeanette or Mary Jane or Janet Kelly*
   9 November 1888
   13 McCarthy's Rents, Miller's Court, Dorset Street, Spitalfields

FALSE ALARMS

Annie Farmer
20 November 1888
George Street
(prostitute who pretended to have been attacked by the Ripper)

Rose Mylett, alias 'Drunken Lizzie' Davies or 'Fair Alice' Downey
20 December 1888
Clarke's Yard, Poplar High Street
(murder victim briefly ascribed to the Ripper)

Alice 'Clay Pipe' McKenzie
17 July 1889
Castle Alley, Whitechapel High Street
(murder victim briefly ascribed to the Ripper)

Frances 'Carrotty Nell' Coles, alias Frances Colman or Hawkins
13 February 1891
in Swallow Gardens off Chamber Street
(murder victim briefly ascribed to the Ripper)

PART I
THE LEGENDARY MURDERER

1

Whitechapel Murders

Jack the Ripper is a mythic figure comparable with Frankenstein's monster and Dracula, with Dick Turpin and Dr Crippen. Everybody knows his name, and most people have heard the strange suggestions that have been put forward to identify him. Rumour and ingenuity have proposed a plethora of celebrated or distinguished names as the uncaught murderer. Bizarre and unlikely solutions have seized public attention. Only the most probable answer, propounded at the time by those in the best position to know, has been inexplicably overlooked.

The first three murdered whores believed in 1888 to be victims of a single hand were found respectively in Brick Lane, George Yard and Buck's Row, all in the parish of Whitechapel. The murders therefore became referred to as the Whitechapel Murders, even though subsequent victims were found in the adjacent parish of Spitalfields, and it seemed that the true centre of the grisly events might lie there where the women lodged, rather than in Whitechapel and Aldgate where they plied their trade.

Until it was destroyed by fire, the parish church of St Mary Matfellon (called 'the White Chapel' after one repainting in the Middle Ages) stood on the south side of Whitechapel High Street almost opposite Osborn Street. Around it, narrow streets of run-down brick terraced houses and tiny shops ran south to Commercial Road, and the parish extended farther south in similar fashion until it abutted on St George's-in-the-East. Only one of the Ripper murders occurred in this southern territory contained by the two great arteries running east, Whitechapel Road and Cable Street.

The majority of the 'Whitechapel murders' took place further north, where Commercial Street led to Spitalfields, and Osborn Street/Brick Lane ran north to Bethnal Green between a warren of lanes and alleys packed with overcrowded humanity. In Spitalfields lay three of the blackest slum streets of the capital: Thrawl Street, Flower and Dean

Street, and Dorset Street. All were noted for cheap doss-houses frequented by thieves and prostitutes. Some houses allowed women to entertain men overnight in the crowded rooms where lodgers were packed, two to a vermin-infested bed, in unlit dormitories.

The term 'East End' entered the language around 1880, as the nation realized that the eastern suburbs of the City had degenerated to slumland rivalling St Giles and Paddington. Hoxton, Shoreditch and Bethnal Green suggested criminal dens – Fagin and Bill Sikes had plotted in this neighbourhood. The dockland parishes of Wapping, Shadwell, Limehouse and Poplar were a byword for the drunken night-life of sailors ashore.

Whitechapel had long been settled by poor Jews who sold secondhand clothes in its street markets. They dominated Petticoat Lane, and renaming the road Middlesex Street neither inhibited the popular Sunday market, nor affected the colloquial usage.

The Mediterranean Sephardic Jews admitted to England by Cromwell had settled around Aldgate on the Whitechapel/City boundary. The two oldest synagogues in London stood here in Duke Street and Bevis Marks. The mid-European Ashkenazim, fleeing in their tens of thousands from the Russian pogroms of 1881 and Bismarck's clearance of Silesia in 1886, flooded the old Jewish quarter and spilled out in a half-mile long triangle, north of Whitechapel Road. George R. Sims, author of the popular *Christmas Day in the Workhouse*, observed that the notorious Spitalfields streets of doss-houses and brothels were little oases of Gentile squalor in a miniature Yiddish town running across Brick Lane, Wentworth Street and Goulston Street. The Jewish Cemetery was very near to Buck's Row where Ripper victim Polly Nichols was found. The Jews' Free School was in the heart of the district.

Jewish immigration at a time of unemployment was unpopular with the Gentile citizenry. Anti-semitism had a long history in English culture, starting from traditional Christian belief that 'the Jews' were responsible for Christ's death. Hatred was fuelled by various foul myths implying that Jews thought it right to murder Christian children, and developed into the prejudiced and erroneous belief that Jews were characteristically dirty and criminal.

Yet a journalist recording a visit to Spitalfields in 1888 found to his surprise that Fashion Street, popularly believed to be as filthy as Flower and Dean Street, was as clean and decent as any poor lower-middle class road in the West End. Its children were well turned out and polite, its housekeeping immaculate. These were the signs that Jews had ousted Gentiles.

Despite the essentially law-abiding nature of orthodox Jewish communities, and their strict taboo against mutilating corpses, the threat of anti-semitism was to play a major part in the police investigation of the Ripper murders.

Crime was rife in the East End streets. Just north of Spitalfields lay 'the Nichol', the western extremity of Bethnal Green: criminal territory in native English hands. Gangs from the Nichol and Hoxton made forays into Whitechapel and Spitalfields, mugging and terrorising streetwalkers, stealing from them, and demanding money in return for 'protection' from violence which they would themselves inflict.

This dangerous district required heavy policing. H Division, Whitechapel, was the ideal proving ground for a young constable with ambition to rise in the detective service. He would encounter habitual crime including so much casual street killing that throughout the 1890s inquest juries preferred not to describe bodies found on the streets as murder victims unless they carried obvious marks of violence; the files were already full of unsolved homicide.

H Division's central station was at Leman Street, a rather gloomy road running gently downhill south from Whitechapel High Street to Royal Mint Street. Away to the north side of the High Street was Commercial Street, winding up to Shoreditch through three-quarters of a mile of the worst slums of Whitechapel and Spitalfields. The construction of this reasonably broad carriageway had done less than its builders had hoped to improve the neighbourhood of Spitalfields Market. As one left the open High Street and climbed the barely perceptible incline to the market, one passed on the right Thrawl Street, Flower and Dean Street and Fashion Street. Next to Fashion Street lay 'Itchy Park', the miserable patch of grassland off Christ Church burial ground; dusty in summer, muddy in winter, infested at all times with sleeping vagrants and drunks.

Christ Church, Spitalfields itself is a dominating Hawksmoor building of Portland stone. In 1888 it gazed majestically and coldly over Dorset Street. One of three or four claimants to the title of 'the worst street in London,' Dorset Street was known locally as 'the do-as-you-please.' Its doss-houses were little better than brothels. Its male population included pimps and pickpockets, burglars and bully-boys. Policemen chasing villains were foolish to enter the street alone. Severe beatings and even murder in the course of duty were occupational hazards for the constables of Spitalfields, and Dorset Street was the most dangerous in their territory.

Pursuing Commercial Street further north one passed narrow terraces of formerly gracious eighteenth-century houses whose wide attic windows proved them to have been built for the prosperous Huguenot weavers, once a flourishing community in Spitalfields. But industrialization and the frenzied movement of trade cycles in the nineteenth century had broken the silk-weaving trade. The weavers' houses had degenerated into over-crowded slums; a status from which some are now escaping as their excellent lines and sound structure make them suitable for gentrification by the childless.

Beyond the weavers' houses come the southern fringes of the Nichol – drab, blind lanes, even after expensive rebuilding in the 1890s. And here, on the triangular island Fleur-de-Lis Street makes with Elder Street, the Commercial Street police station stood until a year or so ago. Embarrassingly close to the Ripper's territory. Staffed by officers who knew and often cared deeply for the district, recognized Ripper victims by sight, yet were helpless to save them.

It was among the H Division police that questions about a murder sequence first started to be asked. Polly Nichols was found with her throat cut and her abdomen slashed in Buck's Row on 31 August 1888. Could there be any connection with Martha Tabram, found in rather similar circumstances in George Yard Buildings just over two weeks earlier? What about Emma Smith, brutally defiled in Brick Lane the previous Easter? Was Whitechapel the stalking ground of a maniac murderer?

Police fears of a Whitechapel murderer spread. The rumours reached the public. They were voiced in the press, and rose to urban panic when Annie Chapman was found dead in Hanbury Street on 8 September. But just before the Whitechapel murderer claimed two more victims on 30 September, he had been given a memorable name. *Jack the Ripper*.

25 Sept.1888.

Dear Boss

I keep on hearing the police have caught me but they wont fix me just yet. I have laughed when they look so clever and talk about being on the right track. That joke about Leather Apron gave me real fits. I am down on whores and I shant quit ripping them till I do get buckled. Grand work the last job was. I gave the lady no time to squeal. How can they catch me now. I love my work and want to start again. You will soon hear of me with my funny little games. I saved some of the proper _red_ stuff in a ginger beer bottle over the last job to write with but it went thick like glue and I cant use it. Red ink is fit enough I hope _ha_ _ha_. The next job I do I shall clip the ladys ear off and send to the police officers just for jolly wouldnt you. Keep this letter back till I do a bit more work, then give it out straight. My knife's nice and sharp I want to work right away if I get a chance. Good luck.

yours truly
Jack the Ripper

So ran the red-inked main text of the most important of the many anonymous letters about the Whitechapel murders sent to the police, newspapers, and prominent murder-watchers. Its importance was emphasized in a post script: 'Don't mind me giving the trade name.' And a subsidiary message at right angles ran:

wasnt good enough to post this before I got all the red ink off my hands curse it. No luck yet. They say I'm a doctor now _ha ha_.

This hoaxer's 'trade name' completely replaced the nickname 'Leather Apron', which some Whitechapel whores had given to their principal suspect. After the police had made one erroneous arrest that pseudonymous local faded out of the popular mind, though the owner of the apron remained to the end the man the police most wanted to have 'helping them with their enquiries'. But Jack the Ripper was a name to strike a chill to the bone. Of all the hundreds of letters posted during the Whitechapel terror and purporting to come from the murderer, this was the first to use the opening 'Dear Boss' and the signature 'Jack the Ripper'.

But it is no more likely than any of the others to have been written by him. Sir Melville Macnaghten, who entered the senior ranks of the police shortly after the murders, always felt he could detect 'the stained forefinger of the journalist' in the correspondence. Dr Robert Anderson, head of the CID during the investigation, claimed that he was tempted to identify him, 'but no public benefit would result from such a course, and the traditions of my old department would suffer.'

Prima facie the letter supports this interpretation. It was posted on

27 September to the Central News Agency, indicating a writer who knew just where to send his missive for maximum publicity. A letter to Scotland Yard might have gone silently into the files. A letter to an individual newspaper might have been splashed as an individual scoop. But a letter to the agency would be distributed as widely as possible. And who would have known this better than a journalist?

Again, the letter was posted in London EC, not London E: in the Fleet Street/Gray's Inn Road/Farringdon Road district where the newspaper offices lay, not Whitechapel or Spitalfields, Stepney or Bethnal Green.

Internal evidence shows it to be the work of an educated man. There is not a single spelling mistake, even though quite demanding words like 'laughed' and 'knife' are used. Sentences start with capitals and end with full stops. The first person singular 'I' is capitalized, like the nickname 'Leather Apron'. True, there are no question marks, and five apostrophes are omitted. Three others, however, are correctly included. All in all, it suggests a casual attempt to imitate a lack of education, but a deep unfamiliarity with the actual literary practices of the uneducated.

There is just a hint that it is the work of a very young man indeed. The 'ginger beer bottle' seems an unlikely possession for a fiendish maniac prowling the slums (though victim Marie Kelly had several in her room). And both the slang and the jocularity of the words 'just for jolly' seem distinctly juvenile.

But the name was brilliantly chosen. And a follow-up postcard after the double murder of 30 September, worse punctuated but definitely by the same hand, read:

> I was not codding dear old Boss when I gave you the tip, you'll hear about saucy Jacky's work tomorrow double event this time number one squealed a bit couldnt finish straight off. had not time to get ears for police thanks for keeping last letter back till I got to work again,
>
> Jack the Ripper

This card was the second most important item of the mighty Ripper correspondence which followed. The knowledge it showed of the first letter's contents (the promise of an ear) proved that it came from the same person. And for years it was believed that it had been posted on the day it purported to have been written – Sunday 30 September, the actual day of the 'double event'. Details of the murders of 'Long Liz'

Stride and Catherine Eddowes were not published until Monday 1 October. So only the murderer, it was argued, would have known immediately that he had struck twice and had been interrupted after the first killing, thus leaving Stride unmutilated. Moreover, a small nick in Stride's ear gave rise to the belief that an attempt really had been made to carry out the grisly collection of a souvenir promised in the first letter.

Actually the card was postmarked 1 October, when the murders were fully reported in the morning papers. And the writer was wrong about the 'squealing'. Annie Chapman had cried out; Elizabeth Stride did not.

Disregarding the fact that Eddowes still possessed both her ears, though her murderer had enjoyed time and privacy to disembowel her and remove a kidney and her womb, some police at first took this as proof of the authenticity of these missives. The first 'Jack the Ripper' letter was widely publicized in handbills and posters. But far from eliciting useful information, these only evoked a host of imitations in a variety of hands posted from all parts of the country. Many followed the original writer's practice of addressing 'Dear Boss'. Some mocked the police – many exploited private or public information about the course of the investigation. The writer who knew in July 1889 that the police had listened to the dreams of spiritualist clairvoyant Robert Lees must have heard it on the grapevine. ('Dear Boss/You have not caught me yet you see, with all your cunning, with all your "Lees" with all your blue bottles/Jack the Ripper.') The widely reported fact that Eddowes' kidney had been removed was reflected in a missive to the Commissioner of the City Police: 'Have you seen the devle with his mikerscope and scalpul a-looking at a kidney with the slide cocked up?' Some formal verses scanned less well:

> Eight little whores, with no hope of heaven,
> Gladstone may save one, then there'll be seven.
> Seven little whores begging for a shilling,
> One stays in Hen|e|age Court, then there's a killing.

> Six little whores, glad to be alive.
> One sidles up to Jack, then there are five.
> Four and whore rhyme aright, so do three and me.
> I'll set the town alight ere there are two.

Two little whores, shivering with fright,
Seek a cosy doorway, in the middle of the night.
Jack's knife flashes, then there's but one.

And the last one's the ripest for Jack's idea of fun.

The nasty, sadistic jeering jocularity is common to a large part of the correspondence, especially those 32 letters which the late Dr Thomas Dutton believed were the work of the real murderer.

Few subsequent investigators have agreed that so many might be authentic. Richard Whittington-Egan's recognition of the postmark on the signed postcard undermined the persistent belief that the name 'Jack the Ripper' had been invented by the murderer himself, and he threw reasonable doubt on the one other letter once accepted as genuine by most students. This did not use the Ripper signature. But it was accompanied by part of a human kidney which the head of the City Police accepted as probably having come from Eddowes' body. The letter, addressed to the Mile End businessman who headed the local Vigilance Committee, runs as follows:

> From hell

> Mr Lusk
>   Sor
>   I send you half the Kidne I took from one woman prasarved it for you tother piece I fried and ate it was very nise. I may send you the bloody knif that took it out if you only wate a whil longer
>   Signed Catch me when
>   you Can
>   Mishter Lusk.

This shows crude attempts to imitate a stage-Irish accent ('Sor' and 'Mishter'). Its frequently convincing illiteracies ('whil' and 'nise') are accompanied by a surprisingly correctly spelled 'bloody', and words which look like a hoaxer's disguised orthography – 'prasarved' and 'knif'.

Obviously anyone capable of writing such a letter and enclosing part of a human kidney was at least mildly abnormal and distinctly unpleasant. The same might be said of most of the other Ripper letter-writers. The true support for the 'Catch me when you Can' letter as a genuine Ripper item is the kidney. And that is gravely suspect, as we shall see when we examine Eddowes' death.

One signatory of two Jack the Ripper letters was discovered. On 21 October Maria Coroner, an apparently respectable mantle-maker's employee, was charged with a breach of the peace in Bradford. She had sent letters to the Chief Constable and a local newspaper, signed 'Jack the Ripper' and declaring his intention of coming to Bradford to 'do a little business'. She said she did it for a joke, and no doubt the other grim letters were a bit of a giggle for equally juvenile writers. Miss Coroner was 21.

The real importance of the famous Jack the Ripper letters lies in their creation of the name. The recurrent Americanism 'Boss' does not point to the murderer's nationality. Their sadistic humour does not necessarily reflect his temperament. The similarity of some to the handwriting of the poisoner Neill Cream does not mean that he wrote them. But they burned into the public mind a name for a nightmare.

PART II
THE VICTIMS

2

Prelude: Emma Smith, Ada Wilson and Martha Tabram

Bank Holiday night, Easter Monday 3 April 1888, found forty-five-year-old prostitute Emma Elizabeth Smith weaving her drunken way home along Osborn Street towards Brick Lane, making for her lodgings at 18 George Street, Spitalfields (between Thrawl Street and Flower and Dean Street). Emma was something of a mystery woman. She was better spoken than the normal run of East End prostitutes. She claimed to be a widow. She also claimed to have left her husband in 1877 and broken all her former ties.

As smartly dressed as her means allowed, Mrs Smith had evidently been in search of trade as well as drink that night. When she reached Wentworth Street, where Taylor Brothers' big cocoa factory formed the corner with Brick Lane, she was stopped by a gang who had followed her from Whitechapel High Street. Three or four young men, one of them aged no more than nineteen in her estimation, set about her, beat her, raped her, and bestially jabbed a blunt stick in her vagina, tearing the perineum. She staggered home bleeding and was rushed to the London Hospital on Whitechapel Road. She gave a description of her assailants before passing into unconsciousness, but her death was inevitable and occurred four days later. Her purse was empty, and H Division police had no doubt that an Old Nichol gang had claimed another victim.

Aspects of Emma Smith's fate, confused with those of other women over the next two years, led to widespread belief in a mythical first victim, left to die on the Whitechapel streets after a stake had been thrust through her abdomen on Boxing Day, 1887. Her identity was said to be unestablished, but from somewhere she acquired the nickname 'Fairy Fay'. The mode of her death obviously derived from Emma Smith; the date from Rose Mylett, killed in Christmas week

1888. The place was sometimes suggested as near George Yard, where Martha Tabram was soon to die.

The so-called 'first victim' never existed. The only unidentified woman to die on the Whitechapel streets in December 1887 perished from starvation and exposure. Three Whitechapel women with names faintly suggestive of the nickname died naturally in hospitals: Sarah Fayer and Alice Farber in December 1887, and Emma Fairy in December 1886. There never was a murdered 'Fairy Fay'.

In the last week of March 1888, however, there was a murderous assault which nearly killed a 'sempstress' (pretty certainly a working prostitute) named Ada Wilson in her room at 19 Maidman Street, Mile End. By her account, a strange man of about thirty with a sunburnt face and fair moustache came to the house, demanded money and, drawing a knife from his pocket, stabbed her twice in the throat. He was five foot six inches tall and dressed in a dark coat, light trousers and wideawake (broad-brimmed soft felt) hat. As far as this description goes, it is similar to those later given of a man or men seen with or near Ripper victims shortly before their deaths, and it is by no means impossible that Ada Wilson was the first target of the East End's multiple murderer.

Another Bank Holiday. Monday 6 August 1888, and Martha Tabram, a fat prostitute in her late thirties, went with her friend Mary Ann Connolly to ply her trade. Miss Connolly, another big woman, was known to her friends as 'Pearly Poll' and she knew Mrs Tabram as Emma Turner. Complicated lists of nicknames, aliases and 'marital' names adopted from successions of common-law husbands abounded among the Whitechapel whores, and identifying the victims was not always easy.

Pearly lodged at Crossingham's doss-house, 35 Dorset Street. Both women hired themselves to soldiers for cheap 'knee-tremblers', leaning up against the walls in backstreet courts and passages.

August Bank Holiday was a good day for trade. Martha and Pearly picked up a couple of guardsmen and went drinking with them in the Whitechapel Road. The little party came out on the street at about 11.30 and immediately fell to bargaining. At the entrance of George Yard (a dark archway in Whitechapel High Street; today's Gunthorpe Street) they came to agreement, and separated for a modicum of privacy. Martha and her soldier turned into George Yard. Pearly and hers went to the next parallel lane, Angel Alley, where prostitutes frequently worked, and where a couple of years later an unmarried mother would dump her unwanted baby.

Like any competent streetwalker, Martha knew places where a couple could hope for ten undisturbed minutes, preferably with a trace of cover. The north-eastern end of George Yard was marked as one of the blackest poverty spots in Booth's survey of London. And a comparison of Booth's designated black spots with other writers on Victorian London suggests that he was influenced by the presence of prostitution as well as destitution in deciding which slums were the worst.

George Buildings, a former weaving factory, had been closed down, sold, and turned into cheap tenements. When Mrs Hewitt, the deputy's wife, extinguished the staircase lights at eleven o'clock, the passages and landings supplied dark corners for hasty use by the erotically inclined.

In the middle of the night Mrs Hewitt was awakened by a cry of 'Help! Murder!' She paid no attention. Husbands constantly beat their wives in her society. Bank Holiday night was a time for heavy drinking, and drunken men and women often fought and screamed. Mrs Hewitt turned over and went back to sleep.

At 2.00 am Mr and Mrs Mahoney came home to George Buildings. They went quietly to their room, and noticed nothing amiss in the darkness. At the same time, Pc Barrett saw a soldier loitering near George Yard who said he was waiting for a comrade who had gone up to a building.

An hour and a half later, cab-driver Alfred Crow made his way back to bed after an exhausting night's work. The very faintest glimmer of dawn was shedding its grey light through the grimy windows, and on the first floor landing Crow dimly saw a shape. He took it for granted that if it was a person, it was a drunk sleeping off her holiday celebrations under cover. Not wanting any distraction from his own sleep, he passed without investigating and went straight to bed.

At five in the morning stevedore John Reeves was preparing to go to work. On the landing he slipped in congealing blood and found the body of Martha Tabram, killed by thirty nine separate stabs in the neck, chest and belly. Her heart, lungs, liver and spleen were all punctured. She had never had a chance of surviving the furious onslaught.

Police investigations quickly turned up Pearly Poll who, rather unwillingly, told them of the night's trade. It was quite probable that Martha had been killed by her soldier customer: prostitutes are always at risk from their clients. And most of Martha's wounds could have been inflicted by a bayonet.

Pearly said that one of the customers had been a corporal, so the authorities organized a parade of all non-commissioned officers and privates at the Tower who had enjoyed leave on Bank Holiday night. Miss Connolly perfunctorily reviewed the parade, and announced that the men were not there. The authorities (probably rightly) thought she was lying, and she failed to increase their confidence in her by absconding and hiding out with her cousin Mrs Shean in Fuller's Court, off Drury Lane.

She claimed that the soldiers had worn white cap-bands. This meant they were Coldstream Guards, and when she was run to earth, she was taken to the Wellington Barracks in Birdcage Walk and confronted with a full parade of the regiment. This time she tried to get the police off her back by picking two men at random. They easily established unshakeable alibis, and the police reluctantly gave up trying to force the truth out of Pearly Poll. The authorities ordered that men garrisoned in the Tower should be forbidden to carry their bayonets or sidearms when off duty. And the military context of Martha's death was quickly forgotten.

Henry Samuel Tabram, a foreman furniture packer of Greenwich, was discovered. He was Martha's husband, and although they had been separated for thirteen years, she still used his name on occasion. Tabram had not seen Martha for nine years. At first he had paid her an allowance of twelve shillings a week. Then she took up with a Spitalfields carpenter named Henry Turner, and Tabram dropped all association with her.

A sad pattern that was to be repeated in the Ripper killings had appeared: respectable working men found drunken wives intolerable, and after separation the women changed their names and sank to the streets.

Turner was lodging at the Working Men's Home in Commercial Street. Like Tabram, he was disgusted by Martha's drunkenness and left her from time to time. Turner had last seen Martha the previous Saturday night, in Leadenhall Street.

With her 'spouses' eliminated, police thoughts turned to the other common source of prostitute murders: the 'blackmailing' gangs of extortionists. The name of the Hoxton 'Hi-Rips' began to be whispered, bringing the word 'ripping' into the Whitechapel murder scene of 1888. The suggestion of their involvement also silenced many possible witnesses. Nobody wanted to incur the gangs' savage revenge on informers.

Enterprising policemen noted the similarities between Martha's death and Emma Smith's. Both were wounded in the abdomen. At night. In the same locality. After Bank Holidays. Rumour and suspicion were abroad by the time the first unquestionably mutilating 'ripping' occurred.

3

Mary Ann Nichols

Polly Nichols was a drab little woman. Forty-two years old, her brown hair turning mousily grey, with two bottom teeth and a top front tooth lost in fights, she stood five foot two inches tall, and maintained an alcoholic brightness and pugnacity.

Born Mary Walker, she married printer's machinist William Nichols, bore him five children, drank his wages, quarrelled with him, and left him in 1881. For the next few years she moved in and out of workhouses and doss-houses, following an erratic path towards the Spitalfields streets. A year spent with her father in Camberwell was not a success; he was glad to see her go. Nichols continued to hear from her, as parish authorities tried to squeeze maintenance money for the children from him. He countered that she had deserted him, leaving him to look after them, and won his case when it was established that she was practising prostitution.

Early in 1888 she was found sleeping rough in Trafalgar Square, and was sent to Princes Road Workhouse in Lambeth, leaving it in April to accept an offer of employment as a maid in the teetotal religious household of Mr Cowdry at Ingleside, Rose Hill Road, Wandsworth. Such respectability quickly bored her. Within a month she had absconded, stealing clothes worth £3.10.0d from the Cowdrys, and retreating to the dark sanctuary of 18 Thrawl Street.

Here she shared a surprisingly neat and clean room with Emily or Nelly Holland, (who seems also to have used the name Jane Oram) occasionally varying her residence by stopping at the more raffish 56 Flower and Dean Street, where women could share their beds with men.

At 1.40 on the morning of 31 August Polly was in the kitchen which served as a residents' common-room in the Thrawl Street doss-house. The deputy noticed her, and demanded the fourpence she owed for the night's rent. When she could not produce it, he ordered

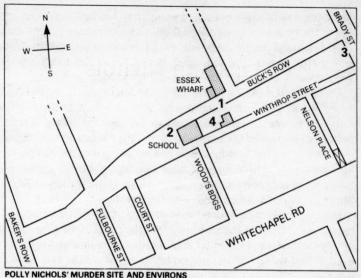

POLLY NICHOLS' MURDER SITE AND ENVIRONS

1 The murder site	3 Unconfirmed bloodstains and	4 Barbers' Yard, slaughterers
2 Drops of blood on the road	reported cries during the night	working through the night

her out. Polly was unabashed and asked him to save her bed for her. 'Never mind!' she cried, 'I'll soon get my doss money. See what a jolly bonnet I've got now!'

Fifty minutes later she was reeling drunkenly down Osborn Street to Whitechapel Road. She met Emily Holland, who had gone out to watch a fire at Ratcliff Dry Dock (the second on the docks that night). Emily urged her to come back home, drawing attention to the church clock striking 2.30. Polly refused, boasting that she had made her doss money three times over that day and drunk it away. She intended to return to the Flower and Dean Street doss after another attempt to find trade, and lurched away eastward along Whitechapel Road.

At about 3.40 Charles Cross, a carman, was making his way to work at Pickfords in the City Road. Not far from his home in Bethnal Green he passed westward along Buck's Row. This long, straight cobbled street ran parallel to the Whitechapel Road from Brady Street to Baker's Row (as the southern end of today's Vallance Road was then). Ten minutes walk away from Osborn Street and Brick Lane, it was well in the east of Whitechapel parish and the farthest of the murder sites from the Spitalfields doss-houses. Large warehouses to the north faced the nearby railway lines running up to the Bethnal Green and Shoreditch tracks. On the south there was a terrace of decent brick cottages, and a great grim Board School, a strange deserted building which still stands. The railings surrounding its flat rooftop play-ground eerily decorate the skyline in wavy wrought iron.

Cross entered Buck's Row from Brady Street. As he walked past Essex Wharf (which still stands) he noticed a bundle like an old tarpaulin lying in the gateway opposite between the school and the cottages. He crossed the narrow road to see if it was worth salvaging, and discovered the huddled body of a woman. Her skirt was pulled up, and he thought she might have passed out after being raped. When he heard footsteps approaching from the direction of Brady Street he stepped back quickly into the shadows.

The newcomer was understandably wary of the figure which had moved abruptly from the pavement into the cover of the gateway as he approached. He was Robert Paul, another carman who, like Cross, lived in Bethnal Green and was on his way to work. The two did not know each other, but Cross called Paul over to have a look at the unconscious woman, and decided as they bent over her that she was dead. Paul noticed her raised skirt, and decorously pulled it down. In so doing he accidentally pressed her breast and thought he felt her stirring. But Cross thought that she would never come round again, and the two hurried on towards Baker's Row to report their find to a policeman.

Within a few minutes of their departure, Pc John Neil of the nearby J Division (Bethnal Green) police station passed on his beat. He too stopped to examine the bundle in the gateway – it had not been there half an hour earlier on his previous round – and flashed his bull's-eye lantern over it. The dim light revealed what Cross and Paul had overlooked: the woman's throat was cut from ear to ear, and blood was still oozing darkly from the wound. She was only just dead; her arm was still warm when he grasped it, even though Paul and Cross had found her hands and face cold to the touch.

His call for assistance was heard by Pc Mizen of H Division who had been met by Cross and Paul and was hurrying along Buck's Row. The two carmen had gone on to their work, leaving the police to deal with the find, and Cross was mystified by Paul's diving suddenly into Corbett's Court, Hanbury Street and deserting him. In fact, that was Paul's workplace.

From the other direction, Pc Thain heard Neil's summons as he passed along Brady Street, and he too joined his colleagues. Thain was despatched to Whitechapel Road to rouse Dr Llewellyn, while Mizen went to Bethnal Green station for assistance and the ambulance (a sort of handcart, really) and Neil guarded the body.

Dr Llewellyn pronounced the woman dead. Not a difficult diagnosis, as the murderer had slashed through her jugular veins, windpipe and half her spinal column; in truth, he had almost cut her head off. She was taken west along Buck's Row in the ambulance to the mortuary (little more than a shed) at the back of the Old Montague Street Workhouse. Here two senile paupers stripped and washed the body, discovering that the skirt concealed a terrible gash down the abdomen through which her intestines bulged. The police advised Dr Llewellyn that the case was serious, and he hurried over to perform his post-mortem.

The throat, he found, had been cut from left to right. Bruises on the right jaw and left cheek suggested to him that the killer had steadied the head. As that on the jaw seemed to be a thumbmark, Dr Llewellyn deduced that the killer was left-handed and had worked from in front of his victim. The great gash ran from the bottom of the ribs, just right of the sternum, to the pelvis. The stomach lining had been lightly slashed, and there were two deep obscene stabs in her genitals.

The police were quickly at work in force on this new and peculiarly horrible murder. It had occurred on J Division's territory, so the Bethnal Green police were involved. But Mizen had reported the incident back in Commercial Street, and H Division maintained an interest. Inspector Abberline, the former head of the Whitechapel CID, was drafted back from Scotland Yard to co-ordinate the investigation.

In the workhouse the dead woman's clothes were examined for clues to her identity. A reddish-brown ulster with large brass buttons bearing the pattern of a woman on horseback accompanied by a standing man was of no immediate help. A brown linsey frock, white chest cloth, short brown stays, flannel drawers, black stockings and men's elastic-sided boots were equally anonymous. But her petticoat carried a Lambeth Workhouse laundrymark, and a young woman called Monk who had resided there earlier in the year suggested that she was Mary Ann Nichols. Soon a tearful Emily Holland was identifying her friend.

The identification was solemnly confirmed by William Nichols. In Abberline's presence he leaned over the body and pronounced lugubriously: 'I forgive you, as you are, for what you have done to me.'

The newspapers were delighted and horrified that the grisly murder was also a mystery. The unknown assailant had carried out his appalling deed remarkably silently. Mrs Emma Green had passed a sleepless night in the adjoining cottage, but she had heard nothing. Mr Walter Purkess, the manager of Essex Wharf, had been in the front bedroom directly overlooking the murder site. His wife had passed a poor night, and had probably been pacing up and down the room when the murder took place. Yet neither of them had been aware of any disturbance until they heard the police at 4.00 am. Since neither Cross, approaching from Brady Street to the east, nor Mizen, working along his beat down Hanbury Street and Baker's Row to the west, had seen any suspicious passer-by hurrying away from Buck's Row, the murderer was thought of as having disappeared mysteriously. (In fact, he could easily have doubled around the Board School into Winthrop Street and away down one of the alleys into Whitechapel Road, or passed west across Baker's Row and along Old Montague Street while Mizen was still checking house doors in Hanbury Street.)

But the myth of a fiendishly cunning, frighteningly silent assassin was in the making. It was particularly feared that he wore rubber soled boots, which held a reputation for some time as sinister silent footwear.

The *East London Advertiser* made a grisly scene grislier by describing 'stains and pools of blood up to 100 yards away', and started a long-lived rumour by suggesting that these proved the murder to have been committed elsewhere and the body dumped in Buck's Row.

The *Evening News* was more detailed. There were some drops of blood in Brady Street, and a Mrs Colwell who lived there claimed to have heard a woman running in the night and screaming: 'Murder! Police!' It had sounded as though she was being struck as she ran, but no pursuers' footsteps were audible. The *News* believed the story, but noted the exceptional difficulty entailed in carrying a dead or mortally wounded woman quite silently from Brady Street to the gateway opposite Essex Wharf. The police searched Brady Street, found no traces of blood, and dismissed the story. For there was no doubt that the murder had been carried out in the Buck's Row gateway.

Two more 'large drops of blood, clear and undeniable' in the words of the *News*, or 'a stain which might have been blood' in Inspector Helson's opinion, were visible on the pavement of the broad part of

Buck's Row to the west of the body. These, the *News* deduced, 'were made by fresh thick blood, and were probably caused by something in the hands of the murderer as he walked away.' Unless, of course, they dripped off the tools and overalls of nightworking slaughtermen from Barber's Yard in Winthrop Street, a sinister narrow lane running parallel to Buck's Row on the south. Three of Barber's knackers had hurried the 150 yards around the Board School to look at the body when a passing policeman told them of its discovery.

The detectives on the ground assumed that this was another extortion gang crime. But doubts about the woman's poverty assailed them, and the superficial similarity between Nichols' wounds and those of Tabram and Smith came to dominate their thinking. The detective forces of H and J Divisions now officially promulgated the idea of a single 'Whitechapel Murderer', responsible for all three cases.

Coroner Wynne Baxter contributed substantially to tension. On 1 September he opened the inquest on Polly Nichols at the Working Lads' Institute in Whitechapel Road, and with repeated adjournments he kept it going until 24 September. There was some reason for the first fortnight's delay: Paul was unwilling to come forward, and it took a little while to trace him. But over the last ten days Baxter seems to have been hoping that a theory of his own might be established, given time, and he came in for some criticism.

Opinions of Baxter relate closely to what commentators want to believe about the identity of Jack the Ripper. Those who need a conspiracy theory – especially one in which the police have been nobbled – describe him as a fearless public servant, determined to carry out his duty at all costs. Others, noting the extraordinary contrast between the lengthy inquests conducted by Baxter, and the expeditious inquests in neighbouring districts, have concluded that he was a long-winded busybody.

Victorian coroners were a touchy breed. The doctors among them thought medical training should be a compulsory prerequisite of office; the lawyers disagreed, and abused the dubious legal practices of the medicos. All were concerned for the dignity of their office, and angry that the police tended to put their authority in second place once they had a secure suspect and could prepare evidence for the magistrates' (or 'police') courts. For coroners' courts were equally empowered to find that a particular suspect had a case to answer, and could send him for trial at the sessions. They deeply resented having this prerogative whisked away from them as soon as an enquiry showed promise of reaching a conclusion.

Moreover, they were elected. And although the office was supposed to be non-political, candidates were usually sponsored by groups representing the major political parties. This left them open to controversial handling in the partisan press.

Coroner Baxter had fought a very dirty election campaign for East Middlesex coroner in 1886 against the Radical MP Dr Roderick MacDonald. Baxter's exploitation of the immunity of coroner's elections from the Electoral Practices Act elicited strong comment: he advertised, canvassed, bribed, made deals to secure the withdrawal of other candidates in his favour, and used improper registration of voters to an alarming extent. He was a lawyer, and effectively a professional coroner (holding three deputy coronerships before his election in Middlesex). MacDonald was a medic whose primary activity was representing impoverished Highland crofters in Parliament. Baxter enjoyed overwhelming support in the middle class neighbourhoods of Stoke Newington and Hackney, while MacDonald comfortably carried the Whitechapel slums. Within a year the coroner's fiefdom had been sub-divided, and Dr MacDonald ruled the North East Middlesex territory.

At Polly Nichols' inquest, Baxter established his ascendancy over the police by using the confused testimony of the senile pauper layers-out to suggest that the police had been casual and incompetent. When the foreman of the jury remarked that decrepit old James Hatfield had just denied that the body wore stays, even though he had personally pointed them out to the jurors on their visit to the mortuary, Baxter testily snapped that the witness had admitted his memory was bad. Preferring Hatfield's evidence to Inspector Helson's, Baxter was severe with the police for not having given direct orders for the washing of the body, and then stayed to observe it. And he rebuked them for failing to observe the mutilated abdomen before the body reached the mortuary. (I don't think Mr Baxter intended to suggest that policemen ought to pull up women's skirts and examine their private parts whenever they find their bodies in the streets, but that is the logic of his criticism.) He encouraged the jury to bring in a critical verdict, which they did, blaming the police for having offered no reward for information.

Dr Llewellyn suggested that the murder weapon was a long knife like a cork-marker's or shoemaker's. He also noted a surprising absence of blood around the body (only about a wine glass and a half spilled in the gutter). This superficially supported the rumour that Polly had been killed elsewhere and carried to Buck's Row, and that her blood must have so bespattered the murderer that he should have presented a most suspicious appearance. But Inspector Helson's evidence contradicted this. The blood from her throat had soaked into the back of her ulster and bodice, and drenched her hair. Nobody involved in the investigation thought for a moment that she had been killed anywhere else.

Dr Llewellyn also stressed the presumed left-handedness of the Ripper. He attributed the victim's silence to the speed with which her vocal cords had been severed.

Buck's Row disliked its new-found notoriety. In a few weeks it successfully petitioned to have its name changed, and it is now Durward Street.

4

Annie Chapman

An hour or two after midnight, in the small hours of Saturday 8 September, Timothy Donovan, deputy of Crossingham's doss-house at 35 Dorset Street, looked into the kitchen. It was his responsibility to see that everyone who intended to stay had paid for a bed: fourpence each if they shared, eightpence for those exclusive enough to want a bed to themselves. A hundred and more people could be packed into some of the narrow four-storey terraced houses in this way, so that the landlords might take up to £140 a week from people who could not afford the 2/4d (12p) that a week's lodging would cost them outright.

Annie Siffey, a short pallid woman of forty-five with dark wavy hair, was sitting alone eating potatoes. She was slightly drunk. Usually her bed was paid for at the weekend by Ted Stanley, a workingman of military bearing known locally as 'the Pensioner', and believed to be an old soldier. The previous weekend the Pensioner had paid for beds for two women: Annie Siffey and Eliza Cooper. Both women also shared the favours of a local character called 'Harry the Hawker', and on Tuesday or Wednesday a fight had broken out between them. Most people believed it was over Harry, but Eliza swore that it was all about her soap, which Annie had borrowed for Ted on the Saturday and not returned. The fight had taken place in Walter Ringer's pub The Britannia on the corner of Dorset Street and Commercial Street, and Annie was nursing the remains of a black eye and a bruised chest she had received. She still felt unwell and depressed; of all the Ripper's victims she most nearly fitted the popular view that they were wretched, prematurely aged drabs.

Donovan asked her for her money, and she replied: 'I haven't got it. I am weak and ill and have been in the infirmary.' Donovan reminded her of the rules and she left the kitchen saying: 'Don't let the bed. I'll be back soon.' She confirmed her intention as she passed John

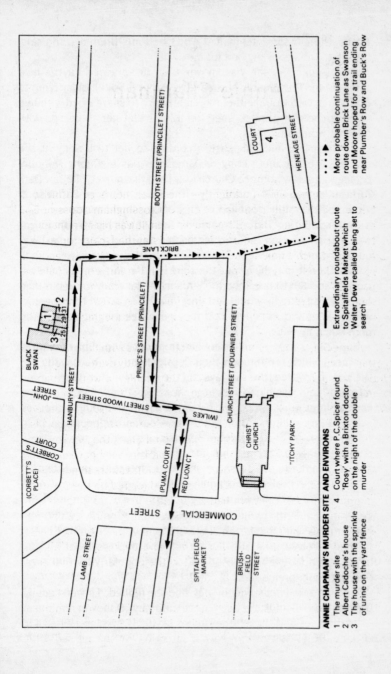

ANNIE CHAPMAN'S MURDER SITE AND ENVIRONS

1 The murder site
2 Albert Cadoche's house
3 The house with the sprinkle of urine on the yard fence
4 Court where P.C. Spicer found 'Rosy' with a Brixton doctor on the night of the double murder

→ Extraordinary roundabout route to Spitalfields Market which Walter Dew recalled being set to search

⋯▸ More probable continuation of route down Brick Lane as Swanson and Moore hoped for a trail ending near Plumber's Row and Buck's Row

Evans, the elderly watchman. 'I won't be long, Brummy,' she said. 'See that Tim keeps my bed for me.'

'Dark Annie', as she was known, then disappeared for the next three hours. Presumably she wandered round Spitalfields trying to find a man who would either pay eightpence to share a bed with her, or fourpence for a quick 'knee-trembler' to let her share one with another woman.

Between five and half past, according to her testimony at the inquest, Mrs Elizabeth Long or Darrell was passing along Hanbury Street on her way home to Church Row from the market. She saw Dark Annie talking to a short man, only a little taller than her own five-foot. He wore a deerstalker hat and had a shabby genteel appearance. She did not see his face, but estimated his age at around forty. His accent was foreign, though the only words she heard him say were: 'Will you?' to which Annie replied: 'Yes.'

Mrs Darrell may have put the time a little early, for between a quarter and ten to five, John Richardson the landlady's son paid the house a visit, and he would certainly have taken action to disperse a streetwalker and her client had they been negotiating outside the door when he left.

The houses in Hanbury Street had front doors opening on narrow passages which ran through their depth to the tiny back yards. Off these passages led the stairways and the doors into the ground-floor rooms. It was possible to walk from the street straight through to the yard without looking into any occupied room, and with the houses sub-let to a conglomeration of tenants – seventeen people slept in no 29 – the front and back doors were left open at night to allow late-coming lodgers to do just that if they wished.

This also made the passages and yards splendid out-of-the-way places for streetwalkers to conduct their business. Mrs Richardson, a genuinely God-fearing woman, did not approve and pretended she did not know such things ever happened in her house. But her son John, who lodged elsewhere, had found couples fornicating in the passage and even up the stairs. And he was almost certainly checking the premises to make sure intruders were not using them for immoral purposes when he looked in on his way to work, though prudish discretion led him to claim that he was making sure the cellar padlock was all right.

He found everything quiet, and sat down on the steps to the empty yard to trim a piece of loose leather off his boot with a table knife he happened to be carrying. It proved too blunt for the purpose – he kept it to cut up carrots for his rabbit – and he had to borrow a knife from a workmate in the market to finish the job.

At what he estimated as half past, Albert Cadoche, a young carpenter lodging at no 31, went to the outhouse in his own back yard. Passing the four-foot high wooden fence that separated the yards, he heard a woman saying: 'No, no,' followed by sounds of a scuffle, and the noise of a body falling heavily. There was no cry for help, and Mr Cadoche decided to mind his own business and go back into his own house.

At five to six, John Davis, a market porter who lived with his wife and three sons in the third-floor front room of no 29, went out to the back before going to work. To the left of the two steps into the yard, her head against the fence, her skirt pulled up, her legs bent and open in garish red-and-white striped stockings, lay Dark Annie. A handkerchief tied round her neck disguised the savage throat-cutting that had nearly decapitated her. Nothing disguised the fact that her belly had been ripped open and her intestines thrown across her shoulder.

The police were rapidly summoned. They found two pills and part of a torn envelope bearing the crest of the Sussex Regiment in the yard, but disturbed very little, for when Dr George Bagster Phillips the Divisional Surgeon arrived, it was he who picked up Dark Annie's personal property: a piece of muslin and a comb in a paper case which had apparently been taken from her pocket and laid rather carefully at her feet. There were also two farthings, though these were not mentioned at the inquest. Possibly the police believed they were worth keeping secret as a clue, since Inspector Reid referred to them at the later inquest on Alice McKenzie, and Major Smith of the City of London Police decided that they suggested the handiwork of a young medical student, known to pass off polished farthings on prostitutes as sovereigns. Major Smith may have had inflated ideas of the price of a tumble with a Spitalfield whore!

A mystery confronting the police was Annie's rings. Donovan and other occupants of 35 Dorset Street confirmed that she had been wearing three brass rings when she left, and they agreed that in a poor light they might have been mistaken for gold. Their marks were still plainly visible on her hands. The police were very anxious to discover what had happened to them, for if Annie had not herself tried to sell them during the night, they had probably been stolen by her murderer and would provide damning evidence against him when he was found.

The legend that her rings and the farthings (with steadily increasing numbers of pennies added) were piled symbolically at her feet in a significant pattern has grown up over the years, developing from the newspapers' original surprise at the neatness of the pile of muslin, comb and, presumably farthings; and gradually eliminating the muslin and the comb.

The usual difficulty confronted the start of the enquiry. Who was Annie Siffey? Not Siffey, anyway. That name was a corruption of 'Sievey', the craft nickname of a sieve-maker with whom she had lived for a year or so. She herself had boasted of being a vet's widow, and having lived at Windsor before coming to the East End. And a good deal of enquiry at last established that she had been married to John Chapman, a humble Windsor coachman. She had separated from him four years previously, but received an allowance of ten shillings a week until his death in 1886.

Since then she had sold flowers and done occasional crochet work for her meagre living. She drank from time to time. And she walked the streets when necessary.

Mr Wynne Baxter opened the inquest on this second victim on 12 September. With adjournments, it lasted until almost the end of the month, so that new revelations about Polly Nichols and Annie Chapman were continually appearing in the papers, keeping speculation and fear simmering.

The inquest jury quickly showed an interest in 'the Pensioner'. 'Harry the Hawker' was known to some of them. But they wanted the Pensioner identified in case the Sussex Regiment envelope had been his. (The police found that actually Annie had picked it up from the floor in Crossingham's where someone else had discarded it.)

It was a couple of weeks before bricklayer's mate Edward Stanley could be found and made to admit unwillingly that he was not in fact a pensioner and had never been in the Essex Regiment as he pretended. He did, however, endorse deputy Donovan's claim that a man known as 'Leather Apron' was sometimes to be seen around the doss-house, and had been wearing a deerstalker hat on his last appearance. It was widely known that the police had been looking for this man following their enquiries into Polly Nichols' death, and had in fact made an arrest two days before Chapman's inquest.

The *Star* had run a long piece on 'Leather Apron' the Wednesday before Annie Chapman's death. It described a short thickset Jew with close-cropped hair, a small black moustache and a very thick neck. He habitually wore a leather apron and a close-fitting black cap, and carried a sharp knife. (Previously they had claimed that he carried a revolver.) He was not known to have any fixed abode, but stayed in doss-houses around Brick Lane (one of which denied this) and was frequently seen in the Princess Alice in Commercial Street. He had also been seen skulking in Leather Lane on the other side of the City. 'I'll rip you up!' was his favourite threat. He moved silently, and disappeared rapidly if men approached.

After a lot of random detentions, the police arrested a Jewish shoemaker, John Pizer, and told the press he was 'Leather Apron'.

The inquest was to be used for Pizer's well-reported exoneration, for he was in serious danger of being lynched if he were released from custody without being publicly cleared. Dr George Bagster Phillips, the police surgeon, also used the occasion to undermine one line of enquiry initiated by Dr Llewellyn that had pointed toward Pizer. The wounds, he declared, could not have been made by a leather-worker's knives, which were too short. A bayonet might have been long enough. So would a surgeon's post-mortem instrument. But ordinary surgical instruments would not, and he doubted whether many doctors carried an instrument capable of inflicting the mutilations.

The inquest established that, apart from Cadoche, no one had heard a sound of the murder. Dr Phillips squashed a suggestion that bloodstains on the walls and fences of neighbouring houses to the west, and a piece of bloodstained paper thrown away into Mr Bailey's packing-case works from over the yard wall of no 25, showed that the murderer had climbed across two yards and escaped through no 25. There were no bloodstains, Dr Phillips asserted. Just smears of blood on the fence in no 29. (Inspector Chandler laughingly told the press that the 'smear or sprinkle' of blood on the fence of no 25 was urine.)

Dr Phillips also went out of his way to state that Chapman's teeth were excellent, although the police and press reported two missing from her bottom jaw. Otherwise, although a strongly-built woman, Annie was in miserable condition, undernourished, with chronic disease in the lungs and brain membranes. The bruises from her fight with Eliza Cooper were still visible, though quite distinct from the marks left by her murderer. But Phillips was impressed by her swollen face and protruding tongue which, coupled with bruising on her neck, led him to believe that asphyxia induced by throttling had occurred before the throat was cut.

On the mutilations, Dr Phillips reserved his evidence, and clearly hoped he would not be called upon to describe them in open court.

Despite his clear warning against suspecting medical men in general, Dr Phillips' resumed testimony gave rise to one of the longest-standing beliefs about the Ripper: the notion that he must have possessed some degree of surgical skill. The account of Annie's mutilations was wrung from him by Wynne Baxter. It is not clear whether Phillips prudishly disliked describing such obscenities to laymen or whether he was trying to preserve special information which the police might find to be the 'guilty knowledge' of a suspect. But he argued vehemently that the wounds had been caused after Chapman's decease, and so were not proper matter for an inquest into the cause of death. Baxter firmly overruled him. He had a theory of his own to air, which would require the presentation of this evidence.

A very important revelation Dr Phillips made about Annie's throat has been almost overlooked ever since. 'There were two distinct clean cuts on the body of the vertebrae on the left side of the spine,' he told the inquest.

> They were parallel to each other and separated by about half an inch. The muscular structure between the side processes of the vertebrae had an appearance as if an attempt had been made to separate the bones of the neck.

In other words, the murderer tried to cut Annie's head off. And failed.

The following year, in his report on the beheaded Pinchin Street torso, Dr Phillips commented that the Pinchin Street murderer was more familiar with the structure of the spine than the Ripper, though he made the defensive point that medical students were not trained in severing spinal columns. For Dr Phillips swiftly and dangerously committed himself to the misleading suggestion that the Ripper had some surgical expertise.

This conclusion was based on the sensational posthumous mutilations. Her abdomen had been ripped open; her intestines cut away from the back wall and laid over her shoulder. Her uterus and its appendages had been removed, together with two-thirds of her bladder. And, in Dr Phillips' view, 'obviously the work was that of an expert – of one, at least, who had such knowledge of anatomical or pathological examinations as to be enabled to secure the pelvic organs with one sweep of the knife, which must therefore ... have been at least five inches long.'

That misleading phrase 'one sweep of the knife' has led to the persistent belief that the Ripper was a doctor. Obviously more than one sweep was involved in severing the womb at top and bottom, and the top cut was pretty inexpert, unless we imagine the Ripper particularly wanted two-thirds of a bladder! What really impressed Dr Phillips was that the clean cut at the lower end had severed the vagina so precisely as to leave the cervix intact with the extracted uterus, and the knife had avoided slashing through to the rectum. In view of other victims' injuries, I think we may reasonably conclude that this was more luck than judgement.

But knowledge of the missing uterus spread fast and the idea of a man with medical training took wing. Within twenty-four hours, Coroner Baxter had been approached by a London medical school, where the sub-curator of the pathology museum had a strange story to tell. On Monday 24th, when Polly Nichols' inquest wound wearily to its close, Mr Baxter's summing-up linked her death with those of Smith, Tabram and Chapman, and suggested that theft of the organ missing from Chapman might also have been the motive for Nichols' murder, though the miscreant had been disturbed before he could extract it.

Three days later, as he summed up on Annie Chapman, he went further. He brought together the facts in the case cogently. But he also stated his new theory:

> There were no meaningless cuts. The organ had been taken by one who knew where to find it, what difficulties he would have to contend against, and how he should use his knife so as to abstract the organ without injury to it. No unskilled person could have known where to find it or have recognized it when it was found. For instance, no mere slaughterer of animals could have carried out these operations. It must have been some one accustomed to the post mortem room.

Mr Baxter was summarizing Dr Phillips' views accurately, and they influenced all his subsequent thinking on the Ripper murders. So we must note immediately that most other medical men disagreed, and the authorities were perturbed by Wynne Baxter's deductive interpretation of the data laid before him.

Their mistrust was justified by the reliance Mr Baxter placed on the cock-and-bull story he had heard from the hospital. There was, he told the jury, a market for the missing organs. An American had approached the pathology museum requesting specimens, pre-served in glycerine so that their flexibility would be retained. The American proposed publishing a limited edition of a physiological monograph, twenty or so copies of which would be distributed with sample organs.

Mr Baxter praised himself for having put this strange information before the public. He praised Dr Phillips for having discovered the theft of the organs. And he criticized the detectives for not having made a successful arrest.

This proved the coroner's high-point in public esteem. The press generally accepted his theory, and lauded him for having announced it. Some pointedly contrasted Baxter's shrewdness with Scotland Yard's incompetence.

But the *British Medical Journal* in a hitherto unpublicized report completely exploded Mr Baxter's story. It said:

It is true that enquiries were made at one or two medical schools [University College Hospital and the Middlesex Hospital, in fact] early last year by a foreign physician, who was spending some time in London, as to the possibility of securing certain parts of the body for the purpose of scientific investigation. No large sum, however, was offered. The person in question was a physician of the highest reputability and exceedingly well accredited to this country by the best authorities in his own, and he left London fully eighteen months ago. There was never any real foundation for the hypothesis, and the information communicated, which was not at all of the nature which the public has been led to believe, was due to the erroneous interpretation by a minor official of a question which he had overheard and to which a negative reply was given. This theory may be dismissed, and is, we believe, no longer entertained even by its author.

Certainly Mr Baxter did not revive it at the later Ripper inquests where he presided.

The sensational publicizing of 'Leather Apron' had given the murder scare an anti-semitic turn. There was nothing inherently prejudiced in suggesting that the murderer might have been a Jew: a huge proportion of the population between Buck's Row and Spital-field Market was Jewish, so that it was a reasonable statistical possibility. But the *Daily News* was severe with its fellow-journalists:

The public are looking for a monster, and in the legend of 'Leather Apron' the Whitechapel part of them seem to be inventing a monster to look for. This kind of invention ought to be discouraged in every possible way or there may soon be murders from panic to add to murders from lust of blood. A touch would fire the whole district in the mood it is now. Leather Apron walks without making a noise. Leather Apron has piercing eyes and a strange smile, and finally Leather Apron looks like a Jew. The last is brutal as well as foolish, and it has already had its effect in a cry against the Whitechapel Jews. Already, as our columns show today, the list of savage assaults in the neighbourhood has shown an alarming increase since the discovery [of Chapman's body] on Satur-day. Every man who can say a reasonable word ought to say it, or worse may follow than we have already known. Much depends on the police. It is hardly too much to say that the peace of a whole quarter of London is now, in an especial manner, in their hands.

The paper did not exaggerate. That weekend Dr Phillips and his assistant were kept up for most of Saturday night binding up wounds. The *Daily News* reported 'cases of assault, some of them of the most serious character, arising directly or indirectly out of the intense excitement caused by discussion of the Murder.' The *East London Observer* described explicitly

A PLOT AGAINST THE JEWS

On Saturday in several quarters of East London the crowds who assembled in the streets began to assume a very threatening attitude towards the Hebrew population of the District. It was repeatedly asserted that no Englishman could have perpetrated such a horrible crime as that of Hanbury Street, and that it must have been done by a JEW – and forthwith the crowds began to threaten and abuse such unfortunate Hebrews as they found in the streets. Happily the presence of a large number of police ... prevented a· riot actually taking place.

And the *Jewish Chronicle* observed that:

> There has been forcibly brought to us the genesis of the anti-Jewish outbreaks which still occasionally occur abroad, and which were not unknown in England in ancient times. It is so easy to inflame the mind when it is startled by hideous crime, that sensation-mongers incur a fearful responsibility when they add to the excitement by giving currency to every idle rumour.

Chaim Bermant has remarked that the scare saw 'the nearest thing to an East End anti-Jewish pogrom, prior to the advent of Mosley.'

This had a significant effect on police enquiries. Pizer was hurried before the inquest, solely to clear a name that had never been blemished until an over-zealous sergeant decided that he was Leather Apron, and as quickly hurried away. Understandably, the authorities feared the massive threat that a riot posed to innocent lives, limbs and property more than the limited threat to a handful of streetwalkers represented by one maniac. And so, although house-to-house enquiries had pointed toward a Jewish suspect, Scotland Yard toned down its public releases, altered a description of a 'Jewish-looking' man to 'foreign-looking', ordered policemen not to talk to the press, and generally undertook a responsible campaign to damp down anti-semitic hysteria which has suggested to some later historians a sinister cover-up.

It was three weeks since Annie Chapman had died. But the revelations of wonderfully nicknamed slum-dwellers like Dark Annie, Harry the Hawker and Leather Apron, not to mention the mysterious theories of Coroner Wynne Baxter, all contrived to see that life did not revert to normal. And as the month ended, the murderer struck again.

5

The Night of the Two Murders

Long Liz dossed in Flower and Dean Street like so many other whores. But she worked a beat well clear of the Brick Lane/Wentworth Street district where four had now died violently in six months. All the Whitechapel murders had been north of Whitechapel Road. Berner Street sloped gently south from Commercial Road to Ellen Street, about two blocks farther south than the point where, as Henriques Street, it terminates today at Boyd Street. Halfway along its length Fairclough Street crossed it. Three houses up from Fairclough Street a pair of large wooden gates, which provided the only access to a yard, were normally left open. The yard took its name from Messrs Dutfield's cart-making business, next to a stable at its western end. To the north (on the right as you entered the gates) no. 40 Berner Street was a two-storeyed wooden structure housing the barn-like premises of a social and discussion club for (mostly Jewish) Socialists, the International Workers' Educational Club. Three artisans' dwellings converted from an older building lay on the south of the yard.

To the east, Berner Street was paralleled by Batty Street, itself the site of a notorious murder the previous year. Israel Lipski, lodging in the attic of no 16, had forcibly poisoned pretty young Miriam Angel, one floor below, and then swallowed acid himself. The murder, involving an overcrowded house full of Jewish immigrants and two Jewish journeymen dragged in by Lipski's accusations, fuelled anti-semitism.

Brunswick Street, just south of Batty Street and Fairclough Street, was known as 'Tiger Bay' — a nickname given to dangerous dockland roads all over the English-speaking world. And the reputation for toughness was rubbing off onto Berner Street.

But to Long Liz it was a quiet street offering easy access to the passing traffic of Commercial Road, the privacy of doorways where

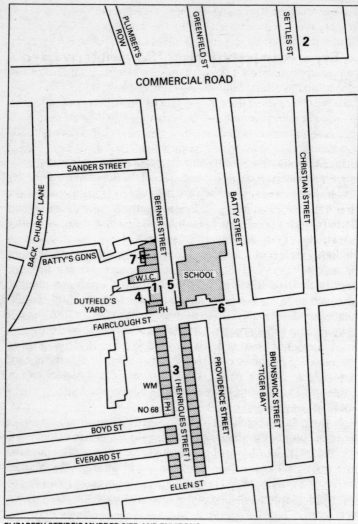

ELIZABETH STRIDE'S MURDER SITE AND ENVIRONS

1   The murder site
2   Stride and client at Bricklayers Arms 500 yards north of this point at 11.00pm
3   Marshall saw Stride and client here
4   Packer's shop
5   Stride and client seen here by Packer and P.C. Smith

6   Stride refusing long-coated man's proposal here five minutes before the murder
7   Mrs Mortimer's house
PH Public houses
WM Marshall's house
WIC Workers' International Club

bargains could be struck, and the hidey-hole of Dutfield's Yard where they might be consummated behind the heavy gates.

Around midnight on Saturday 29 September, various people including a policeman saw her chatting up a man or a succession of men. At approximately 1.00 am, Louis Diemschütz, steward of the International Workers' Educational Club, clattered his pony and cart down the empty street. He hawked gimcrack jewellery, and had spent the afternoon and evening selling his wares at Sydenham. Saturday night was an active club evening. A debate on 'The Necessity for Socialism among Jews' had been succeeded by community singing, and a few members were still making music as Diemschütz turned his pony's head in at the gate.

As he did so, the beast shied, and refused to go on into the yard. Diemschütz prodded around in the darkness with his long-handled whip to see if there was any obstruction, and discovered a soft bundle on the ground to the right of the pony's head. At this, he leaped down and struck a match to investigate. He found a woman lying against the wall, and assumed she was drunk. It crossed his mind that she might be his wife, and he hurried into the club to make sure she was inside. When he came out with another member called Kozebrodske (but conveniently known as Isaacs) they made the horrifying discovery that she was dead. A pool of blood ran from her newly-slit throat. Instantly the Socialists were racing up to Commercial Road screaming 'Murder!' at the tops of their voices, until they encountered Pc Lamb, whose initial impression was that they had either caused or been the victims of a disturbance.

This was not an improbable notion. Immigrant Jewish Socialists were perceived as over-excitable, unreliable and generally undesirable. Within six months Diemschütz would find himself tried and convicted for losing his temper with a mob. On Saturday 9 March 1889, Dr Adler the Chief Rabbi preached at the Duke Street Synagogue behind Aldgate, and firmly declared that Socialism was incompatible with Judaism. The following week, Diemschütz and the Club activists marched to the synagogue in protest. The *East London Advertiser* made clear its distaste for Jews and Socialists, and its objection to poor men being allowed to express political opinions, saying:

> on the principle that even 'a worm will turn' we have been treated to a Hebrew demonstration, which reminded one....

of those hubbubs in the Temple when anything occurred to displease the Israelites of old. . . .

[T]he concourse [was] headed by a German band and a repulsive looking black and white banner bearing the words 'Jewish Unemployed and Sweaters' Victims'. . . . A more abject and miserable set of men it would have been impossible to see anywhere. Ill-clad, dirty, unwashed, haggard and ragged, they looked in the bright sunlight a picture of misery. Everything was done by the police to facilitate their progress. The traffic was stopped, notwithstanding that it was just the busiest part of the haymarket.

When the demonstrators returned to Berner Street, a small crowd followed, hooting and jeering at them. The Jews locked themselves into the clubhouse and sent for the police. But it was some time before they arrived. In the interim Diemschütz, goaded beyond endurance by the taunting, declared that he would rather die than put up with it, and led a charge of the members to scatter their enemies. The Jews were armed with a motley collection of umbrellas, broomsticks and saucepans, and a frenzied fight was taking place on the streets when policemen at last arrived. They immediately set about to quell the Jews, and Detective Constable Frost forced his way into the clubhouse, where some of the members fought with him, taking him as a reinforcement of their tormentors.

In consequence, Diemschütz and two other members found themselves in Thames Magistrates' Court, charged with running out of their premises to threaten and belabour innocent passers-by. Diemschütz was refused permission to bring charges against Inspector Ferret for failing to prevent a breach of the peace, and lost a charge of assault which he brought against Frost. The Berner Street residents suggested that a handful of innocent children had made harmless sport of the Socialists and knocked mischievously at their door, to suffer a murderous onslaught in retaliation. When this case was put to a jury in April, it was thrown out without hesitation. But Diemschütz's defence against the charge of assaulting the police (that the police had in fact attacked the Jews) was stigmatized by the judge as a wicked lie, and he was given three months hard labour for his part in the affray. His co-defendant Kozebrodske was given a £4 fine or one month's imprisonment. It was not a very good time to be a Jewish Socialist in the East End.

On the showery night of 29–30 September, however, the club members suffered no more harassment than detailed interrogation and thorough body searches – treatment which they found sufficiently insulting to honest citizens who had reported the discovery of a corpse. Nor were they pleased when the police tried to buy drink and tobacco during the night's investigation, shrewdly suspecting that this was an attempt to entrap them into contravening the club's licence.

While all this was going on, another perky little streetwalker was making her way south from Bishopsgate Police Station. Catherine Conway (to give her the married name she insisted was legitimately 'bought and paid for') was just five foot tall with dark auburn hair, a turning-up nose, and a cheeky outlook which belied the general fecklessness, malnutrition and destitution to which a grasshopper life of drinking and singing had brought her.

Around eight o'clock in the evening she was in Aldgate High Street, gloriously drunk and 'imitating a fire-engine', by one account. By the time City Pc Lewis Robinson arrived she had sunk to the pavement in a happy stupor, gave her name as 'Nothing', and had to be supported away from the crowd that had gathered. She was put to rest in the cells at Bishopsgate, and observed every half hour by Pc George Hutt who supervised them. By a quarter past midnight she was heard to be awake and singing softly to herself. By half past she called out to know when she could be let out. (She knew that the City Police did not clog up their courts with pointless drunk-and-disorderly cases, but released most drunks when they sobered up.)

'When you are capable of taking care of yourself,' Pc Hutt told her.

'I can do that now,' she replied, unabashed.

At one o'clock Hutt released her. 'What time is it?' she asked.

'Too late for you to get any more to drink,' replied the policeman.

When she asked again he told her it was just on one, and she remarked: 'I shall get a damn fine hiding when I get home!'

'And serve you right!' answered Hutt. 'You have no right to get drunk!'

As she left, he asked her to pull the outer door to behind her. And with a cheery 'All right. Good night, old cock!' she wove off in the direction of Aldgate, rather than Church Street, Spitalfields, where she was lodging.

At 1.35 Joseph Lawende with his friends Joseph Hyam Levy and Harry Harris left the Imperial Club in Duke Street beside the eastern

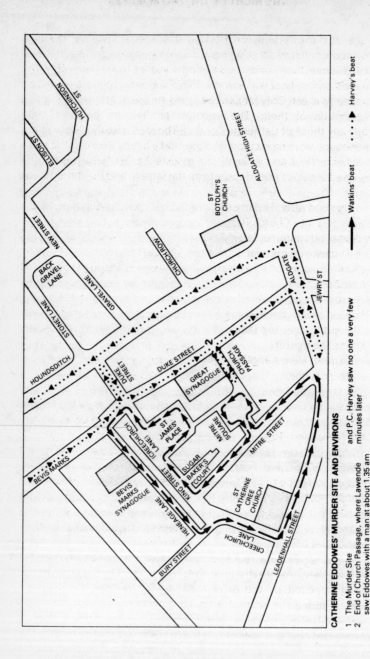

CATHERINE EDDOWES' MURDER SITE AND ENVIRONS

1 The Murder Site
2 End of Church Passage, where Lawende
  saw Eddowes with a man at about 1.35 am

▲ Harvey's beat

······ Watkins' beat

and P.C. Harvey saw no one a very few
minutes later

edge of the City between Bevis Marks and Aldgate. At the dark covered Church Passage which led southwest out of the street into Mitre Square they noticed a man and a woman talking amicably. The woman, whose back was towards them, was seen to place a hand on the man's chest. Only Mr Lawende paid sufficient attention to give a description of them. The woman's clothes, he believed, were certainly those of Catherine Conway. The man, clearly visible in the moonlight, wore navy coloured serge and a deerstalker cap. He had a red neckerchief and a small fair moustache. Mr Levy was a little alarmed at seeing licentiousness on the streets, and the three moved away.

Very soon after, Pc James Harvey's beat brought him down Duke Street and into Church Passage. He saw no one.

About ten minutes later, Pc Edward Watkins came right into the small square on his beat. Shining his lantern into its darkest corner – he saw the sprawled body of a woman in a pool of blood. Immediately he rushed into Kearley and Tonge's warehouse whose door into the square was ajar, and cried out to the ex-policeman night-watchman: 'For God's sake, mate, come to my assistance!'

'Stop till I get my lamp,' replied George Morris the watchman. 'What's the matter?'

'Oh dear! Here's another woman cut up to pieces!'

'Where is she?'

'In the corner.'

As soon as Morris shone his light on the body he blew his whistle and ran out into Mitre Street. In Aldgate he found Pc James Harvey and Pc Holland. They came back with him to the square.

George Clapp, night-watchman at 5 Mitre Square, had heard nothing. Pc Richard Pearse, who lived in the cottage at 3 Mitre Square, had gone to bed twenty minutes after midnight. He too had heard nothing. Watkins swore that he had passed through the square on his beat at 1.30 and it had been empty. (Lawende's testimony implicitly confirms this, making it needless to speculate that Watkins might have been scamping his rounds.)

The murderer had struck again with amazing speed and silence. He had travelled nearly half a mile from Whitechapel to the City without being impeded by the extra Metropolitan police patrolling the streets during the scare. He had not encountered any constable hurrying to the summons of their colleagues' whistles in Berner Street. He had killed a woman in the tiny yard without disturbing the

Jews in the club-house or the cottagers opposite. Apparently alarmed by Diemschütz's approaching pony, he had slipped away unseen. From Henriques Street to Mitre Square is now about fifteen minutes walk with traffic on Commercial Road and at Aldgate to contend with. But the police estimate in 1888 was that the two sites were eight minutes apart. The murderer enjoyed half an hour to skulk somewhere between Duke's Place and Bishopsgate, pick up Catherine Conway, and go with her to Church Passage. But Watkins' beat allowed him no more than ten minutes to cut her throat and complete his frightful mutilation. Harvey's hitherto unnoticed presence cuts the murder time to about five minutes.

Catherine had been ripped up with a new brutality. The full medical report given by Dr Frederick Gordon Brown to her inquest has been preserved in the Corporation of London archives among the coroner's papers, and recently made available to the public. It is well worth reproducing his account of the discovery in full. (For convenience I have punctuated the coroner's notes.)

> The body was on its back, the head turned to left shoulder. The arms by the side of the body as if they had fallen there. Both palms upwards, the fingers slightly bent. A thimble was lying off the finger on the right side.
>
> The clothes drawn up above the abdomen. The thighs were naked. Left leg extended in a line with the body. The abdomen was exposed. Right leg bent at the thigh and knee.
>
> The bonnet was at the back of the head – great disfigurement of the face. The throat cut. Across below the throat was a neckerchief. The upper part of the dress was pulled open a little way. The abdomen was all exposed.
>
> The intestines were drawn out to a large extent and placed over the right shoulder – they were smeared over with some feculent matter. A piece of about two feet was quite detached from the body and placed between the body and the left arm, apparently by design. The lobe and auricle of the right ear was cut obliquely through.
>
> There was a quantity of clotted blood on the pavement on the left side of the neck round the shoulder and upper part of the arm, and fluid blood-coloured serum which had flowed under the neck to the right shoulder, the pavement sloping in that direction.

> Body was quite warm. No death stiffening had taken place. She must have been dead most likely within the half hour. We looked for superficial bruises and saw none. No blood on the skin of the abdomen or secretion of any kind on the thighs. No spurting of blood on the bricks or pavement around. No marks of blood below the middle of the body. Several buttons were found in the clotted blood after the body was removed. There was no blood on the front of the clothes. There were no traces of recent connection.

The observations that there were no traces of recent connection and no secretion of any kind on the thighs are fascinating. They prove that these Victorian investigators were not naive innocents, but fully understood that mutilating murderers are driven by a sexual obsession which *may* lead them to copulate with or masturbate over the dead or unconscious bodies of their victims. Dr Brown deliberately looked for evidence of these practices.

Dr Phillips had estimated it must have taken half an hour to carry out the crude mutilation of Chapman. Yet here was a worse-mutilated body which had been worked on for no more than five minutes at most. The serious disagreements of the doctors were about to begin.

The rest of the night was filled with frantic police activity. Dr William Sequeira had been fetched from his home in Jewry Street, and arrived at 1.55. He confirmed the death, but did not touch the body until police surgeon Brown arrived twenty five minutes later.

Inspector Edward Collard hurried down from Bishopsgate Station, reaching the square just after 2.00 am. A sergeant gave him the buttons and thimble found beside the body, and the most useful clue to the woman's identity, a small mustard tin containing two pawn tickets. He sent constables out to search the neighbourhood and stop any men on the streets, but they found nothing of any importance.

Acting City Police Commissioner Major Henry Smith took a hansom cab and raced over to Mitre Square from his shakedown bed at Cloak Lane Police Station. In the absence of the City Commissioner he took direct control of this, the first Whitechapel murder to fall within the domain of his force.

Superintendent M'William, head of the City CID, ordered a fresh search of the streets when he arrived, and directed men to go into the common lodging houses. They found nothing of any importance.

Detective Constable Halse worked his way east across Hounds-ditch and Middlesex Street as far as Goulston Street, which he reached at 2.20 in his estimation. Then he turned back and returned to Mitre Square. He accompanied Collard and the body to Golden Lane Mortuary, where he observed that part of the victim's apron was missing. Major Smith had also gone to the mortuary, and he and Halse returned to Mitre Square, where they learned that the missing piece of apron might have been found by the Metropolitan Police. Halse and Detective Hunt went to Leman Street Station, and were directed back to Wentworth Model Dwellings, Goulston Street, a vast gaunt range of new brick tenements which lined the south side of Wentworth Street, and extended briefly down both sides of Goulston Street. The apartments were planned on the staircase system, with access from the streets and the inner courtyards through open doorways, surmounted by heavy pre-cast ornamental latticework in vaguely Moorish ball-and-circle patterns. Each doorway revealed a solid central pillar supporting the first flight of stone stairs to one side, and leaving a dank space on the other. In the doorway to apartments 108–119 on the eastern side of the street, which Halse had passed at 2.20, Pc Alfred Long had found the missing piece of apron, filthy with blood and faecal matter, thrown into the empty space. Above it on the wall was a blurry chalked message:

> **The Juwes are**
> **The men That**
> **Will not**
> **be Blamed**
> **for nothing**

From the outset, this discovery was to be a matter for discord between the responsible police forces. Long, like Halse, asserted that he had passed the doorway at 2.20, and the apron had not been there. It seems far more probable that both men overlooked the insignificant discarded rag at that point, since the doorway is at most five minutes walk from Mitre Square, which the murderer had certainly left by 1.45.

It was 2.55 when Long found the cloth. He thereupon blew his whistle for assistance, and began a quick search of the staircases and passages. He did not set off in pursuit of the miscreant who might be supposed to have dropped the cloth, for he did not believe the street harboured a murderer; he expected to find the body of another victim somewhere on the darkened landings.

When another constable arrived, Long left him to watch the building and hurried up to Commercial Street Station to hand over the cloth to the inspector there. It proved definitely to have come from the murdered woman, and as such is the only certain clue we know to have been left by Jack the Ripper.

Halse criticized the Metropolitan man for not having set off in pursuit at once. And he disagreed with him about the wording on the wall. Long had failed to observe the mis-spelling and capitalizations. His notebook recorded simply: 'The Jews are the men that will not be blamed for nothing.' Halse noted down: 'The Juwes are not the men that will be blamed for nothing.' Later officers on the scene recorded other variants. The detailed wording and lay-out given above, and accepted by most scholars today, is that filed by the Metropolitan Police and the Home Office.

Long was an A Division man from Westminster, drafted into unfamiliar territory as part of the police effort against the White-chapel murders. He seems to have been confused by the strident demands of the City Police who promptly invaded Metropolitan territory to pursue their own case. And when pressed, he tended to stick rigidly to what he had noted down close to the time of events. He persistently refused to acknowledge any recollection of the mis-spelling of Jews, though he admitted that an inspector had noted the spelling JUEWS. He was in the unfortunate situation of having instantly formulated a theory which had proved wrong (that a body was in the building) and was confronted with indignant officers whose theories had not been tested at all, but who all assumed that the Ripper had wiped his hands in the doorway, left a cheeky message, and then headed north, either up Bell Lane and Crispin Street, or along Wentworth Street and Commercial Street, making for the vicinity of Flower and Dean Street.

Long was so uncomfortable with his fast-thinking seniors that he tended to contradict himself and one of his most important pieces of evidence has been consistently reversed. He could not, he told the inquest which was pressing him, form an opinion as to whether the writing was recent. He did not, in fact, know whether it had been there or not when he passed the doorway before finding the piece of apron. It was the cloth and its bloodstains that had attracted his attention – not mere graffiti, of which there were all too many on the walls of Whitechapel. Much quarrelling and recrimination might have been avoided had this simple fact been taken in at the time (and since).

The Goulston Street doorway was soon visited by the most important policeman at hand. With the half-apron definitely proven to be the victim's, Major Smith hurried to inspect the writing (although it was in Metropolitan and not City territory) and, by his own account twenty years later, left orders for it to be guarded and photographed. By Halse's account at the inquest, however, it was erased before Smith saw it, and it was Halse who had protested that it should be preserved for the Major's inspection and preferably photographed.

Smith, meanwhile, raced away towards Spitalfields, to spend the remainder of the night 'detecting', for all the world like Inspector Clouseau after the Pink Panther.

In a small court off Dorset Street he found a little public sink with some red-tinged water running out of it. Instantly the Major assumed that the murderer had stopped here to wash his hands. Since the bloody water had not all flowed from the basin, he could have left no more that five minutes earlier. Major Smith always believed that he had been nearer to catching the Ripper at that moment than any policeman in London.

Major Smith was obviously quite wrong in imagining that the Dorset Street 'clue' had anything to do with the murder. It takes two and a half minutes to pass from Wentworth Model Dwellings up Bell Lane and Crispin Street to the multi-storey car park at the old site. Major Smith's proposal suggests that the murderer spent at least forty minutes – probably a great deal longer – hanging around the immediate vicinity. Then, just as the detectives were about to fan out and search Spitalfields, he left cover and went to a semi-public place to wash his hands. Such a man would not merely be mad, he would be caught!

Besides, Smith's suggestion makes nonsense of the position of the cloth and writing. Anyone heading from Mitre Square to Dorset Street would not cross over to the eastern side of Goulston Street. There was a Wentworth Model Dwellings doorway on the western pavement of Goulston Street, which would have been passed by the north-travelling fugitive if he wished to stop and wipe his hands or, more likely, throw the incriminating cloth quickly into the dark corner as he hurried by. It would be most unnatural to cross the road at that point, when the direct left turn would carry him straight up to Bell Lane and the narrower, darker crossing points at White's Row and Crispin Street. Major Smith presumably found a basin in which a market porter had washed his hands, or a local resident had rinsed off some stained clouts or bandages.

It must have been morning by the time Collard started a house-to-house enquiry. In Hutchinson Street (running obliquely across the recent site of the P & O Building) this turned up Mr Joseph Hyam Levy, who confirmed that he and his friends had seen a man and a woman outside Church Passage the previous night, and he had said: 'Look there! I don't like going home by myself when I see those characters about.' Levy's testimony led the police on to his friend Mr Lawende in Dalston, who provided the City Police with the only description of the murderer they ever revealed to the public.

As dawn approached, market hawkers were appearing to set up their stalls in Petticoat Lane. Sir Charles Warren, the Metropolitan Police Commissioner, arrived to survey the scenes of the latest outrage. He quickly assessed the graffiti as meaningless, and ordered that it should be erased. Superintendent M'William of the City Police apparently protested (though Long, who returned to Goulston Street at 5.00 am testified that he heard no serious protest). But Sir Charles refused even the suggestion that it be hidden behind a blanket until the photographer arrived, or its top line erased (which Halse claimed to have recommended). He had little doubt that the consequences would be a violent anti-semitic riot if street-traders saw the words, and he was probably right.

He has been severely criticized for this prompt action. So it is worth noting the considered judgement of Walter Dew who, at the time, was a Whitechapel Detective Constable, thoroughly familiar with goings-on at street level and the likelihood of any such writing emanating from the Ripper. The message's destruction 'was certainly unfortunate,' he conceded.

> But I doubt if it made a lot of difference anyway. There was no reason, so far as I can see, why this particular message should have proved more useful than many others which Jack the Ripper was supposed to have written.
>
> As I have said before, it is questionable whether these messages were the work of the murderer at all. Why should he fool around chalking things on walls when his life was imperilled by every minute he loitered?

What Dew says is sound sense. Moreover, had the message not been found at the same time as the apron, it is unlikely that it would ever have been connected with the murders. Swanson's report to the Home Office observed that the chalk was blurred, and so, we may infer, old. Its interpretation has given all commentators some difficulty: was it a boast by the murderer that he, the Jew, was avenging himself on the anti-semitic population? Or was it a cunning bid by a Gentile murderer to cast suspicion on the Jews? If so, his cunning over-reached itself, as his message was so ambiguous.

But consider what the message says, and how it might be interpreted if we never imagined that it had anything to do with the murders. It was chalked on the wall of a tenement building occupied almost entirely by Jews, so it was probably intended as a gesture of hostility to the neighbourhood; perhaps to specific occupants of Wentworth Model Dwellings.

And what do the words mean? With the dialect double negative taken into account, surely 'The Jews are the men that will not be blamed for nothing' is tantamount to saying: 'Jews are people who will not accept responsibility for anything they have done.' It sounds like the exasperated racist generalization of some Gentile who feels he has just come off badly or been cheated in a deal with a Jew. And on going back to complain, he has been blandly dismissed without the Jew accepting any responsibility. The calm spiritual certainty of a man who spends an hour or so in prayer at dawn every day provokes the Gentile to think: 'Jews are people what won't take the blame for nuffink they've done!' And he writes it up on the wall as a relief to his feelings.

Bear in mind that there is no evidence that the writing and the apron appeared at the same time and it seems that the chalked clue lost for ever as day broke over the night of the double murder was no clue at all.

6

Elizabeth Stride

In Dutfield's Yard, the police and surgeon William Blackfield were examining the body of a woman in her early forties. 'Traces of prettiness remained in her face,' according to Walter Dew, who saw the body, 'and there must have been a time when she had been exceedingly proud of her curly black hair.' Her complexion was dark. Her height of five foot five inches was enough (as they soon learned) for her to be known as 'Long Liz' among the stunted slum-dwellers. She wore a black cloth jacket to which was pinned a red rose set in a spray of maidenhair (or, more probably, asparagus) fern, a black skirt, velveteen bodice, white stockings, spring-sided boots and a crepe bonnet. A check scarf around her neck concealed the gash in her throat. It ran from left to right, and penetrated to a depth of three inches. But unlike those on Nichols and Chapman it was not a deep cut to the spine; indeed, it tailed off so markedly at the end that her right jugular vein was intact.

Bruising on her face and neck suggested that she had been pulled from behind by her scarf. It seemed likely that she had been forced to the ground before her throat was cut: the wound had bled profusely where she lay.

An early rumour alleged that her left ear had been nicked, as though the murderer started cutting it off before he was disturbed. The story was quite untrue. As Dr Bagster Phillips told the inquest, her only injury was the cut in her throat. 'The lobe of the left ear,' he reported, 'was torn as if from the removal or wearing through of an ear ring, but it was thoroughly healed.' A common enough accident; it had also happened to Frances Coles, who in 1891 was the last woman (wrongly) suspected of being a Ripper victim.

In her left hand she still grasped a tissue paper containing cachous. Some of these had fallen into the gutter at her head. Her right hand loosely held a few grapes or their stalks. These have acquired legendary status, largely because they were not saved by the police as evidence, but swept away into a drain, where two detectives employed by the *Evening News* ultimately recovered them. The only mention made of them at the inquest was Dr Phillips' testimony that despite the fruit stains on her handkerchief, he was prepared to swear that she had not swallowed grape pips or skins within hours of her death, and that he did not himself see any grapes in the yard. The police were evidently embarrassed by their careless destruction of this evidence, and hoped to minimize reference to it.

This has been blown up into the wild allegation that the grapes were an important clue incriminating a prominent physician, and that the CID and Dr Phillips united in an unholy attempt to conceal their existence by elimination and perjury. The simpler explanation that the woman was fastidious and spat out all but the flesh of her grapes is supported by Walter Dew's recollection that 'detectives searching every inch of the ground came upon a number of grape skins and stones.'

To some local policemen she was a familiar figure. She appeared eight times on drunk and disorderly charges at Thames magistrates court in the 20 months before her death, always giving her real name and not, as the press alleged the alias Anne Fitzgerald.

But a drunken vagrant's past self-identification on minor charges was not sufficient for the inquest. Someone had to identify the body. And the identification of Long Liz was to prove more laborious than that of any other Ripper victim. Not only was she herself an habitual self-dramatizing liar, but the enquiry was hopelessly entangled by the appearance of Mrs Mary Malcolm, who made Long Liz seem relatively truthful.

At 1.20 on the morning when Long Liz was killed, Mrs Malcolm was lying in her bed at 50 Eagle Street, Holborn. To her surprise she felt a strange pressure on her breast, and three kisses on her cheek. She heard the kisses quite clearly, too. At once she had a presentiment that something had happened to her sister Elizabeth Watts, and when she read about the murders in the papers she hurried over to Whitechapel to see the body.

In the mortuary at St George's-in-the-East she took Long Liz for a stranger by gaslight. But by daylight she was sure it was her sister and positively identified a black mark on her leg as having been caused by an adder bite in childhood.

Long Liz had disgraced her family, according to Mrs Malcolm. She had married a wine merchant named Watts in Bath, but he left her when he found her in bed with a porter. Her little boy was maintained in boarding school by Mr Watts' sister. Liz had lived in Poplar with a man who kept a coffee-shop. In about 1885 he had gone to sea, and died in a shipwreck. From then on Liz's progress had been downhill. She had begged from Mrs Malcolm, who gave her two shillings every Saturday when they met at the corner of Chancery Lane. Once Liz had handed a naked baby over to her. Its father was said to be a policeman.

This positive identification put the police in a quandary. Mrs Malcolm seemed to bear a physical resemblance to Long Liz and clearly knew things that other people corroborated. Liz had, for example, lived with a man named John Stride who kept a coffee-shop at 187 Poplar High Street in 1872. She always claimed that he had drowned, though in the notorious *Princess Alice* disaster off Woolwich in 1878, and not at sea.

But there were other witnesses who offered rather different accounts of Long Liz. They asserted that she still used the surname Stride, for example, whereas Mrs Malcolm stoutly denied that she had ever used the name, or that her coffee-house keeper had been so called. Mrs Malcolm denied that her sister was Swedish, yet everyone in Whitechapel who had known her believed that she was, though all agreed that her English was unmarked by a foreign accent. Nobody had heard of a little boy from Bath at boarding school. Some had heard that nine children of hers and Stride's had drowned on the *Princess Alice*. Others believed that several were being supported by the Swedish church at a school south of the river.

It was generally understood that Liz had worked on the *Princess Alice* (a Thames pleasure steamer which collided with a coaster and sank because both captains habitually disregarded river navigation rules) and had suffered from a speech impediment ever since the accident, when a man had kicked in the roof of her mouth as they both struggled up to safety.

Michael Kidney, a docker from 38 Dorset Street, had lived with her 'nearly all the time' for the last three years. He believed her to have been born in Stockholm and to have come to England as a servant. Nonetheless, he understood her to be of high-class Swedish parentage and to speak Yiddish as well as Swedish. He was sure she had no relatives in England, though he was aware of friends of her mother. John Stride had been a ship's carpenter from Sheerness before he took up the coffee-house in Chrisp Street, and Liz had indeed enjoyed a liaison with a policeman whom she used to meet in Hyde Park before she met Stride. But her children were all Stride's, and seven of them had survived the *Princess Alice* and attended school under Swedish church sponsorship. Kidney admitted that Mrs Malcolm looked very like Liz.

He was greatly distressed by the loss of his woman. He arrived, drunk, at Leman Street Police Station on Monday 1 October and announced that he would shoot himself if he were the policeman on whose beat the murder had occurred. He also insisted that he could find the murderer if the police would give him a body of detectives. The police declined his offer.

Bereavement affected his health. He was in Whitechapel Workhouse Infirmary with syphilis the following June, and again in August and October with lumbago and dyspepsia.

The authorities could not dissuade Mrs Malcolm from telling her story at the inquest which Wynne Baxter opened in Cable Street Vestry on 1 October. The coroner clearly disbelieved her, yet he was powerless to dismiss a witness who claimed under oath to make a positive identification as next of kin. Meanwhile the inquest had to be adjourned while a definite attempt was made to prove or disprove the victim's identity.

It took more than three weeks to do so. On 24 October Wynne Baxter was able to hold the final sitting. Pc Walter Stride testified that he recognized in the mortuary photographs of Long Liz a woman who had married his uncle, John Stride, a carpenter of Poplar. And Inspector Reid, head of the Whitechapel CID, said that Stride had died in the Poplar and Stepney Sick Asylum in 1884. So much for the *Princess Alice* disaster!

And, once and for all, so much for Mrs Mary Malcolm! That extraordinary lady's testimony was vehemently rebutted by Mrs Elizabeth Stokes of Tottenham, the former Mrs Watts of Bath. She limped in on the foot which had been crippled by the adder's bite and denounced her sister's story as a pack of lies. Mrs Stokes had suffered a mental breakdown when Mr Watts died, but there had been no adultery or separation, no upbringing of children by a spinster aunt. Neighbours were now accusing Mrs Stokes of living bigamously with her brickmaker husband while her first husband was still alive. She was understandably distressed. Equally understandably, Mrs Malcolm was not to be found to give the explanation of her conduct the coroner wanted.

The pastor of the Swedish church in Prince's Square confirmed that Long Liz was known to them as Elizabeth Stride, née Gustafs-dotter, born in 1843 near Gothenburg. The church had no record of any children, and was certainly not supporting any south of the river.

And Dr Bagster Phillips nailed another of Long Liz's extraordinary lies. The roof of her mouth had never been damaged in any way. Dr Phillips's other interesting evidence was that Long Liz's right hand was covered with blood. He could give no explanation for this.

In the intermediate hearings, a number of witnesses gave a picture of the woman's movements around midnight. In addition, five people who were not called before the coroner gave relevant statements to the police and the press. Put together, they summarize a busy night of professional whoring:

11.00 pm. Two labourers named Best and Gardner went into the Bricklayers' Arms on Settles Street, north of Commercial Road and almost opposite Berner Street. As they went in, Stride emerged accompanied by a short man with a dark moustache and sandy eyelashes wearing a morning suit and coat and a billycock (bowler) hat. They stood in the doorway for some time, hugging and kissing, until the labourers started chaffing them. They urged the man to come in and join them for a drink, and when he refused, they called out to Stride: 'That's Leather Apron getting round you!' After a while the man's embarrassment overcame him, and he and Stride moved away towards Commercial Road and Berner Street. Best and Gardner were quite certain he was an Englishman and no immigrant.

11.45 pm. William Marshall, a labourer of 64 Berner Street (on the west side of the street, between Fairclough Street and Boyd Street) stood outside his door between a quarter and ten to twelve, and noticed a woman he later identified as Stride talking to a man in a short black cutaway coat and a small round peaked sailor's cap. He had a respectable, clerkly look, and carried no gloves or stick. The pair were kissing and carrying on, and he heard the man say in a mild, educated voice: 'You would say anything except your prayers.' This took place about three doors away from him, after which they moved away up the road passing the club-house, and he paid no more attention. If Marshall observed the cap correctly, this could not be the man who had been in the Bricklayers' Arms. But everything else about him agrees with the description.

Midnight. Around this time, greengrocer Matthew Packer claimed to have seen Stride and her companion. His various statements to the press and police were so contradictory, and he seemed so willing to alter his testimony to meet his questioners' needs, that he was set down as unreliable and never called to the inquest. Yet he was so important that Sir Charles Warren, the Metropolitan Commissioner, interviewed him personally, and left the following notes that have not been published before (they are barely legible):

Matthew Packer
Keeps a small shop in Berner Street with a few grapes in window. Black and white.

On Sat night about 11 p.m. [this was the hour to which marginal notes show the CID wanted Packer's original testimony altered] a young man 25–30, about 5.7 with a long black coat buttoned up, soft felt hat, kind of hawker hat, rather broad shoulders, rather quick in speaking. Rough voice. I sold him ½ pound Black grapes 3d. A woman came up with him from Back Church end (the lower end of street) she was dressed in black frock and jacket, fur round bottom of jacket a black crape bonnet, she was playing with a flower like a geranium white outside & red inside. I identify the woman at the St George's Mortuary as the one I saw that night.

They passed by as though they were going up Com. Road, but instead of going up they crossed to the other side of the road to the Board School & were there for about ½ an hour till I shd say 11.30 [again, Packer originally said 12.30] talking to one another. I then put up my shutters. Before they passed over opposite to my shop they went near to the club for a few minutes apparently listening to the music.

I saw no more of them after I put up my shutters. I put the man down as a young clerk.

He had a frock coat, no gloves.

He was about ½ inch or 2 or 3 inches [illegible] but higher than she was

These notes show that the police were either working to a confused timetable, or dishonestly decided to distance the grapes as far as possible from Stride's death. They also seem determined to establish that Packer's man was the same seen by Best, Gardner and Marshall. Warren clearly pressed final questions to bring the man's coat and clerkliness in line with their testimony.

Packer was not averse to publicity. After telling Detective Sergeant

Stephen White that he saw nobody relevant on the murder night, he made a long statement to the *Evening News*'s detectives who found the grape-stalks, in which he set the time Stride came to his shop as midnight to 12.30, and described the man as heavy and middle-aged. This publicity led to his questioning by Warren.

Twice in the month Packer returned to the press with stories of seeing his suspect on Commercial Road, and hearing from a man buying rabbits that the Ripper was his cousin from America.

12.30 am. William West, a Socialist printer, left the club-house and was sure there was nobody behind the gates at that time.

12.35 am. Pc William Smith now saw Stride talking to a man where Packer had seen his customers – on the pavement opposite the International Workers' Club and a little way up the road. He described the man as being about twenty-eight years old, of medium height, wearing a dark overcoat and a hard deerstalker hat, and carrying a parcel, about eighteen inches by six inches, wrapped in newspaper.

It seems most likely that the man Smith saw was the man who bought the grapes, and, loosely wrapped, they were the newspaper 'parcel' from which he and Stride might have eaten them like fish and chips. If this was not the same man, then Stride changed her companions very quickly indeed, but wasted a lot of time with the grape-purchaser. It seems possible that the cap, billycock, hawker hat and hard deerstalker were all the same double-peaked or floppy-brimmed hat seen inattentively from different angles under in-different lighting. Packer gave the *Evening News* the additional epithet 'wideawake'. Stride seems to have spent about an hour and a half with a congenial client who bought her drinks and grapes. If the men were all different, then she probably serviced at least two and possibly three men (seen by Best, Marshall, Packer and Smith) in Dutfield's Yard that night.

12.40 am. Morris Eagle, a club member, returned to Dutfield Yard which he had left at midnight, but found nothing amiss.

12.45 am. At this point two different witnesses describe two completely different situations involving Stride. One of them must be wrong about the time, though the error need only be one of about two or three minutes. The most dramatic of them was never told to the inquest, but stayed on the Home Office files in Chief Inspector Swanson's report until discovered by Stephen Knight in the 1970s. It runs as follows:

12.45am. 30th Israel Schwartz of 22 Helen Street, |sc. Ellen Street| Back-Church Lane stated that at that hour on turning into Berner Street from Commercial Road and had got as far as the gateway where the murder was committed he saw a man stop and speak to a woman, who was standing in the gateway. The man tried to pull the woman into the street, but turned her round and he threw her down on the footway and the woman screamed three times, but not very loudly. On crossing to the opposite side of the street, he saw a second man standing lighting his pipe. The man who threw the woman down called out apparently to the man on the opposite side of the road: 'Lipski' and then Schwartz walked away, but finding that he was followed by the second man he ran as far as the railway arch, but the man did not follow so far. Schwartz cannot say whether the two men were together or known to each other. On being taken to the Mortuary, Schwartz identified the body as that of the woman he had seen and he thus describes the first man who threw the woman down:- age about 30, ht. 5ft. 5in. comp. fair, hair dark, small brown moustache, full face, broad shouldered; dress, dark jacket and trousers, black cap with peak, had nothing in his hands.

Second man age 35, ht. 5ft. 11in. comp. fresh, hair light brown, moustache brown; dress, dark overcoat, old black hard felt hat, wide brim, had a clay pipe in his hand.

Notes in Chief Inspector Swanson's hand show that the police thought Schwartz's statement was reliable, though they doubted whether the man who attacked Stride on the pavement was her murderer.

The *Evening News* had also seen and interviewed Schwartz, and revealed that he was Hungarian and spoke almost no English. Their reporter understood that the tall man with the pipe came out from a public house to witness the scene. Abberline, too, had observed that Schwartz spoke no English, and one wonders whether the difficulty of questioning this recent immigrant led to his description of Stride's assailant being so close to that of the variously described man of medium height in a black coat and indeterminate headgear who seems to have spent so long with the woman.

This was a dramatic scene. Yet at exactly the same time, James

Brown told the inquest, he was going home to his supper at 35 Fairclough Street. As he passed the Board School in Fairclough Street (between Berner Street and Christian Street) he saw Stride with her back against the wall talking to a stoutish man, about five feet seven inches tall in a long coat which almost reached his heels. The street was dark, and he did not even see whether the man had a hat on, let alone what his face was like. But he had his arm up against the wall, and Stride was saying to him:'No, not tonight. Some other night.'

About fifteen minutes later, before he had finished his supper, Brown heard the cries of 'Murder!' as the club members rushed out to Commercial Road in search of the police.

12.49 am. (Or, in his words, about a quarter of an hour before the body was found) Joseph Lave passed through the courtyard, finding it so dark that he had to grope his way along the club-house wall. There was definitely no body there.

One last witness was not called before the inquest. As Diem-schütz's pony turned into Berner Street it was heard by Mrs Mortimer from no 36, two doors above the club. She had come out into the street between 12.30 and 1.00 to listen to the community singing and saw nothing unusual for the twenty minutes or more she stood there. As she turned to go back into her house she saw a man of about thirty, dressed in black and carrying a small shiny black bag, walk quickly down the street from the Commercial Road direction, glancing up at the club-house as he passed, and proceeding towards Ellen Street. He was, however, shown to be an ordinary member of the club going about his legitimate business. Mrs Mortimer really only testified to the murderer's stealth. As she told the *Morning Post*: 'There was certainly no noise made, and I did not observe any one enter the gates.'

What are we to make of all this testimony? First of all, it is astounding that nearly all commentators hitherto have assumed that Stride spent the midnight hours with one man, probably the Ripper. Even allowing for the possibility that one hat acquired three or four different descriptions, it is obvious that the man in the short cutaway coat could not possibly be Brown's man in an overcoat that almost reached his heels!

But there are many common features between the 'different' men of medium height observed. A short black coat, a morning suit and coat and a cutaway coat all sound like the same garment. The clerkly manner or soft voice recurs, as do the fresh complexion and moustache.

Since Stride was twice seen hugging and kissing the man she seems to have been with from 11.00 pm to about 12.40, and once overheard listening to suggestive badinage, there can be no doubt that she was actively soliciting. And since Marshall and Packer both saw her moving towards or looking at Dutfield's Yard, it is a reasonable surmise that she serviced him there.

Unless, of course, the same man was her assailant as observed by Schwartz. Again the 'cap' is the dubious point of identification. The black coat, empty hands, fair complexion and dark moustache are all decidely compatible with the sandy-eyelashed man described by Gardner and Best. But Schwartz's scanty English made him vulnerable to leading questions, and Warren's note of Packer's interrogation shows that the police were actively looking for common details in the witnesses' descriptions.

Did Long Liz, then, quarrel with her client after the amicable evening? Did a villain or bully persuade her of his good intentions for a long hour and forty minutes? Or was he definitely different from the 'clerkly' and gently-spoken man or men of similar appearance?

And since Long Liz was engaged in a working night, why did Brown overhear her turning away a trick, and what happened to her takings? Surely this is explained by the assault. The man who threw her onto the street pavement (not, be it noted, the darkened yard) was not killing her, but robbing her. It would be most extraordinary for the Ripper himself to start an attack in the open, in the presence of two witnesses, and to have the temerity to shout an insult at them. It would be surprising if Stride screamed *softly* if she had any inkling that her attacker was the dreaded murderer. But one of the regular robbers from the local gangs would be a different matter. Liz would have been familiar with this occupational hazard. Making the minimum of fuss could save her a lethal beating up. Her quiet calls for help were presumably directed to the nearby Schwartz and the tall man with a clay pipe. The Dutfield's Yard cottagers and high-minded Socialist Jews might ignore prostitutes on their territory, but if she shouted loudly for help, they might arrive too late to be of real help, and could subject her to abuse. And the unpleasant experience could well have decided her to go somewhere else without looking for any more trade. Brown's observations that the man in Fairclough Street had his hand up against the wall suggests that he was hindering her from hurrying on as she would have liked. And she had gone in the opposite direction from her way home to Spitalfields (south-east rather than north-west).

Interestingly, she was talking to the overcoated man almost opposite the entrance to 'Tiger Bay'. Surely this must have been where her assailant came from? It seems likely that she was following him, hoping, presumably, to identify him or his house for a time when she could come back with Michael Kidney and other male friends to duff him up. But someone – possibly the man in the long coat, probably Jack the Ripper, certainly a murderer – persuaded her to turn one more trick in the dark yard.

Though the police believed Schwartz's testimony, there was good reason why Sir Charles Warren, at least, might have preferred his story to remain undisclosed. The anti-semitic tension generated by the earlier murders was still a real threat to law and order and it was being promoted by a powerful source. In the most gentlemanly manner, *The Times* was keeping Jewish association with the crime before its readers' attention. It went to the trouble to report that the Socialists at the inquest all made affirmations instead of taking the oath. Readers could infer that they refused the oath as Jews (even if godless ones willing to demonstrate politically and sell jewellery on Saturdays). It was not a necessary or universal practice to report that Jewish witnesses affirmed. No other paper did so, and *The Times* itself omitted the information when describing Diemschütz's trial the following March. But at the time of the Stride inquest the paper was conducting a nasty little campaign to revive a particularly unpleasant form of the 'legend of blood' – the slander that Jews kill Christians for religious reasons.

On 2 October it published a suggestion from Vienna that a superstitious reading of the Talmud required Jews who defiled themselves by fornicating with Christian women to atone by killing and mutilating their partners after the manner of the Whitechapel murderer. This, it was alleged, had emerged in the repeated trials of a Jew named Ritter and his wife for the murder of their maid, Frances Maich.

Every other newspaper which printed this story added the alternative that Gentile Galician thieves also mutilated women for their sexual parts to make into 'corpse candles', which were supposed to ensure the continued sleep of those who were passed by their light. Most omitted the anti-semitic version altogether. *The Times* was unabashed, and continued to print occasional embroideries of the story from Vienna. On 16 October an Austrian MP, Dr Josef Bloch, wrote categorically that the Ritters were transparently innocent, although prejudiced local juries had convicted them three times, compelling the High Court to step in and quash the convictions. There was no evidence that Ritter had ever been intimate with Maich, and abundant evidence that she had a lover who was a Gentile thief.

Shamelessly, *The Times* opposed Dr Bloch's contribution with an unsupported assertion from an unnamed correspondent in Vienna who claimed that the juries had been right, and the trials proved the existence of the superstition among Jews. It was not until 25 October, the day after the inquest ended, that a sulky editorial note closed any further correspondence and confessed that an undefined superstition seemed to be held by Galician thieves, and not Jews.

The *Jewish Chronicle* protested without avail. On 5 October, *The Times*'s Vienna telegram seemed to it 'as dangerous a piece of composition as could be imagined. Of course it is not correct.' And on 12 October it went further:

> There are not wanting signs of a deliberate attempt to connect the Jews with the Whitechapel murders . . . . But if [the Goulston Street] inscription . . . . was the work of the murderer, it was written to throw the public off the scent, not to put them on. The peculiar horror entertained by Jews of any mutilation of the human body after death is either unknown to, or concealed by, the theorists. To us it seems wrong for respectable newspapers to lend their columns to such suggestions, which are the work of ignorance, if not of malice.

Sir Charles Warren agreed. At this time he issued a statement that 'Juwes' was not Yiddish for Jews, nor had it been possible to find any language in which it meant 'Jews'. He probably preferred not to have additional tension supplied by the introduction of Schwartz as a Jewish witness to an unprovoked assault who had been afraid to take any action, and ran away with the taunt 'Lipski' ringing in his ears. Feelings were running high and irrational in Whitechapel.

Mr Baxter's summing-up put the right question to the jury. Was this really one of the Whitechapel murders? There was no characteristic abdominal slashing. But in other respects, the coroner quickly pointed out, the murder seemed to be part of the sequence. The victim was a middle-aged prostitute, killed motivelessly at dead of night in a gateway which might be used for quick coupling. The throat was cut from left to right so that the woman's vocal cords were severed before she could cry for help. And the murderer made a rapid and silent escape.

It is clear that Mr Baxter very much wanted this to be a Ripper murder. He was starting to feel a rather vain proprietorship over the Whitechapel murders, as he showed when he dismissed the 'unskilful injuries' in Mitre Square as the probable work of an imitator. This shows what enormous weight he placed on Dr Phillips' evidence in the Chapman case. But would Phillips have postulated expert surgery carried out over half an hour had he known that Lawende, Harvey and Watkins were to prove circumstantially but conclusively that the Mitre Square murderer must have completed his work in very little more than five minutes?

There was, in fact, more to cast doubt on Stride as a Ripper victim than Mr Baxter conceded. Her bloodsplashed right hand, for example, suggested that this murderer's expertise had not prevented the woman from making a last attempt to defend herself or try to stanch her bleeding. Baxter claimed that all the victims were too poor to make robbery a plausible motive (though Emma Smith had undoubtedly been robbed of her night's paltry takings). Elizabeth Stride was better looking than any of her predecessors. Dew (fifteen years or so younger than her at the time) saw 'traces of prettiness' even in her bloodless cadaver, and the evidence before the inquest strongly suggested that at least one client had gone with her that night. Yet her takings were not on her person.

Remembering that Mr Baxter assumed Smith and Tabram to be part of the sequence, he should also have been confronted with suspicious topography. Osborn Street, George Yard and Hanbury Street were all in the immediate neighbourhood of Brick Lane. Indeed *The Times*, with some exaggeration, placed the first four murders (including Smith's and Tabram's) at no more distance than three hundred yards away from each other. Buck's Row was actually much more out of the way, but accessible in a very direct line along Wentworth Street and Old Montague Street. But Berner Street was farther from Brick Lane than Buck's Row, and really in a different part of Whitechapel altogether. Two twentieth-century theorists who both believed the Ripper to be a woman agreed, on different grounds, that Stride was not a Ripper victim.

Yet there is no doubt that, after initial hesitation, the official police view (that of those who directly headed the enquiry from Scotland Yard) was that Elizabeth Stride had been killed by the same hand that struck Polly Nichols, Annie Chapman, Catherine Eddowes and Marie Jeanette Kelly. Why did they reach this firm conclusion, while confidently discounting Smith, Tabram and several later murder victims? Perhaps because Schwartz's evidence sufficiently explained the theft of her night's takings. But mainly, as Chief Inspector Swanson's report would show, because they already had their own ideas about the topography of the murders.

7

Catherine Eddowes

The body in Mitre Square gave the police less trouble than the one in Berner Street. The mustard tin contained two pawn tickets issued by Mr Jones of Church Street, Spitalfields, to Emily Birrell and Anne Kelly against a man's shirt and a pair of boots.

These would lead to the victim's identification after the City Police discovered that although she was certainly the woman who had been in the cells at Bishopsgate Police Station until 1.00 am, calling herself Mary Anne Kelly of 6 Fashion Street, she was not known by that name at that address. On Tuesday unemployed market-porter John Kelly presented himself to the police, fearing rightly that the owner of those particular pledges must be his common-law wife Catherine Kelly, alias Conway, alias Eddowes.

She was forty three years old, and came from the Midlands. One of her arms was tattooed TC for Thomas Conway, her first husband. He had been a soldier and she had borne him two sons and a daughter. Neither Kelly nor the daughter knew whether, as she claimed, an actual ceremony of matrimony had been performed. And when Conway presented himself to the authorities, ten days after she was buried and the inquest had closed, no one was interested any more. They had decided to use her maiden name of Eddowes, by which she has been known ever since.

All her acquaintances knew that she and Conway had separated eight years earlier and she rarely if ever saw him. It was believed that he was a teetotaller and had left her because of her drinking. He drew his army pension under the pseudonym Quinn, specifically to avoid her contacting him. The couple's daughter lived in Southwark, married to a gun-maker. The sons' addresses had been deliberately withheld from their mother. The Conway family knew her essentially as a hopelessly feckless and persistent scrounger.

Her more immediate acquaintances described a brighter side. She was cheerful and lively, often singing. She and Kelly rarely quarrelled, except when she had been drinking. Her sister Mrs Gold of Thrawl Street and the deputy of 55 Flower and Dean Street both denied knowing that she ever prostituted herself. Kelly was evasive on the subject.

But he, too, was patently honest, though desperately poor, and he gave a picture of their last days together that was at once pathetic and attractive in their mutual need and sympathy.

They had been hop-picking in Kent with Emily Birrell for several weeks. Catherine's head and arms had acquired a healthy suntan on this working holiday. Mrs Birrell had left them on their way back to London the previous week, and asked them to pawn her man's shirt for her. On their return they spent Thursday at 55 Flower and Dean Street. On Friday they were broke, and stayed in Shoe Lane Casual Ward. On Saturday they pawned the boots and shirt, bought a late breakfast together, and then split the remaining sixpence. Catherine gave fourpence to Kelly to get himself a bed in Flower and Dean Street again, and took the remaining twopence to try her luck at Mile End Casual Ward. This was a business-like division of their resources. If Kelly, an able-bodied man, went to a Casual Ward, he would have to pay for his accommodation with a morning of useless labour. And Catherine had to walk to Mile End to establish her *bona fides* as a 'traveller', entitled to casual overnight accommodation in 'the Spike' and not required to enter the workhouse as a resident.

Of course she never reached Mile End. Somewhere she found enough money to fuel her imitation of a fire engine, and thereafter her movements were known, apart from the gap between 1.00 am and 1.35, and the last ten minutes of her life.

Her body was taken to the City Mortuary in Golden Lane. The official police list of her clothes and property attached to the coroner's papers is interesting, offering more detail and some variants from the familiar inventory published in the press. The often-alleged spectacles and chrysanthemum pattern on the chintz dress are not mentioned by the police. But there are copious petticoats and loose pockets to make up for them.

Black straw bonnet trimmed with green & black Velvet and black beads, black strings. The bonnet was loosely tied, and had partially fallen from the back of her head, no blood on front, but the back was lying in a pool of blood which had run from the neck.

Black Cloth Jacket, imitation fur edging round collar, fur round sleeves, no blood on front outside, large quantity of Blood inside & outside back, outside back very dirty with Blood & dirt. 2 outside pockets, trimmed black silk braid and imitation fur.

Chintz Skirt, 3 flounces, brown button on waistband. Jagged cut 6 ½ inches long from waistband, left side of front. Edges slightly Bloodstained, also Blood on bottom, back & front of skirt.

Brown Linsey Dress Bodice, black velvet collar, brown metal buttons down front, blood inside & outside back of neck and shoulders, clean cut bottom of left side, 5 inches long from right to left.

Grey Stuff Petticoat, white waistband, cut 1 ½ inch long, thereon in front. Edges bloodstained. Blood stains on front at bottom of Petticoat.

Very Old Green Alpaca Skirt. Jagged cut 10 ½ inches long in front of waistband, downward, blood-stained inside, front under the cut.

Very Old ragged Blue Skirt, red flounces, light twill lining, jagged cut 10 ½ inches long, through waistband, downward, blood-stained, inside & outside back and front.

White Calico Chemise, very much blood-stained all over, apparently torn thus ⌐Z_ in middle of front.

Man's White Vest, button to match down front, 2 outside pockets, torn at back, very much Blood-stained at back, Blood and other Stains on front.

No Drawers or Stays.

Pair of Mens lace up Boots, mohair laces. right boot has been repaired with red thread. 6 Blood marks on right boot.

1 piece of red gauze Silk, various cuts thereon found on neck.

1 large White Handkerchief, blood-stained.

2 Unbleached Calico Pockets, tape strings, cut through, also top left hand corners cut off one.

1 Blue Stripe Bedticking Pocket, waistband and strings cut through (all 3 Pockets), Blood-stained.

1 White Cotton Pocket Handkerchief, red and white birds eye border.

1 pr. Brown ribbed stockings, feet mended with white.

12 pieces of white Rag, some slightly bloodstained.

1 piece of White Coarse Linen.
1 piece of Blue & White Shirting (3 cornered).
2 Small Blue Bed ticking Bags.
1 Tin Box containing Tea.
1 do   do   do   Sugar.
1 Piece of Flannel & 6 pieces of Soap.
1 Small Tooth Comb.
1 White Handle Table Knife & 1 Metal Tea Spoon.
1 Red Leather Cigarette Case, white metal fittings.
1 Tin MatchBox, empty.
1 piece of Red Flannel containing Pins & Needles.
1 Ball of Hemp
1 piece of old White Apron.

Dr Frederick Gordon Brown carried out the post mortem, and his full report is possibly the most interesting of all the documents now brought to light in the inquest papers. It is the most detailed and accurate medical account we have of the Ripper's work. (Again, I add punctuation to the coroner's notes.)

When the body arrived at Golden Lane some of the blood was dispersed through the removal of the body to the mortuary. The clothes were taken off carefully from the body. A piece of the deceased's ear dropped from the clothing.

I made a post mortem examination at half past two on Sunday afternoon. Rigor mortis was well marked; body not quite cold. Green discoloration over the abdomen.

After washing the left hand carefully, a bruise the size of a sixpence, recent and red, was discovered on the back of the left hand between the thumb and first finger. A few small bruises on right shin of older date. The hands and arms were bronzed. No bruises on the scalp, the back of the body or the elbows.

The face was very much mutilated. There was a cut about a quarter of an inch through the lower left eyelid, dividing the structures completely through. The upper eyelid on that side, there was a scratch through the skin on the left upper eyelid, near to the angle of the nose. The right eyelid was cut through to about half an inch.

There was a deep cut over the bridge of the nose, extending from the left border of the nasal bone down near to the angle of the jaw on the right side of the cheek. This cut went into the bone and divided all the structures of the cheek except the mucous membrane of the mouth.

The tip of the nose was quite detached from the nose by an oblique cut from the bottom of the nasal bone to where the wings of the nose join on to the face. A cut from this divided the upper lip and extended through the substance of the gum over the right upper lateral incisor tooth. About half an inch from the top of the nose was another oblique cut. There was a cut on the right angle of the mouth as if the cut of a point of a knife. The cut extended an inch and a half, parallel with lower lip.

There was on each side of the cheek a cut which peeled up the skin, forming a triangular flap about an inch and a half.

On the left cheek there were two abrasions of the epithelium under the left ear.

The throat was cut across to the extent of about six or seven inches. A superficial cut commenced about an inch below (and about two and a half inches below and behind the left ear) and extended across the throat to about three inches below the lobe of the right ear. The big muscle across the throat was divided through on the left side. The large vessels on the left side of the throat were severed. The larynx was severed, and below the vocal cord all the deep structures were severed to the bone, the knife marking intervertebral cartilages. The sheath of the vessels on the right side was just opened. The carotid artery had a fine hole opening. The internal jugular vein was opened an inch and a half – not divided. The blood vessels contained clot. All these injuries were performed by a sharp instrument like a knife, and pointed.

The cause of death was haemorrhage from the left common carotid artery. The death was immediate and the mutilations were inflicted after death.

We examined the abdomen. The front walls were open from the breast bone to the pubes. The cut commenced opposite the enciform cartilage. The incision went upwards, not penetrating the skin that was over the sternum. It then divided the enciform cartilage. The knife must have cut obliquely at the expense of the front surface of that cartilage.

Behind this, the liver was stabbed as if by the point of a sharp instrument. Below this was another incision into the liver of about two and a half inches, and below this the left lobe of the liver was slit through by a vertical cut. Two cuts were shewn by a jagging of the skin on the left side.

The abdominal walls were divided in the middle line to within a quarter of an inch of the navel. The cut then took a horizontal course for two inches and a half, and made a parallel incision to the former incision, leaving the navel on a tongue of skin. Attached to the navel was two and a half inches of the lower part of the rectus muscle on the left side of the abdomen. The incision then took an oblique direction to the right, and was shelving. The incision went down the right side of the vagina and rectum for half an inch behind the rectum.

There was a stab of about an inch on the left groin. This was done by a pointed instrument. Below this was a cut of three inches going through the peritoneum [*sic*, sc. perineum] about the same extent.

An inch below the crease of the thigh was a cut extending from the anterior spine of the ilium obliquely down the inner side of the left thigh and separating the left labium, forming a flap of skin up to the groin. The left rectus muscle was not detached.

There was a flap of skin formed from the right thigh, attaching the right labium, and extending up to the spine of the ilium. The muscles on the right side inserted into the frontal ligaments were cut through.

The skin was retracted through the whole of the cut in the abdomen, but the vessels were not clotted. Nor had there been any appreciable bleeding from the vessels. I draw the conclusion that the cut was made after death, and there would not be much blood on the murderer. The cut was made by someone on the right side of the body, kneeling below the middle of the body.

I removed the content of the stomach and placed it in a jar for further examination. There seemed very little in it in the way of food or fluid, but from the cut end partly digested farinaceous food escaped.

The intestines had been detached to a large extent from the mesentery. About two feet of the colon was cut away. The sygmoid flexure was invaginated into the rectum very tightly.

Right kidney pale, bloodless, with slight congestion of the base of the pyramids.

There was a cut from the upper part of the slit on the under surface of the liver to the left side, and another cut at right angles to this, which were about an inch and a half deep and two and a half inches long. Liver itself was healthy.

The gall bladder contained bile. The pancreas was cut, but not through, on the left side of the spinal column. Three and a half inches of the lower border of the spleen by half an inch was attached only to the peritoneum.

The peritoneal lining was cut through on the left side and the left kidney carefully taken out and removed. The left renal artery was cut through. I should say that someone who knew the position of the kidney must have done it.

The lining membrane over the uterus was cut through. The womb was cut through horizontally, leaving a stump of three quarters of an inch. The rest of the womb had been taken away with some of the ligaments. The vagina and cervix of the womb was uninjured.

The bladder was healthy and uninjured, and contained three or four ounces of water. There was a tongue-like cut through the anterior wall of the abdominal aorta. The other organs were healthy.

There were no indications of connexion.

I believe the wound in the throat was first inflicted. I believe she must have been lying on the ground.

The wounds on the face and abdomen prove that they were inflicted by a sharp pointed knife, and that in the abdomen by one six inches long.

I believe the perpetrator of the act must have had considerable knowledge of the position of the organs in the abdominal cavity and the way of removing them. The parts removed would be of no use for any professional purpose. It required a great deal of knowledge to have removed the kidney and to know where it was placed. Such a knowledge might be possessed by one in the habit of cutting up animals.

I think the perpetrator of this act had sufficient time, or he would not have nicked the lower eyelids. It would take at least five minutes.

I cannot assign any reason for the parts being taken away. I feel sure there was no struggle. I believe it was the act of one person.

The throat had been instantly severed so that no noise could have been emitted. I should not expect much blood to have been found on the person who had inflicted these wounds. The wounds could not have been self-inflicted.

My attention was called to the apron. It was the corner of the apron, with a string attached. The blood spots were of recent origin. I have seen the portion of an apron produced by Dr Phillips and stated to have been found in Goulston Street. It is impossible to say it is human blood. I fitted the piece of apron which had a new piece of material on it which had evidently been sewn on to the piece I have, the seams of the borders of the two actually corresponding. Some blood and, apparently, faecal matter was found on the portion found in Goulston Street. I believe the wounds on the face to have been done to disfigure the corpse.

This detailed and fascinating account tells us a lot about the Ripper, and about the men who investigated him. His attack on Catherine Eddowes subdivides into five different kinds of assaults:

(i)   The rapid assassination by throat-cutting.
(ii) The 'ripping', or opening up of the abdomen and disembowelling (moving intestines out of his way over the shoulder).
(iii) Random fierce hacking, slashing and stabbing, especially in and around the groin and upper thighs, but also inside the abdomen (the liver), and across the face (nose and right cheek).
(iv) Removal of internal organs (kidney and uterus). It is not apparent whether the two-foot section of colon placed between the arm and the body was also deliberately cut out for its own sake, or furiously removed during the disembowelling as a particularly stout impediment to the abdominal cavity. Certainly there is fury implicit in the forceful doubling back into the rectum of the sygmoid flexure, which connects colon and rectum.
(v)   The precise marking of the eyelids and cheeks.

It is impossible to tell the order of the posthumous mutilations, but we can see how Baxter justified his belief that the Mitre Square murderer was an unpractised incompetent compared with Annie

Chapman's assailant. Eddowes' womb was incompletely removed; the cervix remained in place. And the clumsy cutting around the rectum both slit it and (to judge from the intestines and the apron) soiled the murderer's hands with her faeces.

Gordon Brown, on the other hand, was unduly impressed by the current opinion that any missing organs had been deliberately sought, and while he obviously describes a lot of uncontrolled and uninformed grubbing and hacking about inside the poor woman's body, he takes it that the kidney was found and removed by someone who knew what he wanted rather than someone who did not know what he had come across.

But Brown is quite correctly impressed by the extraordinary and obsessional marking of the cheeks and eyelids. The neat Vs pointing up to the eyes, and the delicate nicks through the eyelids point to a murderer who was precisely and quasi-artistically putting his personal mark on his victim's face, mastering her human personality in a way quite different from the frenzy with which he tore at her bowels and sex organs. This precise mutilation, carried out in a dim light and with very little time to spare is peculiarly striking. The coroner proposed a rational but implausible motive: that the face was mutilated to impede Eddowes' identification.

Two other doctors who had examined the body thought the wounds were utterly inexpert. Dr Sequeira saw no especial skill in the injuries, and he did not think that the stolen organs had been deliberately sought. Dr Sedgwick Saunders, the City Public Analyst, who (like Dr Phillips) attended Dr Brown's autopsy, agreed with Sequeira. These two did not even go so far as to suggest a butcher or veterinary student. What they saw suggested to them a completely unskilled ghoul cutting and removing whatever he came across that appealed to him in the abdomen. Moreover, at the inquest both asserted that in this they agreed with Dr Brown. It seems that Brown's willingness to attribute limited expertise to the Ripper was little more than professional courtesy to the hapless Dr Phillips, who had nailed his colours to the mast of the murderer's skill in mutilating Annie Chapman.

If the doctors were in disarray, the City Police force was superbly marshalled. Whereas the Met were content to leave one or two Inspectors to attend inquests on behalf of the Commissioner, the City force sent in Mr Crawford, the City Solicitor, to represent them when Mr Langham the coroner opened the inquest at the mortuary.

He began his hearing two days later than Baxter opened that on Stride, so that the identification by next of kin was ready as well as the report of the autopsy. The police produced a surveyor called Frederick Foster to testify that Goulston Street lay in a direct line between Mitre Square and Flower and Dean Street. Without being offensive they could hardly have stated more positively that the murderer was a resident of Spitalfields, and the responsibility of the Met's H Division.

Foster also helped the police as far as he could in their mind-boggling claim that the murderer took forty-five minutes or more to get from Mitre Square to Goulston Street. 'It would take within a quarter of an hour to get there,' he asserted; a truthful but misleading way to describe four minutes slow walk!

Mr Crawford carefully led Foster through an account of the route, and it may be significant that of the two possible routes he mentioned, only the longer one leading out from Church Passage was described. The City Police had reason to suspect that the murderer actually left through St James's Place, and may have wished to keep this information from the public.

At the second hearing Dr Brown was recalled to crush a rumour. With the coroner's permission, Mr Crawford examined him:

Q: The theory has been put forward that it is possible for the deceased to have been taken to Mitre Square after her murder. What is your opinion about that?

A: I think there is no doubt on the point. The blood at the left side of the deceased was clotted and must have flowed from her at the time of the injury to her throat. I do not believe the deceased was moved in the slightest way after her throat was cut.

Q: You have no doubt that the murder was committed at that spot?

A: I feel quite sure it was.

After that positive evidence, it is astonishing that the suggestion that the body was transported to the square should ever again have been made.

Constables Watkins and Harvey described their beats, and timed their visits to the square by reference to Aldgate Post Office clock. Probably Eddowes already lay there dead when Harvey walked the length of Church Passage, but he did not notice her in the darkest corner of the square. Her assailant must already have left – and since Watkins saw no one as he came down Mitre Street, and Harvey saw no one as he came down Duke Street, he must have left by St James's Place and King Street.

Inspector Collard's testimony is very important. The press wrongly ascribed it to M'William, Head of the City CID (who did not testify). And no one has realized that it completely eliminates the idea that Lawende's rough description of the man outside Church Passage could have been in police hands before the night was out.

Collard's first direction to his men was to search the streets. This turned up nothing useful. M'William, when he arrived, then sent detectives to enquire in lodging-houses, which again produced no important information. Meanwhile (as we know from Halse's testimony) Collard was in the mortuary supervising the preliminary examination of the body. The house-to-house enquiry in the neighbourhood which followed this cannot have been undertaken until the following morning. It turned up Levy who lived nearby, and he directed the police on to Lawende, a mile away in Dalston.

Lawende's own description of the man with Eddowes was vaguer than has been assumed. He asserted that he would not know the man again, and described little more than his clothes. Nonetheless, the City Police found it precise enough for Mr Langham to stop him from giving details of the face.

The evidence on the writing in Goulston Street was heard, and Long, the Metropolitan constable, seemed the most slow-witted of the witnesses. Mr Langham closed the proceedings without having attracted Mr Baxter's notoriety for long-windedness. And the City could congratulate itself on having appeared efficient.

The return of City Commissioner Sir James Fraser from two months' leave added to the City's public popularity. For he was able to obtain from the Lord Mayor the offer of a £500 reward for information – an action that was being urged on the Met and firmly refused by the Home Office.

The Whitechapel Vigilance Committee demanding this reward was starting to attract attention to itself, and the name of its chairman, Mr George Lusk of Alderney Road, Mile End, became familiar to the public. This was unfortunate for Mr Lusk. When the first two 'Ripper' letters were published, immediately after the double event (of which the second letter seemed to show instant knowledge), he became one of the recipients of the spate of imitative letters. He came to fear that he and his son were being watched by a sinister man with a beard, and had his house put under police guard. And on 16 October he received the notorious parcel containing half a kidney and the letter 'From hell' signed 'Catch me when you Can'.

Sensibly enough, Lusk assumed it was a hoax, and the kidney probably a dog's. Other members of the Vigilance Committee urged that it be examined by a doctor. The initial medical observation was that it was human and had been preserved in spirits of wine. It was taken on to Dr Robert Openshaw, curator of the London Hospital Museum, and from him to Leman Street Police Station, whence it was passed by the Met to the City Police, who sent it to various doctors. On 19 October the press carried some curious information purporting to derive from Dr Openshaw. He was quoted as believing it to be 'a ginny kidney . . . the organ of a woman of about forty-five years of age, and . . . taken from the body within the last three weeks.' The following day Dr Openshaw corrected this elaboration, telling the press his microscopical examination proved it to be the anterior part of a human kidney. It had been preserved, in his opinion, in spirit for ten days. The curator further added that all other statements which had been made were entirely erroneous.

The most enthusiastic believer in the kidney was Major Smith. In his memoirs, written twenty two years after the event, Smith gave this account of it.

> **It was posted to the office of the Central News, together with a short note of a rather jocular character unfit for publication. Both kidney and note the manager at once forwarded to me.**

This, of course, was utter garble. Smith then gave the substance of the police surgeon's report as follows:

> **The renal artery is about three inches long. Two inches remained in the corpse, one inch was attached to the kidney. The kidney left in the corpse was in an advanced state of Bright's Disease; the kidney sent me was in an exactly similar state. But what was of far more importance, Mr Sutton, one of the senior surgeons of the London Hospital . . . and . . . one of the greatest authorities living on the kidney and its diseases, said he would pledge his reputation that the kidney submitted to them had been put in spirits within a few hours of its removal from the body, thus effectually disposing of all hoaxes in connection with it. The body of anyone done to**

death by violence is not taken direct to the dissecting room, but must await an inquest, never held before the following day at soonest.

And with that Major Smith crows exultantly over all the newspapers which had maintained that the clue was a hoax.

Making every allowance for the old gentleman's shaky memory, and respecting the fact that he repeats none of the canards attributed to Openshaw, it must still be asserted that his claim is worse than inconclusive. He is the only witness to the alleged Bright's Disease.

Moreover, as Richard Whittington-Egan points out, the respective lengths of renal artery on the kidney and in the body are both exactly what would be expected if the kidney were simply removed, without any calculated attempt to retain or reject the artery.

But the Major's last and decisive 'proof' is a bare-faced reversal of the conclusion reached by the medical report he actually received. Chief Inspector Swanson summarized it at the time in the report he sent to the Home Office (which Stephen Knight found in their files):

The kidney was at once handed over to the City Police, and the result of the combined medical opinion they have taken is that it is the kidney of a human adult, not charged with fluid as it would have been in the case of a body handed over for purposes of dissection to an hospital, but rather as it would be in a case where it was taken from the body not so destined. In other words *similar kidneys might and could be obtained from any dead person upon whom a post mortem had been made for any cause, by students or dissecting room porter.*

[My italics]

Dr Sedgwick Saunders had been even more devastating in his dismissal of the organ. It was a pity, he told the *Evening News*, that

some people have not the courage to say they don't know. You may take it that there is no difference whatever between the male and female kidney. . . . You may take it that the right kidney of the woman Eddowes was perfectly normal in its structure and healthy, and by parity of reasoning you would not get much disease in the left. The liver was healthy and gave no indication that the woman drank. Taking the discovery of half a kidney and supposing it to be human, my opinion is that it was a student's antic. It is quite possible for any student to obtain a kidney for this purpose.

To summarize the evidence of the kidney: at a time when letters were pouring in to the authorities at a rate of 1,000 a month, many of them hoaxes, over a hundred of them purporting to be from the murderer, part of a human left kidney was sent with one such. The letter showed no special knowledge of any of the murders to stamp it as genuine. Its handwriting, style and signature differed from the two which, on inadequate evidence, have been claimed as genuine. It arrived a good fortnight after it was common knowledge that Eddowes' left kidney was missing – but when it was *not* equally well known that her uterus had been taken too. Its condition was such that it could easily have been obtained by any medical student or from a hospital porter. The competent medical authorities and the Metropolitan Police did not believe it to have come from Eddowes, and there is no evidence that anyone but Major Smith ever did. Please may we forget about the kidney?

The Metropolitan Police, unlike the City force, made the mistake of ignoring proper public relations, and they paid for it in press attacks. The *Star* drew a comparison. 'The City police,' it observed, 'from the Major downwards, try to oblige the representatives of the press rather than to frustrate them in their enquiries, like Sir Charles Warren's men.' The *Daily Telegraph* complained as early as September:

> It is clear that the Detective Department at Scotland Yard is in an utterly hopeless and worthless condition; that were there a capable Director of Criminal Investigation, the scandalous exhibition of stupidity and ineptitude revealed at the East End inquests, and the immunity enjoyed by criminals, murder after murder, would not have angered and disgusted public feeling as it has undoubtedly done.

Within a week, the *Pall Mall Gazette* had taken this broad hint. W. T. Stead, its brilliant editor, combined evangelical prurience and radical fervour with a gift for imaginative serial features in a very dignified layout. The Ripper murders caught his eye, and he was not unhappy to tell the world that the head of the CID was enjoying leave at his leisure while his men failed to catch the criminal.

> The chief official who is responsible for the detection of the

murderer is as invisible to Londoners as the murderer himself. You may seek Dr. Anderson in Scotland Yard, you may look for him in Whitehall Place, but you will not find him. Dr. Anderson, with all the arduous duties of his office still to learn, is preparing himself for his apprenticeship by taking a pleasant holiday in Switzerland.

It was perfectly true. Dr Robert Anderson, a Home Office civil servant, had been newly appointed Assistant Commissioner in charge of the CID, and took up his post the day after Polly Nichols was found. He spent a week organizing his office and then left for the continent on his doctor's orders, only to learn that Annie Chapman had died the night he left. As the pressure on the force increased, he moved from Switzerland to Paris so as to be closer at hand if needed, but he was still abroad on the night of the double murder. He came back in response to an urgent summons the following day.

As we shall see, Anderson was undoubtedly under great stress at that time, and his doctor's recommendation of two months complete rest away from it all was very wise. But it certainly looked bad.

Luckily for Anderson, there was still greater hostility to his chief, Sir Charles Warren. The Vigilance Committee was furious that the Met and the Home Office stubbornly refused to post a reward. They blamed the Commissioner, and mass meetings in Victoria Park, Hackney and Mile End Waste condemned Warren and the Home Secretary, demanded their resignation, and threatened to string up Sir Charles if he ventured into the East End. *Fun* caricatured him as a helplessly stiff-necked Blimpish buffoon in an over-ornate uniform, and demanded his and the Home Secretary's dismissal. *Punch* extended the abuse to bobbies in general, with a cartoon of sinister, jeering ragamuffins playing blind man's buff with a hopelessly befuddled constable.

Certainly the uniformed branch made a large number of arrests of innocent people, some of whom, however, needed to be stopped from behaving bizarrely or drunkenly. The CID had followed information leading to the arrests of a couple of certifiable lunatics, but its most widely publicized operation had been the tracing and arrest of the innocent John Pizer. It was still more unfortunate that the Aldgate Post Office was burgled at the very time when the City Police were examining the body in Mitre Square, a stone's-throw away. An impression grew that the police were drafting so many of their number into obtrusive but useless street patrols around White-chapel that ordinary crime could flourish unimpeded.

The most useful and impressive police work was unspectacular and went almost unnoticed. Collard and M'William's house-to-house investigation had only turned up Lawende and Levy, but it was a far more professional and useful operation than Major Smith's night passed in haring all over Spitalfields believing himself to be one jump behind the murderer. And the Met was likewise carrying out a massive house-to-house enquiry over a large and densely populated area. The bulk of the reports were in when Anderson returned from the continent, though the work was not completed to the department's satisfaction until a couple of weeks later. It produced information from which the Scotland Yard chiefs made some definite deductions. But as Dew complained, they kept them to themselves. They not only refused to tell the press, but left their own juniors uninformed. Security was at a high premium with Dr Anderson. The public, unfortunately, was only made aware of such things as the 'Ripper' letters (soon to be discounted as worthless by the detectives) which were reproduced on handbills.

Sir Charles Warren later complained that the many hundreds of suggestions which poured in to Scotland Yard usually boiled down to the same four unimaginative proposals.

The most noisily canvassed recommendation was that blood-hounds should be brought in. The Commissioner's response to this produced further adverse publicity.

The silliest offer of help came from Mrs Henrietta Barnett, wife of the Vicar of St Jude's, who persuaded 4,000 women to sign a petition to the Queen urging stronger government action, and pledging in return that 'each woman of us will do all she can to make men feel with horror the sins of impurity which cause such wicked lives to be led.' This well-publicized plea forced the overworked senior detectives to prepare a brief for the Home Secretary noting that they knew of sixty two permanent brothels in Whitechapel, and suspected many more intermittent ones; that there were 233 common lodging houses with 8,530 occupants in the district; and an estimated 1,200 prostitutes.

A patent medicine company proved amazingly opportunistic. The following advertisement appeared in *The City Press* on 24 October:

THE WHITECHAPEL MYSTERY – It is said this fearful crime was committed by an insane person. Insanity springs from divers causes, and more often can be traced to bodily ailments unregarded. Romanalicum, the liniment of the Ancients, is the best safeguard. It cures all bronchial affections, pleurisy, pneumonia and many other diseases. No house should be without it, and no stable, as it is also good for horses and dogs. Its price is within the reach of all. To be obtained of all Chemists and Saddlers, price 2s 6d per bottle.

Observers who did not expect their horses and dogs to graduate from pleurisy to serial murder were watching the dates anxiously. Martha Tabram had died on 7 August, Polly Nichols on the 31st. Annie Chapman had been found on 8 September, the double event had occurred on the 30th. Would the last week of October end in murder?

8

Marie Jeanette Kelly

Nothing happened on 31 October. The pattern had been broken.

This does not mean that the tension relaxed. Stride's long drawn-out inquest saw to that. The police sealed off Clerkenwell Green on 5 November to prevent some socialists from burning Sir Charles Warren in effigy. And when, on a wet 9 November the Lord Mayor's Show passed resplendent through the streets, Alderman Whitehead's headlines in the afternoon papers were stolen by the murderer. The radical *Star*, unwilling to allow even an unostentatious Liberal Lord Mayor's procession to pass without a sneer, commented that 'while the well-stuffed calves of the City footmen were being paraded for the laughter of London [Jack the Ripper's] victim was lying cold in a foul, dimly lit court in Whitechapel.'

The worst and last of the actual Ripper murders involved the youngest and most quickly identified victim. For the previous eight months Mary Jane or Janet or Marie Jeanette Kelly had rented the squalid room in Miller's Court, Dorset Street, where her remains were found. Her rent was now five weeks in arrears, but as long as her man, Joe Barnett had been in work the four shillings and sixpence a week had been kept up. So she had a fixed address, and the identificatory testimony of Barnett and her landlord and neighbours was accepted. The search for confirmation and next-of-kin which had drawn out earlier inquests was eschewed, and we are left with some unverified details. Even the surviving coroner's papers add little to the information given to the press.

According to Joseph Barnett, the fish porter who had lived with her for eighteen months, up to the previous two weeks, she was twenty five years old. She was born in Limerick and while quite young moved with her family to Wales. In 1879 she married a collier called Davis who was killed in a pit explosion two years later. Marie spent eight months in an infirmary in Cardiff and then joined a cousin with whom she took to whoring in that town. On coming to London in 1884 she found immediate employment in a Knightsbridge gay house (brothel) and then went to France for two weeks under a gentleman's protection. But she disliked the country and returned to London to live with a man called Morganstone in Pennington Street near the Stepney gasworks. She left him to live in Bethnal Green Road with a plasterer called Joseph Flemming, for whom she professed great affection.

Barnett picked her up one Friday night when she was soliciting in Commercial Street, and made a further appointment for the following day. On this they agreed to live together, and took lodgings in George Street, Spitalfields, where Flemming still visited her at first.

The two lived together at various addresses culminating in Miller's Court, Dorset Street, until Marie insisted on having a prostitute called Julia to live with them. Barnett objected and moved out. So, quite soon, did Julia. But she was succeeded by Maria Harvey who stayed with Kelly on the Monday and Tuesday before her death, and left some men's clothes in her room. Oddly enough, Mrs Harvey's name was wrongly given as Julia by *The Times* when it first interviewed her.

According to Julia Venturney, who lived opposite in Miller's Court (and might, of course, have been the Julia in question) Barnett disapproved of Marie's walking the streets. So he moved into a lodging house in Bishopsgate, though he continued on friendly terms with Marie. After her death he moved again, to live with his sister in Portpool Lane, Gray's Inn Road.

The mundane elements of this narrative have been accepted without quibble by most commentators. But the interlude in France and the West End has provoked questions. Since nearly all her neighbours knew her as Mary Jane, but she was buried under the names Marie Jeanette, it has been suggested that she fancied the French connection and assumed Frenchified versions of her given names. It has also been proposed that she invented the stories of the 'gay house in the West End' and the 'gentleman in France' to give a posh explanation of her existence as a streetwalker. I think this overestimates the class value of the term 'West End'. Not all commercial sex in Mayfair and Marylebone was as stylish as the 'pretty horsebreakers' of Rotten Row. Barnett Rotto, who kept grubby assignation rooms above his grocery in Charlotte Street twenty years later, might have been described as running 'a gay house in the West End'.

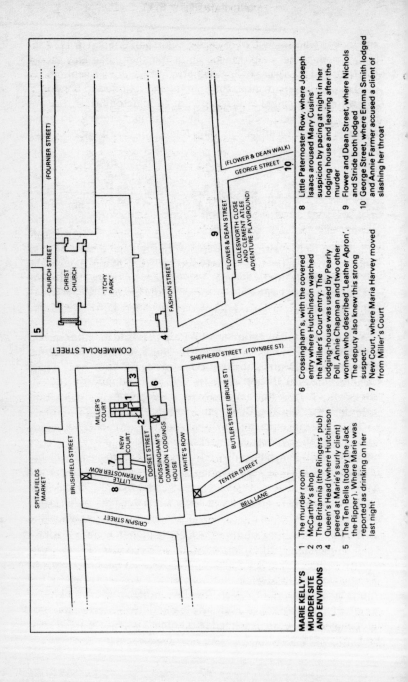

MARIE KELLY'S MURDER SITE AND ENVIRONS

1 The murder room
2 McCarthy's shop
3 The Britannia (the Ringers' pub)
4 Queen's Head (where Hutchinson peered at Marie's surly client)
5 The Ten Bells (today the Jack the Ripper). Where Marie was reported as drinking on her last night

6 Crossingham's, with the covered entry where Hutchinson watched the Miller's Court entry. The lodging-house was used by Pearly Poll, Annie Chapman and two other women who described 'Leather Apron'. The deputy also knew this strong suspect.
7 New Court, where Maria Harvey moved from Miller's Court

8 Little Paternoster Row, where Joseph Isaacs aroused Mary Cusins' suspicion by pacing at night in her lodging house and leaving after the murder
9 Flower and Dean Street, where Nichols and Stride both lodged
10 George Street, where Emma Smith lodged and Annie Farmer accused a client of slashing her throat

So it had better be said at once that we simply do not know how accurately Marie Jeanette told her lover her life story, and we do not know whether she was christened Marie Jeanette and simplified it for convenience, or Mary Jane and elaborated it for pretension. Nor does it matter, unless we are propounding some far-fetched motive for the Whitechapel murders.

Marie's room was known as 13 McCarthy's Rents. It was actually the back ground-floor room of 26 Dorset Street, but it had been partitioned off from the rest of the little house and could only be entered by the first door on the right-hand side in Miller's Court, a pokey yard of six dwellings entered through the first archway on the right in Dorset Street, coming from Commercial Street.

The twelve-foot square room held a bed, a table, a bedside table, a little square table above the bedhead and a chair. There was room for little else. The difficulty the first doctor had in entering has led some commentators to think the table had been pushed against the door so that the murderer must have left by the window. But the doctor was only negotiating the narrow space available to Marie and her friends at the best of times.

An engraving of 'The Fisherman's Widow', hung above the fireplace opposite the door. Chipped crockery, empty ginger beer bottles and a little stale bread were in the wall-cupboard next to it.

The window was at right angles to the left-hand side of the door. Two panes of glass had been broken a few weeks previously, and since Kelly had lost her door-key it was her practice to reach through the hole to bolt the door on the inside when she went out. A man's pilot coat hung over the window in lieu of a curtain.

John McCarthy ran a small grocer's shop just outside the court at 27 Dorset Street. He was also landlord of the majority (at least) of the Miller's Court rooms.

Two other tenants of 'McCarthy's Rents' were active prostitutes. Mrs Mary Ann Cox of no 5 at the top end of the court told the police: 'I am a widow and an unfortunate.' Elizabeth Prater who lived in the room immediately above Marie Jeanette described herself as a married woman living apart from her husband for five years, though she now walked the streets.

Julia Venturney, the German woman who lived at no 1 Miller's Court, called herself a laundress, and said that although a widow, she was living with a man named Harry Owen. None of which need have prevented her from being on the game. She knew Kelly and Barnett well, and gave him a good character. They lived together without quarrelling. He was kind to Kelly and gave her money. Mrs Venturney revealed that Marie Jeanette had broken the window when drunk a few weeks previously, though she was only occasionally tipsy. (Joe Barnett insisted so loyally, firmly and improbably on Marie's sobriety that the coroner had to push him to admit that he had ever seen her drunk in his presence!)

Mrs Venturney had become something of a confidante of the dead woman, who revealed that she had another lover named Joe, a costermonger who ill-used her for living with Barnett. This might explain Barnett's uncertain feeling that she was frightened of someone, not necessarily the Ripper.

A couple called Keyler lived in Miller's Court upstairs at no 2, and the court possibly housed another married couple called Kennedy, whose daughter was reported as having visited them at 3.30 on the night of the murder.

Clearly McCarthy was not a super-pimp running a stable of prostitutes in Miller's Court. His tenants were a mixture of the respectable and the disreputable poor, who shared an ability to pay four and sixpence a week for rooms of their own rather than fourpence a night for a doss. Four of them left immediately after the murder. But he had no illusions about Marie Kelly's profession.

At about seven o'clock on the evening of 8 November Joe Barnett dropped in to Miller's Court to see how Marie was. Maria Harvey, who had found a room of her own in New Court, Dorset Street, was also visiting, and said that the two were on the best of terms. Both Barnett and Mrs Harvey left by eight o'clock.

In the course of the evening Marie certainly had several drinks. It may have been while she was in a public house that she spoke to her nineteen-year-old friend Lizzie Allbrook and confessed that the Ripper business was frightening her. She intended to go back to her mother in Wales, she said.

At 11.45 Mrs Cox was coming home along Commercial Street and into Dorset Street. She saw Marie just in front of her, walking with a stout man in a billycock hat. He had a long overcoat, blotchy face and a carrotty moustache, and carried a quart can of beer. Marie hardly needed this as she was already very drunk. As she went into her room she said 'Good night' somewhat incoherently to Mrs Cox, and announced that she was going to sing. Strains of the sentimental ballad 'Only a violet I plucked from mother's grave' emerged from

13 McCarthy's Rents, and could still be heard when Mrs Cox went out again fifteen minutes later. At 1.00 am Mrs Cox came home again for a few minutes and Kelly was still singing.

After Mrs Cox had left Mrs Prater came home and stood around at the bottom of the court for about twenty minutes waiting for a man who was supposed to be living with her. Despite published claims that she was talking to McCarthy, she told the coroner at the inquest that she spoke to no one and saw no one. The singing had stopped by the time Mrs Prater went to bed in the room above at half past one.

By 2.00 am Kelly seems to have sobered up and got rid of the blotchy-faced man with the carrotty moustache. An acquaintance called George Hutchinson saw her in Commercial Street and made a detailed statement placing all her movements very precisely within a couple of hundred yards of her home.

About 2.00 am on the 9th I was coming by Thrawl Street, Commercial Street, and just before I got to Flower and Dean Street I met the murdered woman Kelly and she said to me: 'Hutchinson, will you lend me sixpence?'

I said: 'I can't. I have spent all my money going down to Romford.'

She said: 'Good morning. I must go and find some money.'

She went away towards Thrawl Street. A man coming in the opposite direction to Kelly [i.e. from Aldgate] tapped her on the shoulder and said something to her. They both burst out laughing. I heard her say 'All right' to him and the man said: 'You will be all right for what I have told you.'

He then placed his right hand round her shoulders. He also had a kind of small parcel in his left hand with a kind of strap round it. I stood against the lamp of the Queen's Head public house [on the north corner of Fashion Street and Commercial Street] and watched him. They both then came past me and the man hung down his head with his hat over his eyes. I stooped down and looked him in the face. He looked at me stern. They both went into Dorset Street. I followed them. They both stood at the corner of the court for about three minutes. He said something to her. She said: 'All right, my dear. Come along. You will be comfortable.'

He then placed his arm on her shoulder and she gave him a kiss. She said she had lost her handkerchief. He then pulled his handkerchief, a red one, and gave it to her. They both then went up the court together. I then went to the court to see if I could see them, but I could not. I stood there for about three quarters of an hour to see if they came out. They did not, so I went away.

He followed this with a really remarkable description of the man:

Age about thirty four or thirty five, height five feet six inches, complexion pale. Dark eyes and eyelashes. Slight moustache curled up each end and hair dark. Very surly looking. Dress, long dark coat, collar and cuffs trimmed astrakhan and a dark jacket under, light waistcoat, dark trousers, dark felt hat turned down in the middle, button boots and gaiters with white buttons, wore a very thick gold chain with linen collar, black tie with horseshoe pin, respectable appearance, walked very sharp, Jewish appearance. Can be identified.

At about 2.30 am Sarah Lewis, a laundress of 24 Great Pearl Street, came into the court. She had quarrelled with her husband and decided to spend the remainder of the night with the Keylers. In Commercial Street, by the Britannia, she saw a short pallid man with a black moustache who carried a little black bag and wore a short coat and pepper-and-salt trousers. He was accompanied by a woman and paid no attention to Mrs Lewis. But she recognized him as one who had accosted her and a friend in Bethnal Green Road the previous Wednesday, repeatedly asking either one of them to come up a lane alone with him, frightening them, and finally undoing the overcoat he was then wearing and feeling for something. It might have been money for a bribe; he might have intended to expose himself; but she and her friend feared a knife and ran away at the time, and she felt scared on seeing him again.

As she passed through Dorset Street she saw a man in a black wideawake hat standing in the shadow of the lodging house opposite Miller's Court, watching the entrance. According to his statement, this should have been Hutchinson. She also saw a young man pass along the street with a woman.

Mrs Cox came home for the night finally at 3.10. The court was silent and she saw nobody.

At 3.30 a woman called Kennedy told the newspapers she went to her parents' home in the court and saw a woman who might have been Marie Kelly talking either to two men or to one man while an older woman stood in the background. Soon after this she heard a cry of 'Murder!'. But she also added a story identical to Sarah Lewis's of having seen the alarming man in Bethnal Green Road the previous Wednesday while in company with a friend, and neither the press nor the police seem to have thought her trustworthy. In any event, after giving elaborate statements to newspapermen (which the *Star* explicitly queried) she was not called to the inquest, unless in fact she *was* Sarah Lewis and gave a different name to the press.

The cry of 'Murder!' was also heard by Sarah Lewis and by Mrs Prater, who had been woken up by her kitten, Diddles, walking across her neck. None of them paid any attention. Mrs Venturney, who said she had been awake all night, heard nothing. But she had not heard the singing either.

At 5.30 Mrs Prater woke up and went out to the Ten Bells in Church Street (where the Jack the Ripper now stands on the corner of Fournier Street) for a breakfast of rum. Apart from a couple of carters harnessing their horses in Dorset Street she saw no one.

An hour later Mrs Cox awoke to hear a man's footsteps leaving the court. She thought it might be the policeman on beat duty.

The most puzzling statement about Marie Kelly's last hours came from Caroline Maxwell, the wife of the deputy at 14 Dorset Street. She swore that she saw Marie standing in the entrance to Miller's Court at 8.30, and said to her: 'What brings you up so early?'

Kelly replied: 'I have the horrors of drink upon me, as I have been drinking for some days past.'

Mrs Maxwell thoughtfully suggested the hair of the dog. 'Why don't you go to Mrs Ringer's [the Britannia] and have half a pint of beer?'

Kelly replied: 'I have been there and had it, but I have brought it all up again.' And she pointed to some vomit in the street.

Mrs Maxwell then went to Bishopsgate to do some shopping. She claimed that she was sure of the time and date because she was returning plates her husband had been looking after for a neighbour. So she was certain it was about nine in the morning when she returned to Dorset Street and saw Marie standing outside the Britannia talking to a shortish stout man in a plaid coat. The clothes Marie wore included a distinctive maroon wool crossover shawl, which Mrs Cox had seen her wearing the night before, though Mrs Maxwell had not seen her wearing it for some time.

According to *The Times* of 12 November this story was supported by another young woman who saw Kelly on the street between 8.30 and 8.45.

At about 10.45 McCarthy told his assistant Thomas Bowyer to go to 13 Miller's Court and collect Marie's outstanding rent. McCarthy's shop was in the Dorset Street house on the other side of the court entry from Marie's and Mrs Prater's, so Bowyer had only to go immediately round the corner. He found the door bolted (or locked, as he imagined) and pushed back the coat behind the broken pane. What he saw sent him running back to McCarthy.

'Governor!' he said. 'I knocked at the door and could not make anyone answer. I looked through the window and saw a lot of blood!'

McCarthy went back to the window with him, saw an appalling spectacle, and said quickly to Bowyer: 'Don't tell anyone. Let's fetch the police!'

Inspector Beck was chatting to Walter Dew in the Commercial Street Police Station when Bowyer burst in, crying: 'Another one! Jack the Ripper! Awful! Jack McCarthy sent me.'

Beck took Dew and two more uniformed constables to the little crib. What they saw on the bed when they pulled back the coat is fully described in Dr Bond, the westminster Divisional Police Surgeon's report, which came to light among papers anonymously posted to Scotland Yard in November 1987.

> Notes of Examination of body of Woman found Murdered & multilated in Dorset St.
>
> Position of body.
> The body was lying naked in the middle of the bed, the shoulders flat, but the axis of the body inclined to the left side of the bed. The head was turned on the left cheek. The left arm was close to the body with the forearm flexed at a right angle & lying across the abdomen. The right arm was slightly abducted from the body & rested on the mattress, the elbow bent & the forearm supine with the fingers clenched. The legs were wide apart, the left thigh at right angles to the trunk & the right forming an obtuse angle with the pubes.
> The whole of the surface of the abdomen & thighs was removed & the abdominal Cavity emptied of its viscera. The breasts were cut off, the arms mutilated by several jagged wounds & the face hacked beyond recognition of the features. The tissues of the neck were severed all round down to the bone.
> The viscera were found in various parts viz: the uterus &

kidneys with one breast under the head, the other breast under the Rt foot, the Liver between the feet, the intestines by the right side & the spleen by the left side of the body.

The flaps removed from the abdomen & thighs were on a table.

The bed clothing at the right corner was saturated with blood, & on the floor beneath was a pool of blood covering about 2 feet square. The wall by the right side of the bed & in a line with the neck was marked by blood which had struck it in a number of separate splashes.

The air passage was cut at the lower part of the larynx through the cricoid cartilage.

Both breasts were removed by more or less circular incisions, the muscles down to the ribs being attached to the breasts. The intercostals between the 4|th|, 5|th| & 6|th| ribs were cut through & the contents of the thorax visible through the openings.

The skin & tissues of the abdomen from the costal arch to the pubes were removed in three large flaps. The right thigh was denuded in front to the bone, the flap of skin, including the external organs of generation & part of the right buttock. The left thigh was stripped of skin, fascia & muscles as far as the knee.

The left calf showed a long gash through skin and tissues to the deep muscles & reaching from the knee to 5 ins above the ankle.

Both arms & forearms had extensive & jagged wounds.

The right thumb showed a small superficial incision about 1 in long, with extravasation of blood in the skin & there were several abrasions on the back of the hand |Moreover?| Showing the same condition.

On opening the thorax it was found that the right lung was minimally adherent by old firm adhesions. The lower part of the lung was broken and torn away.

The left lung was intact: It was adherent at the apex & with a few adhesions over the side. In the substances of the lung were several nodules of consolidation.

The Pericardium was open below and the Heart absent. In the abdominal cavity was some partly digested food of fish & potatoes and similar food was found in the remains of the stomach attached to the intestines.

Dr Bond's description of the body as naked is slightly inaccurate. What remained of the poor woman's chemise still lay around her shoulders and upper arms.

The clenching of the hands is similar to the finding on Annie Chapman's body. The complete multilation all round the neck indicates a last attempt to cut the head off, and once again it failed completely, so that one may reasonably dismiss the whole notion of a medically skilled murderer.

And to his grisly collection of a kidney and two wombs, this appalling murderer now added a heart.

A drawing in *Reynold's Newspaper* for 18 November shows that Kelly's clothes were on the broken-backed chair, and her boots lay in front of the fireplace. It was a traumatic sight, vividly remembered with horror by everyone who saw it.

Beck sent for Superintendent Arnold, the Chief of H Division. Arnold telegraphed the Commissioner's Office, and had a window removed. Inspector Reid, head of H Division CID, was soon on the spot, followed shortly by Inspector Abberline from Scotland Yard, who cleared the court of onlookers and refused to allow the occupants of the other houses to leave until 5.00 pm. But no immediate attempt was made to enter the room as the Commissioner might want to use bloodhounds and the scent must not be confused.

Dr Anderson arrived on the scene of the only Ripper crime to transpire while he was both in office and in England. It became known that Sir Charles had no bloodhounds at his disposal had he wanted them used, and Arnold had the bolted door broken in at 1.30. According to Dew the floor inside was slippery with blood and he seems to have fallen over in it.

Dr Bagster Phillips began his examination with ample assistance. As well as his own junior partner, Dr Gordon Brown was present, and Dr Duke of Spitalfields. And, apparently on Anderson's specific request, Dr Bond, a lecturer in forensic pathology who was also medical adviser to the Great Western Railway and A Division (Westminster) police surgeon.

Phillips confidently assumed that death had occurred about twelve hours previous to their examination, and that the mutilations had taken about two hours to perform. Dr Bond, who submitted a personal report on the medical evidence linking all the murders, concurred, but a little more cautiously. The times of death of the

Ripper's victims were never really decisively established. Rectal temperatures were not taken, and the doctors seem to have relied on their own sense of touch to determine body temperature, and to have noted the onset of rigor mortis. This imprecise method had led Phillips to give a time of death that must have been totally incorrect in Chapman's case, placing it an hour or more earlier than John Richardson had found the Hanbury Street yard empty, and the women Darrell and Long had seen her alive.

Dr Bond accepted that the mutilations might have hastened the cooling of Kelly's body. But he observed that rigor mortis had started when he arrived at 2.00 pm, and increased while they worked. As its inception may be anything from six to twelve hours after death, this gave rough limits between 2.00 am and 8.00 am.

So Mrs Maxwell's strikingly circumstantial story was ruled out, and no one had to explain why a murderer who consistently struck in the small hours, only once killing at dawn, should have changed to a long and hazardous operation by daylight from which he escaped undetected through busy streets. It leaves unexplained Mrs Maxwell's error: whether she had mistaken the day or (less probably) the person.

Inside the sparsely furnished room the police found the remains of a fierce fire in the grate. It included the charred wire rim of a woman's hat and the heat had unsoldered the spout and handle of a kettle standing in or by the grate. Mrs Harvey thought the fuel had been clothes she left at Kelly's: a hat and jacket, two men's shirts, a boy's shirt and a child's petticoat. The pilot coat over the window was also hers. Abberline surmised that the fire had been intended to supply light for the murderer to work by. Half a candle of Kelly's was found unburned.

The body was taken to Shoreditch mortuary, which placed it within the jurisdiction of the North-East Middlesex coroner, Dr Roderick MacDonald MP. Mr Wynne Baxter disputed the propriety of this, as the murder had occurred within his territory, and two of the jurors boldly protested when the inquest opened in Shoreditch Town Hall on 12 November. Dr MacDonald suppressed them firmly. He asserted that the murder had happened under his jurisdiction. He invited any jurors who insisted that Mr Baxter was their coroner to disempanel themselves. He changed the ground of his jurisdiction by maintaining that the important question was where the body lay (in the mortuary) and not where it had died. And he reinforced that argument with the observation that Annie Chapman had died within his district, but had been rightly sat on by a jury under Baxter's direction because her body had been taken to Whitechapel mortuary. Altogether the flurry indicates the persistent touchiness of Victorian coroners and suggests that Wynne Baxter believed that he should be *the* coroner handling the East End murder sequence. It is probably relevant, too, that MacDonald and Baxter had fought such a bitter election for the district which Baxter now ruled. But it does not suggest any improper collusion with the police on MacDonald's part.

Nonetheless, he conducted an enquiry which was tailored to police needs. Evidence of identity was taken from Barnett. Inspector Ledger of G Division put in a plan of the room. McCarthy and Bowyer described the discovery of the body. Mrs Cox, Mrs Prater, Mrs Lewis and Mrs Maxwell told what they knew, or thought they knew, of Kelly's last hours. Dr Baxter Phillips gave the briefest possible evidence of the cause of death. Beck and Abberline gave cursory accounts of their actions. And without going any further into details, Dr MacDonald announced: 'There is other evidence which I do not propose to call, for if we at once make public every fact brought forward in connection with this terrible murder the ends of justice might be retarded.' He accepted the jury's finding of murder by some person or persons unknown, and their signatures on a certificate which he never bothered to complete, and closed the proceedings after only one day.

Dr MacDonald's alacrity is a nuisance to historians. He leaves a lot of unanswered questions unanswerable. Wynne Baxter would have extracted a full medical report from the doctor. We should know a little more precisely about the contents of the room, Kelly's clothes and the fire. And Baxter would have proceeded so slowly that Hutchinson would have come to light before the inquest terminated. He might have probed Hutchinson's testimony: how, in underlit Commercial Street, could he identify his man's eyelashes so clearly? Or the colour of his handkerchief in Dorset Street? How unbuttoned was this figure, whose dark overcoat, dark jacket and light waistcoat were all visible to Hutchinson, not to mention his thick gold watch chain? What on earth was he doing wearing spats in the middle of the night? (They were strictly morning wear.)

Altogether Hutchinson's statements suggest that police and journalists asked point by point about possible details of costume and appearance. And Hutchinson helpfully gave a positive answer every time, thereafter having the amazing capacity to fix his asseverations in his mind and repeat them without self-contradiction.

Without a Baxter summation we must be content with some simple observations. Firstly, if Dr Phillips was right in placing the time of death around 2.00 am, then however he was dressed Hutchinson's man must have been the murderer. And in that case the cry of 'Murder' two hours later is irrelevant. We know a good deal more about mass-murderers and mutilators than the Victorians did, and the likelihood of Jack the Ripper sitting around in a darkened room talking peacefully with his victim or enjoying extensive normal sexual activity for an hour and forty minutes can be discounted.

On the other hand, if the cry was Marie's last utterance then Hutchinson's man must be innocent, and we may assume that Marie went out again some time after three o'clock and found another client. She might, then, have been the woman Mrs Kennedy claimed had been talking to two people in the court at 3.30. In either case, as with all the other victims, no proceeds from her professional activities were discovered with her body. Mrs Cox's blotchy-faced man probably paid for his entertainment with more than a share of his quart of beer. Hutchinson's man was overtly a client, and either he killed her without paying, or his fee was removed by the murderer.

As this was the only murder to take place indoors, it was the only one in which the victim was undressed. As her clothes were placed neatly on the chair, she presumably undressed herself for intercourse. The Victorian harlot would normally keep a shift or chemise on, and in such circumstances her client would strip to his shirt. This is the only case where several doctors agreed that the murderer's hands and forearms would have been bloody, and he could not have avoided some splashes of blood on his clothes. His state of undress may explain why there was no evidence of his cleaning himself up as he had done with the piece of apron on leaving Mitre Square. It also suggests another purpose for the fire. Abberline was probably right that he worked by its light. But he may equally have wanted its warmth on a chill November night as he shivered with morbid excitement in a state of undress.

One last observation was made by the police at the time. The crimes were growing worse. The mutilation had escalated from Nichols, slashed, to Chapman disembowelled and robbed of her womb, to Eddowes, disembowelled, robbed of womb and kidney and slashed about the face, to the frightful destruction of Kelly. The increase in savagery pointed to a single hand.

On 12 November Metropolitan Police Commissioner Sir Charles Warren's resignation was announced. There was general rejoicing and a popular assumption that his failure to catch the Ripper had caused his downfall. The news was greeted with cheers in the House of Commons, where partisan MPs hoped that his fall would be quickly followed by that of the unpopular Home Secretary.

And that was the last of Jack the Ripper's murders. It was not recognized at the time. Five more outrages over the next eighteen months would be hailed by the press as evidence that the White-chapel murderer was still at large. But the police quickly concluded in each case that this was not so, though even they did not close the file until 1892. Thereafter, senior officers involved recorded on various occasions their considered opinion that the Ripper's five victims were Nichols, Chapman, Stride, Eddowes and Kelly. So we may now appropriately summarize the distinguishing features of these cases.

All were streetwalkers; all were actively soliciting for trade immediately before they met their deaths. The conclusion that the murderer presented himself as a client is obvious and irresistible. None had any takings on her person, and Annie Chapman's rings were never traced. The conclusion that he was poor enough to rob them is reasonable.

They were not, as is usually stated, prematurely aged harridans. Stride and Kelly were presentable and attractive. Nichols and Eddowes were undernourished, but the former went cheerfully out on the streets in her new bonnet, and the latter had a perky personality which pretty clearly showed itself attractively in her expression and bearing. Chapman was generally run down but was still described as strongly built, which could not have been said of Nichols and Eddowes.

They all had more or less of a drink problem, and most were drunk when murdered. Nichols certainly was; Chapman had been. Eddowes and Kelly were sobering up from what seem to have been pretty hefty drinking sessions. Only Stride was sober.

Stride can only be included on the assumption that the murderer was interrupted before he could mutilate her. If Diemschütz's approaching pony and cart frightened him away, then, noting that he had not been inhibited from mutilating Annie Chapman by the passing market traffic in Hanbury Street, we may guess that he was sufficiently familiar with the Workers' International Club to know that its steward drove a cart, was out that night, and was expected back. Otherwise the abdominal mutilations increased steadily, and facial mutilations were introduced in the last two murders. He also seems to have attempted decapitation at first, but abandoned it as too difficult. This led to quicker and lighter throat-cutting strokes until Kelly's case, when he may possibly have made a last unsuccessful attempt to cut off his victim's head.

It is quite untrue that a surprising absence of blood suggested that the outdoor victims had been killed elsewhere and brought to the murder sites after they were dead. In every case there was quite sufficient bleeding from the neck at the spot to have caused death, and this in itself would have restricted the haemorrhage from the abdominal wounds. Professor Cameron of the London Hospital Forensic Medicine Department and the late Dr Francis Camps both thought the bruising indicated that the Ripper partially strangled or throttled his victims before cutting their throats, as he certainly did in Chapman's case. He could easily have done this while they stood before him with their hands engaged in pulling up their skirts, and it would have ensured their almost instantaneous silence. Medical opinion at the time was that the throats had been cut while the victims were lying down, which seems odd given that Whitechapel's outdoor prostitutes, then as now, are not likely to lie on the cold ground for intercourse. But if partially strangled they would have lain unconscious, and the strangulation too would have restricted the amount of bleeding.

Of course, notwithstanding the widespread impression that the Ripper came, killed and went through constantly travelled streets with mysterious silence and invisibility, on at least one and possibly two occasions his victims (Chapman and Kelly) were heard to cry out. Miller's Court, with its harlots and visitants, behaved like a street that never sleeps, but actual passers-by only came through every half hour or so after midnight. And he was never at any time penned in by potential observers, though Hanbury Street and Dutfield's Yard were very risky sites for a quick getaway and might have proved traps.

All the victims lodged in the Thrawl Street/Flower and Dean Street/Church Street/Dorset Street doss-houses off Commercial Street: a very tight district within two minutes walk of Christ Church, Spitalfields, in any direction. This is not in itself significant. The concentration here of common lodging-houses meant that virtually all East End whores lived there at least part of the time. But it has tended to make us feel a centre of murder rather to the west of the evidence. (This has been encouraged by the inclusion of Tabram and Smith.) In fact, lines drawn from Buck's Row, Dorset Street, Mitre Square, Hanbury Street and Berner Street put the murder sites in an uneven diamond centring on a point east of Brick Lane, to the north of Heneage Street. And if we discount Mitre Square since it was probably visited from a starting point in Berner Street, the diamond becomes a more regular kite, and the centre moved to a point near Green Dragon Yard, south of Old Montague Street. This is worth noting since the City Police certainly believed that the hunt must concentrate around Flower and Dean Street, and it is easy to slip into this slight misdirection.

One last caution. For convenience, we accept the official view that these five were the exact tally of Ripper victims. But subsequent experience of searches for sexual serial murderers shows that we are nearly always inaccurate in allotting victims to them before their arrest. Victims of different imitative murderers may be included; the arrested serialist may confess to unsuspected crimes; other un-solved cases may seem likely to be his. Jack the Ripper might have struck earlier and/or later; he might not be responsible for any given one of the five ascribed victims. We are dealing with strong probabilities rather than certainties.

As far as the East End was concerned, he was still at large and dangerous. Many reminiscences of Jack the Ripper actually refer to subsequent murders, which must therefore be examined.

9

False Alarms: Annie Farmer, Drunken Lizzie, Clay-Pipe Alice and Carrotty Nell

On 19 November Marie Kelly was buried at Leytonstone. The next morning Thrawl Street had cause to believe it saw the Ripper running red-handed along its length.

Annie Farmer, forty-year-old wife of a City Road tradesman, had left her husband and worked her way down to the Spitalfields streets. On the night of the 19th–20th she trudged the Whitechapel pavements unsuccessfully searching for trade, until at 7.30 am she picked up a man whose appearance suggested a shabby version of Hutchinson's astrakhan-collared gent. He was not entirely unknown to Annie, who had seen him a year before. She took him to Satchell's lodging-house at 19 George Street, where they snuggled into an eightpenny doss together, and all was peaceful for two hours.

At 9.30 Annie screamed and the man, fully dressed, raced out of the doss-house door and away along Thrawl Street. As he passed a pair of cokemen working in the street he explained his flight succinctly with the observation: 'What a – – cow!' Annie's throat was bleeding, and it seemed that the Ripper had at last made the serious mistake of leaving a live victim to identify him.

But Annie was hiding coins in her mouth. Her throat had been given a shallow cut with a blunt knife, quite unlike the Ripper's deep penetrations with a sharp six-inch blade. Knowing their Spitalfields tarts, the police concluded that Annie had tried to cheat her client before lightly cutting her own throat and crying murder in an ingenious ploy to frighten him off. Within a couple of days they had stopped searching for him, confident that he would give himself up to them to clear his name if necessary.

That Christmas the most expensive toyshops stocked a game for three called 'How to Catch Jack'. One player had to move his two 'Murderer' pieces from narrow alleys at one end of the board to the safety of 'Alsatia' (a criminal slum) at the other without being caught between two of the dozen 'Policemen' or 'Journalists' pieces held by his opponents. The makers recognized one conflict in the investigation: between a 'Policeman' and a 'Journalist', Jack was safe.

On Thursday 20 December a woman's body was found in the yard between 184 and 186 Poplar High Street, where a builders' merchant called George Clark kept his materials. Pc Robert Goulding discovered her lying in something vaguely like a Ripper victim's attitude, left leg drawn up and right leg stretched out, at 4.15 am. She wore brown and black outer clothes with a dark tweed jacket, but brightened her appearance with a lilac apron, red flannel petticoat and red and blue striped stockings.

Superficially she was no Ripper victim. Her throat was not cut, her clothes were not disarranged and her body bore no wounds. The doctors who examined the corpse were at first at a loss to find a reason for death. Then they detected a faint mark on her neck, and decided that she had been strangled with a piece of string.

This happened two miles away from the centre of the Whitechapel murders. But it was still the East End. The dead woman was certainly a prostitute, and the populace panicked. The press, too, speculated on this as another Ripper murder.

It took a few days to establish who the woman was. She was known in Poplar as 'Fair Alice' Downey. But she was familiar to Whitechapel and Spitalfields, where she frequently lodged in George Street, and was known as 'Drunken Lizzie' Davis or Millett or Mellett. Finally her mother came forward from Pelham Street, north of Hanbury Street, and identified her as Rose Mylett. The difficulties seem to have stumped later commentators, who have either ignored or completely misdescribed her case.

While she lay in the mortuary a succession of doctors trailed in to examine her. Five days after the murder Dr Bond of Westminster found that the mark around her neck had completely disappeared, and taking this with other signs, he concluded that she had not been strangled but had fallen down drunk and choked to death on her own coat collar.

Mr Wynne Baxter took a dim view of this in his summing-up at the inquest:

After Dr Bromfield and his assistant, duly qualified men, came to the conclusion that this was a case of homicidal strangulation, someone had a suspicion that the evidence was not satisfactory. At all events, [the jury] heard that doctor after doctor went down to view the body without [Baxter's] knowledge or sanction as coroner. He did not wish to make that a personal matter, but he had never received such treatment before. Of the five doctors who saw the body, Dr Bond was the only one who considered the case was not one of murder. Dr Bond did not see the body until five days after her death and he was, therefore, at a disadvantage. Dr Bond stated that if this was a case of strangulation he should have expected to find the skin broken, but it was clearly shown, on reference being made to the records of the Indian doctors in the cases of Thug murders, that there were no marks whatever left. Other eminent authorities agreed with that view.

Perhaps the eminent authorities might have felt there was a difference between strangulation with a soft scarf – the thuggees' *rumal* – and strangulation with a piece of doubled string. Mr Baxter had to acknowledge that the case was difficult. No string or any other ligature had been found. Secondary signs of strangulation – a protruding tongue and clenched fists – were missing. The mark on the neck had not even been noticed at first. And although much violent death was associated with Spitalfields, where Mylett had lodged, this was clearly not in sequence with the notorious Whitechapel murders.

Dr Phillips was as keen as Mr Baxter to associate himself with theories of an expert East End killer. He recalled that there had been signs of strangulation on Annie Chapman's body and now suggested that Mylett's supposed murderer 'had studied the theory of strangulation, for he evidently knew where to place the cord so as to immediately bring his victim under control.'

The jury gave Mr Baxter the verdict of wilful murder he half-wanted. Scotland Yard filed Anderson's explanation to the Commissioner for having drawn down the coroner's strictures. Anderson agreed with the uniformed police that Mylett's death was natural; demanded that Bond be despatched to correct Bromfield's view; and was horrified that first Bond's assistant, and then the Senior Police Surgeon intercepted the message, went down on their own accounts, and confirmed the diagnosis of murder. Even Bond had to be sent to Limehouse twice before he returned with the report Anderson expected. But it came and almost persuaded the irritable coroner.

Disregarding the jury, Anderson declined to set the CID searching for a murderer he deemed to be non-existent.

There was relative calm until July. Then total panic broke out in the East End when Pc Andrews found a woman's body in Castle Alley at 1.00 am. She lay out of sight among the parked costermongers' carts in what was then a barely accessible lane running between Old Castle Street and Whitechapel High Street. Her throat had been cut, her clothes were disarranged, and the first report was that a pool of blood had formed from a gash in her abdomen. Andrews whistled up Sergeant Bedham who had just passed the High Street entrance to the alley, and the two came to the hasty conclusion that the Ripper was at work again.

The woman was quickly identified by a man named McCormack who had been living with her at a common lodging house in Gun Street, to the west of Spitalfields Market. Her name was Alice McKenzie, and the property from which she took the nickname Clay Pipe Alice was found underneath her, together with one farthing. A strong-featured not unhandsome woman in her forties, she had gone out on the streets accompanied by another prostitute, gloriously named Mog Cheeks, to earn her rent that night. Mog Cheeks was missing for a couple of days and then turned up to reveal that she had been staying with her sister.

The Times believed that this was the work of the same murderer who had claimed seven victims the previous year. (It included Smith and Tabram in the Ripper's count.) But Dr Bagster Phillips pointed to some marked dissimilarities. The injuries to her throat had been made with a short knife, and her abdomen was not gashed, merely scratched severely by fingernails.

Not even Wynne Baxter claimed this as one of the sequence, despite Inspector Reid's appearance to express interest in the farthing. The coroner was always prone to follow Dr Phillips' lead, and the doctor now firmly disputed the suggestion that the seven Whitechapel murders of 1888 had been by the same hand. The Metropolitan Commissioner, James Monro, personally investigated this case and concluded that there was no sexual motive behind the killing.

The jury returned a verdict of wilful murder by a person or persons unknown and urged that the almost enclosed northern end of Castle Alley be opened up to make a continuous thoroughfare from Wentworth Street to Whitechapel High Street. This was done, and Old Castle Street has now swallowed up the former parking place for barrows.

Nonetheless, Clay Pipe Alice's death prompted a short-lived zenith of the scare in the East End. For the first time *The Times* reported that prostitutes were staying off the streets, a policy that Scotland Yard had urgently recommended to them. (The evening papers thought this had happened sporadically since the double murder.)

The women were back on the streets by September. Assistant Chief Constable Melville Macnaghten, making enquiries in Whitechapel, heard one complain that she had taken 'a bloke' down a suitably dark alley when a policeman in rubber soles appeared silently from behind a wagon and her client ran away. She went on to say that she was going out again in search of trade, regardless of the Ripper scare.

Macnaghten was in the district investigating the Pinchin Street murder. A woman's torso was found under a railway arch in Pinchin Street, south of Back Church Lane. As there was a gash on its abdomen it was briefly thought that this, too, might be the work of the Ripper. Another possibility was that it might be connected with a torso found a year earlier when the foundations for New Scotland Yard were being dug in Whitehall. But neither was ever identified, and neither had any connection with the Whitechapel Murders.

Finally, in the small hours of 13 February 1891, Pc Ernest Thompson found a woman's body in Swallow Gardens, the dismal passage under the railway arches between Chamber Street and Royal Mint Street. A woman who often walked through this and a parallel passageway was to complain to *The Times* that the use of these wretched places as public privies was still more offensive and dangerous to health than their use as public brothels.

As Thompson turned from the 'Gardens' toward Chamber Street, blowing his whistle, he heard a man's footsteps hurrying away in the darkness. Thompson had been a policeman for only six weeks. He was to be criticized for not having given chase at once, and the belief that he had allowed Jack the Ripper to escape preyed on his mind until his own death at the hands of a ruffian he was moving on from a coffee-stall a few years later.

Pc Hart of the uniformed branch came quickly to his assistance, followed by plain-clothesman George Elliot. They fetched a doctor and notified Leman Street. Superintendent Arnold and local CID chief Reid came immediately, and by 5.00 am Chief Inspectors Swanson and Moore who directed the Ripper enquiries for Scotland Yard arrived. The authorities took the case seriously. Anderson came to the site during the morning, accompanied by Macnaghten. The detectives soon found Frances' takings for the night hidden behind a gutter-pipe in the archway wall of Swallow Gardens.

The Times confidently listed this as the ninth of the series. They did not include Farmer, Mylett or McKenzie, but they added 'a woman found on the stairs of an industrial dwelling house' before Smith, ascribing details drawn from Tabram to the mythical 'first victim'.

But within a day the police equally confidently announced that this was not a Ripper murder. They had identified the woman and were in hot pursuit of a suspect. Her name was Frances Coles, also known as Colman or Hawkins, but usually designated 'Carrotty Nell'. She was the good-looking daughter of a former bootmaker in Bermondsey workhouse. Her corpse had been distinguished by the possession of two hats: a new one on her head, and another pinned under her shawl.

This clue led back to a seaman named Thomas Saddler who had bought the new hat for Frances the previous day, and had later been seen quarrelling violently with her in Thrawl Street and threatening to kill her. Still later, he had turned up in a bruised and blood-spattered state at the lodging-house where the two had passed the previous night. But Frances had gone out with another man, he was told.

The police concluded that Saddler had carried out his threats and returned to the lodging-house to establish a weak alibi. It turned out that after spending a happy night and most of a day drinking and fornicating with Frances, Saddler had gone out only to be attacked from behind by a woman in a red shawl and robbed of his watch and money by two male accomplices. His quarrel with Frances had been for not coming to his aid.

After this Saddler went down to Wapping to rejoin his ship, the *Fez*, at London Docks. But in his disordered state after the attack the watchmen refused to let him into the docks. Saddler promptly abused them, calling them dock rats, and was quickly embroiled in another fight. The dockers outnumbered him, hence his sad condition when he returned to Spitalfields. He had his wounds dressed at the London Hospital.

With reasonable evidence before them of Saddler's violent temper, the police held him for a month. But one of Wynne Baxter's very thorough inquests, supported by the efforts of the National Seamen's Union to which Saddler had appealed when he feared that he might be charged with being Jack the Ripper, led to his release. Scotland Yard remained convinced that the ferocious seaman was guilty of Coles' murder.

After Frances Coles, no more victims were to be ascribed to the legendary monster.

PART III
THE POLICE

10

The City and The Met

The London Police developed from the constables who carried out magistrates' orders, arresting suspected criminals and keeping watch to deter crime. The principal magistrates of the City of London were the Lord Mayor and Aldermen. But the most efficient magistrates' office in the metropolis was that at Bow Street, where the Fielding brothers had strengthened the constabulary and encouraged it to detect criminals by investigation as well as simply arresting those who were accused or taken red-handed.

By 1790 it was clear that Bow Street's fashion of policing ought to be extended over the metropolis, but that this could only be carried out under the direction of a paid and professional magistracy. The City fathers objected. They refused to give up their courts, and they delayed the formation of a proper London police force for forty years. Finally they were circumvented, and a Metropolitan Police Force that had no standing within the City of London was created. It rapidly proved itself so efficient that the Lord Mayor and Aldermen were threatened with losing their magisterial powers lock, stock and barrel in the interest of having the City properly policed. To save their courts, the City fathers established their own police force in imitation of the Met. At the time of the Ripper murders it was directed by a Commissioner (Sir James Fraser), an Assistant Commissioner (Major Henry Smith), three Superintendents, controlling respectively the uniformed branch (Executive), supplies and pay (Chief Clerk), and the Detective Department (Superintendent M'William).

The situation was extraordinary. An area completely surrounded by the Metropolitan Police Force and no larger than one of its local divisions was entirely independent. But it suited the British love of anomalies handed down by history, and it confirmed the tradition of constitutional freedom whereby the City of London claimed that it only voluntarily subjected itself to the Sovereign's rule. For the

Metropolitan Police was directly controlled by H.M. Government through the Home Office.

To give it freedom of police action, its highest officers (the Metropolitan Commissioner and three Assistant Commissioners) were all *ex officio* JPs for London and the Home Counties. They could, thus, issue warrants for search or arrest without the necessity of reporting back to a separate magistracy, and prisoners could be remanded direct to police custody. The Commissioner at the outbreak of the Ripper murders was the notorious Sir Charles Warren. He was succeeded on his resignation by a former head of the CID, James Monro. In 1890 Monro resigned, and so the death of Frances Coles occurred early in Sir Edward Bradford's very successful decade as Metropolitan Commissioner.

The Assistant Commissioners held responsibilities equivalent to those of the City Superintendents. The one responsible for the CID was of most importance to the Ripper affair. At the time of the deaths of Emma Smith and Polly Nichols this was still James Monro. But his resignation had been accepted a month before Nichols' death and he withdrew to other duties in the Home Office to be succeeded by Dr Robert Anderson, who remained Assistant Commissioner (CID) until 1901.

There were four Chief Constables immediately under the Assistant Commissioners. In 1888 Monro invited a thirty-five-year-old planter recently returned from India to consider joining the force as Assistant Chief Constable in the CID, and in June 1889 Melville Macnaghten was enrolled in that rank, from which position he rose to become Assistant Commissioner in 1903.

These were the 'classes' of the police in socially stratified Victorian society. Other ranks, even if as senior as Superintendents, were definitely 'masses'. There were six Superintendents attached to the Commissioner's Office at Scotland Yard, and a large number of Chief Inspectors and Inspectors.

Each local division was also headed by a Superintendent, supported by a Chief Inspector who deputized for him. Sub-Divisional Inspectors were in charge of the sub-divisional police stations, and other Inspectors had a roving brief to work between stations. The Local Inspector headed the divisional CID.

Superintendent M'William's official involvement once the City Police had been drawn in was seen as very valuable. But his detailed enquiry turned up no particularly useful information. As befitted a

City policeman, he was particularly noted for his skill in teasing out complicated fraud cases.

There are various listings of the Metropolitan officers in charge of the Whitechapel Murders. Until Polly Nichols' death it was entirely a matter for H Division, and Reid, the Local Inspector, was in command. But the Buck's Row murder brought in J Division and Inspector Helson, while H Division retained an interest (since Mizen had immediately reported the murder back to Commercial Street, and the inquest took place on their territory).

At this point Inspector Abberline was sent over from Scotland Yard to work with Helson and co-ordinate the investigation. He was the most prominent of the police on the ground, and was repeatedly and erroneously described thereafter as being in charge of the Ripper enquiry. He was actually in charge of the individual enquiries into the murders as separate cases. His importance stemmed from the many years he had spent as H Division's Local Inspector before he was transferred to the Commissioner's Office. He knew the district and its villains better than any other officer on the case. But a Chief Inspector and another Yard man were also allocated to it, and outranked him.

Bluff, genial Inspector Moore was understood by Detective Constable Dew of H Division to be heading the enquiry, which suggests that he handled the transfer of material from the East End to Scotland Yard. In fact, Dr Anderson, noting regretfully that he, himself, Warren and Superintendent Williamson of the CID were all too busy to handle the inquiry into Polly Nichols' murder, placed Chief Inspector Donald Swanson in charge, with a special office in Scotland Yard.

This quiet, gentle Scotsman had been a brilliant schoolboy and then a schoolmaster in Thursoe, until he felt that teaching was a dead-end job. So coming to London he joined the police, walked the beat at Leyton, and rose steadily through the ranks.

He was remembered as a man of great humanity, both to criminals and to 'bent' policemen. In his spare time he read philosophical works, took annual fly-fishing holidays in Scotland, and was quite untouched by the heady evangelicalism which his superiors avowed.

All the papers on the Whitechapel murders came to him for processing, and he prepared the final reports that went to the Home Office. He remained the soul of discretion, however, and his family were aware that while he knew everything about the Jack the Ripper case, he was not passing any gossip on to them or anybody else.

Assistant Commissioner Anderson was finally responsible for the case. On his hasty return from the continent after the double murder, Sir Charles Warren and the Home Secretary told him that they looked to him to find the murderer. But Anderson, a canny and experienced civil servant, replied that he would only 'hold myself responsible to take all legitimate means to find him.'

He believed that he succeeded. This belief has been challenged, scoffed at and almost suppressed. But it is manifestly important. The man in charge of the enquiry, commanding the maximum available information, three times printed his belief that the Ripper had been identified, and it would have been possible to publish his name.

11

The Coppers on the Ground

In one way and another, huge numbers of policemen were involved in the activity stimulated by the Ripper murders. H Division constables were on the alert to intervene when mobs threatened to lynch suspects. Some Detective Sergeants were specifically drafted to work on the case. (Thicke, Godley, Enright and McCarthy were listed on different occasions.) Other divisional detectives were sent on the routine house-to-house enquiries which combed the Commercial Street/Hanbury Street/Brick Lane/Osborn Street/Whitechapel High Street triangle. And uniformed constables from other divisions were brought in to step up the nightly patrols until 1891.

Some of those involved published recollections of their participation. F. P. Wensley, who rose to become the first Assistant Commissioner promoted from the ranks, recalled his first year as a uniformed constable, when he was sent from Lambeth to help with the street patrols. 'Not that I had much to do with it,' he observed, honestly, forty years later.

> In common with hundreds of others I was drafted there and
> we patrolled the streets – usually in pairs – without any
> tangible result.

Few of his colleagues confessed to so humble a role. Sergeant Ben Leeson became a close colleague of Wensley's in later years, and began serving as a CID constable in H Division in 1891. This meant he was (by his own account) actively involved in the Frances Coles investigation; indeed, Leeson claimed to have been the first to come to Thompson's assistance when he discovered the body in Swallow Gardens. The inquest shows that at least two other constables arrived earlier, and Donald Rumbelow has pointed out that Leeson's memory was extraordinarily defective when he came to write his memoirs. It is not surprising, then, that Leeson should assume that the Coles case was a Ripper murder. He is no use as a guide to detailed incidents.

He does, however, show us some of the general views and attitudes of the ordinary detective on the ground. He describes Coles as 'young and pretty', which her mortuary photograph proves, but which could never have been believed of any Whitechapel whore if we relied solely upon the impressions of senior officers. He tells us, too, of the vague suspicion held by ordinary coppers.

> I am afraid I cannot throw any light on the problem of the "Ripper's" identity, but one thing I do know, and that is that amongst the police who were most concerned in the case there was a general feeling that a certain doctor, known to me, could have thrown quite a lot of light on the subject. This particular doctor was never far away when the crimes were committed, and it is certain that the injuries inflicted on the victims could only have been done by one skilled in the use of the knife.

Leeson misreports 'the police most concerned in the case', but may well be describing junior detective gossip three years after the events. The doctor rumour, established by Phillips' over-confident assertions at the Chapman inquest, took quick and firm roots.

Leeson was not the only detective to make an unconfirmed assertion that he was 'first on the scene'. Walter Dew states:

> I was the first police officer on the scene of the ghastly crime in Miller's Court.
> What I saw when I pushed back an old coat and peeped through a broken pane of glass into the sordid little room which Kelly called her home was too harrowing to be described.

Yet within a few pages Dew is telling us that Inspector Beck preceded him, and urged him not to look at the horrible spectacle.

The explanation for this self-contradiction is probably commercial. Dew's memoirs have the catchpenny title I *Caught Crippen* and it seems that being first on the spot was a highly marketable reminiscence.

Sergeant Stephen White, whom we have seen interviewing fruiterer Matthew Packer in the house-to-house enquiries at Berner

Street, did not choose that experience as his favourite anecdote of the Ripper affair. Instead (as reported in the *People's Journal* in September 1919) he told how he had been watching 'a certain alley just behind the Whitechapel Road [which] could only be entered from where we had two men posted in hiding, and persons entering the alley were under observation.' As White approached to take the report from the watchers, a well-dressed man with a musical and educated voice emerged from the alley and said 'Good night' to him. Immediately one of the watching police came out of hiding, searched the alley, and found a mutilated body. White was sure he had seen Jack the Ripper, and his evidence is sometimes accepted by those who argue for an educated middle-class murderer. Donald Rumbelow assumes the alley must have been Mitre Square. But this had three exits, did not lie off Whitechapel Road, and was not being watched by hidden detectives on the night Eddowes was murdered. It would not have been patrolled by White, anyway. It was City territory, and he was an H Division Metropolitan man. Despite an erroneous recollection that the night was frosty (probably ghosted in by the sub-editor whose style colours the whole reminiscence) he must have been referring to Castle Alley and Clay Pipe Alice's murder. In which case, even if his educated man had killed McKenzie, he would not have been the Ripper.

An even better known reminiscence is that of ex-Pc Robert Spicer, who apparently resigned from the force in disgust when his superiors refused to acknowledge that he had apprehended Jack the Ripper. On the night of the double murder (so Spicer told the *Daily Express* in 1931) he was patrolling Heneage Street, and investigated a court running off it. At the end of the court was a brick-built rubbish bin, and on the bin he found a local tart called Rosy accompanied by a man with a black bag. Spicer was not satisfied by the account the man gave of himself, and took them both back to Commercial Street station. There the man identified himself as a 'respectable Brixton doctor'. Rosy made no complaint and said that he had given her a florin, and the senior officers at the station hastily sent Spicer's suspect about his business.

Spicer was highly indignant. What, he pertinently asked, was a 'respectable' doctor doing up a Whitechapel back alley with a tart? The question, of course, answers itself, and does not mean that the doctor was Jack the Ripper!

By far the most useful and accurate of constables leaving later memoirs was Walter Dew. You may have noticed that his specious claim to be 'first' at Dorset Street was set in an exceptionally precise, yet concise, description of the broken window with an overcoat serving as a curtain. This is typical of Dew's accurate recollection of things he saw, wherever he can be checked against other sources.

It is obvious, however, that he wrote from memory, and did not consult newspaper cuttings or the Scotland Yard files. He said that he hated the case, so it is unlikely that curiosity would have led him to re-examine the data when seniority put them within his grasp. He was completely unaware that Melville Macnaghten had filed notes which named three suspects. He made unimportant geographical slips – spelling 'Osborne' Street, and calling Berner Street rather than Brunswick Street 'Tiger Bay'.

But it is Dew's total errors which really prove his honesty and usefulness. In his account of the Buck's Row murder, he told of Cross's discovery of the body, his seeing Paul approaching, and their both going to tell Mizen. He gave none of their names, simply describing 'Charles ––, a carman, and 'another man'. Then he commented:

> All this was afterwards told in evidence by the carman. It never had the corroboration of the other man. The police made repeated appeals for him to come forward, but he never did so.

Dew did not regard this silence as evidence of guilty knowledge. The man might have had his own more ordinary crimes to conceal, or he might have feared reprisals by one of the local gangs.

Dew was completely wrong in asserting that the second man refused to come forward. Robert Paul gave evidence on 17 September that fully confirmed Cross's and Mizen's statements. Yet the error in itself demonstrates Dew's honesty and accuracy. For it took two weeks to find Paul. The inquest opened on 1 September and Cross gave his evidence on the second day, testifying that the man appeared to be a carman, but was a stranger to him, and had left without a farewell at Corbett's Court. It was another two weeks before Paul was found, and what Dew obviously recalled was the fact that he and his mates spent some days in fruitless searching for him. Meanwhile Chapman had been murdered, and the detective duties in the division were increased. Clearly Dew never learned that Paul had come forward; he was too busy with other matters (the house-to-house enquiries which began then, for example) and was never told such an unimportant detail. The search for Paul (unmentioned at the inquest) stuck in his mind fifty years later.

He was similarly influenced by his first duties in the Kelly case. For two days he was searching for Mrs Cox's blotchy-faced man in a billycock hat, and believed this was the murderer. When Hutchinson turned up with his story of the man in the astrakhan-collared coat, Dew assumed that Hutchinson, like Mrs Maxwell, had mistaken the day.

Dew's account of Dutfield's Yard indicates that he never went there. He said that Stride was found under an archway leading to some stables. He also said erroneously that Dutfield's Yard had a back exit leading out to Commercial Road.

Assuming there was a way out of the yard, Dew placed Mrs Mortimer's house there, and said that she saw her man with the black bag cross the yard and go out of the non-existent western exit.

He stated that Catherine Eddowes's apron was black, whereas the official list showed it to be white. The *Daily News* noted that it was so filthy as to be barely detectable as white. And, like *The Times*, Dew asserted that Marie Kelly's candles [*sic*] were burned down to the stumps in Dorset Street. These are his outstanding errors. Given the fairly detailed accounts he gives of the major murders, this is an impressively accurate feat of memory.

The combination of acute observation with complete ignorance of some later developments and historical queries that have arisen from them makes Dew an invaluable witness. We have already seen that if he can be trusted, the mystery of Elizabeth Stride's uneaten grape skins and pips is solved. He tells us that the run-down Annie Chapman was nonetheless strongly built. Like Leeson, he was untainted by gentlemanly contempt for the Spitalfields whores. He described Marie Kelly as 'quite attractive' and added:

> I knew Marie quite well by sight. Often I had seen her parading along Commercial Street, between Flower-and-Dean Street and Aldgate, or along Whitechapel Road. She was usually in the company of two or three of her kind, fairly neatly dressed and invariably wearing a clean white apron, but no hat.

It is Dew who tells us of the many graffiti that appeared in Whitechapel, explicitly purporting to be by the murderer. He cited one off Hanbury Street that read: 'This is the fourth. I will murder 16 more and then give myself up'. They frightened children, and like the street patrolling vigilante groups were a nuisance to the police. But they were not clues, and although he recognized the elimination of the Goulston Street graffitus as a mistake, Dew did not believe it would prove to have been done by the Ripper.

He gives us one more interesting hint at a surprising line of enquiry. After the Hanbury Street murder, he suggests that the Ripper probably came out of no 29, turned left on Hanbury Street and went to Brick Lane, where he turned right, and then right again (presumably along Princelet Street and Puma Court) to escape into Spitalfields Market. Now this is a most peculiar route. As the two right turns indicate, Dew proposes that for some unfathomable reason the murderer deliberately set off in a direction he did not want, and made a large loop back. It would have been quicker, and involved less busy streets, to cross over Hanbury Street, go almost immediately down Wilkes Street and thence into Puma Court and to Spitalfields Market. Nor can the odd movement be explained by an uncancelled recollection of the supposed bloodstains on the fences of no 27 (the bloodstains that Inspector Chandler laughed off as urine). That route would have led the murderer directly toward rather than away from Spitalfields Market.

A possible explanation for Dew's recollection would be a confusion of two hypothetical destinations. We have seen that the City Police took for granted an escape route in the direction of Flower and Dean Street or Dorset Street. This (by now the commonest impression) would pull the fugitive back west from Brick Lane toward Spitalfields Market. Only he would hardly have gone there in the first place.

But Dew might have been given an eastward lead to follow at the outset of the investigation. We shall see that there may be reason to suppose that Scotland Yard was interested in locations east and south of Brick Lane. And there is no doubt that the senior men in the Commissioner's Office did not share their conclusions with their juniors.

Dew noted that Inspector Frederick Abberline was an important officer bringing his great knowledge of the district to the investigation. Many writers since have accepted the press belief that he was in charge of the case, and have assumed that his would be the definitive identification of the Ripper.

Unfortunately, he told the *Pall Mall Gazette* his theory in March, 1903, and it was ridiculous.

Abberline described himself as 'the chief of the detective corps' – that is, the organiser of the actual foot-slogging and house-to-house inquiries. But despite his confident claim to be in constant touch with Scotland Yard and to be fully apprised of their state of ignorance, he makes it clear that he was actually still as under-informed as he had been at the time of Annie Chapman's murder, when he revealed to the press that he had not been shown the divisional surgeon's report and did not know what organs were missing from her body.

Abberline thought the wife-poisoner Severin Klosowski, hanged in 1903 under the name George Chapman, had probably been the Ripper. Two of the reasons he offered for this belief completely discredit him as an authority. He thought it was significant that Klosowski had lived or worked in George Yard, because he still imagined that Martha Tabram was a Ripper victim. Worse still, he believed that the murderer evinced expert surgical skill, and that his motive had consistently been the acquisition of the victims' wombs for sale to the American doctor writing the monograph on the uterus.

Abberline confidently dismissed two of the major suspects seriously considered by Scotland Yard: a 'student' or 'young doctor' found drowned in the Thames in December 1888, and 'a man who died in an asylum a few years ago'. He gave two identical reasons for rejecting these theories. The first was that there was no evidence 'of a tangible nature' to support the suspicions. The second, that for some months into 1889, 'the detectives were still told to hold themselves in readiness for further investigations |which| seems to point to the conclusion that Scotland Yard did not in any way consider the evidence as final.'

Abberline's reasoning can be supported. Commissioner Monro's reports to the Home Office on the Castle Alley and Pinchin Street murders show that, while he knew the Ripper had been inactive since December 1888, he was not convinced that he had been found. Assistant Commissioner Anderson,too, carefully indicated in his memoirs that the was accepting Monro's assurance that Clay Pipe Alice's murder (which happened while he was on leave) was not a Ripper case. And he repeatedly stated that the evidence which proved to his satisfaction that the murderer had been found was not of a kind which could be used to charge him. Chief Inspector

Swanson offered as the second most important piece of evidence against the primary suspect the fact that the murders had stopped after he had been identified. And we know that the force as a whole was very careful to state that there was 'only suspicion against' their first major suspect. My own deduction from these pointers is that after the Whitechapel murders had clearly stopped finally, the chiefs went back over the data on the principal suspects, and reached their own conclusions, based on informed judgement, as to which had been the murderer. And they did not share their conclusion with Abberline.

It is easy to see why Abberline was kept underinformed by Warren, Monro, Anderson, Swanson and (probably) Moore. His sound knowledge of professional crime in Whitechapel was seriously offset by his incorrigible habit of talking to the press. And after the first revelations of the search for 'Leather Apron' had almost provoked race riots, Scotland Yard was extremely anxious that the press should have no chance to revive any socially dangerous sensation.

Abberline made one interesting negative statement to the *Pall Mall Gazette*, saying

> You must understand that we have never believed all those stories about Jack the Ripper being dead, or that he was a lunatic or anything of that kind.

On the face of it, this completely eliminates all suspects identified by police sources, except perhaps the vague 'doctors' proposed by Leeson and Spicer. But by 'lunatic', Abberline almost certainly meant only the kind of hallucinatory 'religious maniac' proposed by the alienist L. Forbes Winslow: a theory also eschewed by Sir Melville Macnaghten. Such a man could not have been found fit to plead in court.

All the senior police agreed that the murderer was in fact a 'sex maniac'. And since overwhelming perverted desire did not prevent him from knowing his actions were wrong, it did not preclude his liability to capital punishment, as would have been the case if he genuinely believed (say) God had ordered him to wipe out prostitutes.

12

Heading the City Force: Sir James Fraser and Major Smith

Sir James Fraser had been Commissioner of the City Police for twenty five years when Jack the Ripper struck. Prior to that he had been Chief Constable of Berkshire for nine years. As an old army man (he resigned his commission in 1854 when Colonel of the 54th Foot) his forte was good administration and discipline. It had been his hope that he would become Metropolitan Commissioner in the 1860s, but when that post went to another ex-soldier, Sir Edward Henderson, he accepted his loss with good grace and soon afterwards moved from Berkshire to the City.

His relations with the Lord Mayor and Corporation were excellent. But he was ready for superannuation by 1888. In two years he would retire, and in another two he would be dead. Fortunately he had an extremely active deputy.

Of all the senior police officers who left recollections of the Ripper affair, Major Henry Smith (Lieutenant Colonel Sir Henry by the time he wrote his memoirs) has enjoyed the kindest treatment at the hands of historians. His professional excellence has been perceived in his rapid rise from Detective Superintendent to Acting Chief Commissioner. We have seen that he sensibly propitiated the press during the Ripper investigation, for which he and his force were favourably contrasted with the Met.

Twenty two years later he took up his own pen and sketched a role for himself that has been accepted without question.

'There is no man living who knows as much of those murders as I do,' he boasted. And then, recollecting that the British like their bluff swaggerers to pad out their purer moments of Mr Toad with some hearty modesty, he went on:

I must admit that, though within five minutes of the

123

perpetrator one night, and with a very fair description of him besides, he completely beat me and every police officer in London; and I have no more idea now where he lived than I had twenty years ago.

This disclaimer is peculiar. Evidently Smith means that he had no idea who the Ripper was, so why does he simply deny knowing where he lived? There is reason to suspect that he may have been issuing a covert warning to a rival that he *did* know the former address of an innocent suspect, now being accused again, and would reveal it if the accusations continued.

Despite Dr Sedgwick Saunders' clear testimony, only Richard Whittington-Egan has questioned the Major's evaluation of Eddowes' kidney. We have seen that the Major was unlikely to have been five minutes behind the Ripper on the night of the double murder, although his faith in the blood-tinged water running out of the Dorset Street basin has never been questioned before. The Major is a splendid example of the success of self-advertisement.

He was known to his contemporaries as excellent company and a fine raconteur. This last characteristic is exploited in his memoirs. He knows the value of establishing a personal connection. Eddowes' arrest for drunkenness, for example, is described thus: 'This woman was in my custody at Bishopsgate Police Station twenty minutes before she was murdered.' The twenty minutes should be forty. And the personal custody is a legal fiction. She was in the custody of the City Police, yes. But it seems most unlikely that the Acting Commissioner made the rounds of local lock-ups giving his personal stamp to the drunks! The good raconteur treats truth as elastic; his treatment of time stretches it without apparently breaking it.

The Major, however, reaches breaking point in discussing the Dorset Street sink. His initial account plausibly suggests that he found it on the night of the two murders. Yet a few pages later he suggests that it had been used to clean the red hands that had just mutilated Kelly!

Similar inaccuracy is apparent in his highly-praised account of the imaginative policing he instituted to pick up the Ripper.

In August 1888, when I was desperately keen to lay my hands on the murderer, I . . . put nearly a third of the force into plain clothes, with instructions to do everything which under ordinary circumstances a constable should not do. It was subversive of discipline; but I had them well supervised by senior officers. The weather was lovely, and I have little doubt they thoroughly enjoyed themselves, sitting on doorsteps, smoking their pipes, hanging about public houses, and gossiping with all and sundry.

If the Major was desperate to catch the Ripper in August, he was acting precipitately before the murders had started! On the last day of that month Nichols died, and the Metropolitan Police swiftly decided that they were looking for a Whitechapel man known as Leather Apron. Not until the establishment of John Pizer's innocence did the search widen. And there was still no reason to suppose that the murderer would be found in the City. Only on 30 September did the body in Mitre Square give Major Smith a duty to involve his men in the investigation. But the weather by then was cool and showery, and the fine raconteur's vision of unbuttoned constables gossiping over their pipes and pots of ale in the long summer evenings would have been lost.

Still, the Major did claim to have put in a personal piece of unsuccessful detection in the middle of September.

> After the second crime I sent word to Sir Charles Warren that I had discovered a man very likely to be the man wanted. He certainly had all the qualifications requisite. He had been a medical student; he had been in a lunatic asylum; he spent all his time with women of loose character, whom he bilked by giving them polished farthings instead of sovereigns, two of these farthings having been found in the pocket of the murdered woman. Sir Charles failed to find him. I thought he was likely to be in Rupert Street, Haymarket. I sent up two men, and there he was; but polished farthings and all, he proved an alibi without the shadow of doubt.

Obviously we can place no reliance on Major Smith's assertion that the farthings were polished and were found in Chapman's pocket, though we do know that two farthings were found in her possession. But how came the Major to have a suitable suspect on his books, and to know just where to find him – on Metropolitan territory?

Strangely for a policeman and a son of the manse, Major Smith knew the Haymarket brothels rather well. He devotes one chapter of his memoirs to describing them and regretting their passing. He recalls Kate Hamilton, echoing the descriptions others have left of this fat, ugly procuress presiding over her ornate drawing room of elegant strumpets and fashionable young men. At her house, at Rose Young's and at Sally Sutherland's a very pleasant evening could be passed, as the Major recalled, and he wished such night-life still flourished in 1910.

Major Smith, in fact, was an interesting example of the senior police officer in the days when the upper echelons were recruited direct from the Old Boy network. And among a tribe of Old Boys the Major was something of a Good Ol' Boy. Born in Scotland, he was a cousin of Robert Louis Stevenson and the son and grandson of Presbyterian ministers. His father's loathing of Gladstone was reflected in Henry's vehement opposition to the Liberals. High Toryism seems to have been common among London's senior police officers.

Smith's education at Edinburgh Academy and University did not lead him to continue the family clerical tradition. He became a jovial, worldly man, bluffly convinced that a lot of religion did not necessarily find favour in the sight of God, and cheerfully accepting the assurance of sporting parsonical friends that his own indifferentism was probably a better Christianity than that practised by many devout church-goers. To the distress of his more sensitive parents, he delighted in attending public hangings, and to the end of his life regretted that this free entertainment had been abolished. It was his only indication of an early interest in law enforcement.

He trained as an accountant, and practised for a few years. Then, on the death of his father, he joined the militia and took his mother to live in the north of England. For some time he enjoyed the sporting life of a country gentleman, developing his tastes for horses, billiards, shooting and dogs. At this period he also began to appear as a City Swell on his visits to London, and learned his way around the red light district of Haymarket.

I should make it clear that apart from the unpleasant liking for public hangings, I see nothing inherently unacceptable in Smith's character. A good companion for a night's drinking and whoring (like Falstaff) is someone to be enjoyed on the appropriate occasions. But such a personality would not be one's first choice as a reliable colleague. He is not someone whose reminiscences of times past are normally to be taken as strictly truthful and accurate. And, most important of all, he would have been decidely *persona non grata* with the very different men who headed Scotland Yard.

Smith came into police work when, in his forties, he needed a steady income. Casting around among his circle for suggestions, he hit upon the idea of having himself appointed Chief Constable of Northumberland. He failed. A Detective Department was created in Liverpool, but again Smith's string-pulling failed to secure him its headship. Then his friends suggested that if he went south and took the relatively humble position of Detective Superintendent in the City of London Police Force, he would be well placed for promotion to the Assistant Commissionership which would soon fall vacant. After which, Fraser's longevity gave him a good chance of reaching the Commissionership quite rapidly. Smith accepted the offer at once, and the promotions came his way as promised. Accordingly he entitled his memoirs *From Constable to Commissioner*, a somewhat exaggerated suggestion of ascent from the ranks.

In London he soon made friends with the Reverend 'Bill' Rodgers of St Botolph's Church, and Under-Secretary Godfrey Lushington of the Home Office. These three gave bibulous dinners with copious speeches on the annual occasion of the Police Ball, social events that their cronies greatly enjoyed. The Reverend Bill made the splendidly unclerical suggestion that the Ripper murders might best be impeded by a system of registering and possibly licensing approved prostitutes. He acknowledged that this might appear an unseemly suggestion from the cloth, but reasonably wondered whether objectors seriously wanted the murders stopped.

While the genial ex-Commissioner was enjoying his retirement and penning his memoirs, his claim to know more about Jack the Ripper than any man living suffered a severe challenge. Sir Robert Anderson, the former head of the Metropolitan CID, had his memoirs serialized in *Blackwood's Magazine*, and far from confirming Smith's claim that every policeman in London had been foxed, Sir Robert asserted that the Ripper's identity was known: that he was a Polish Jew who had been protected by his people, and then incarcerated in an asylum. Sir Henry Smith exploded apoplectically.

> Sir Robert Anderson spent, so he tells us, the day of his return from abroad and half the following night 'in reinvestigating the whole case.' A more fruitless investigation, looking to all he tells us, it would be difficult to imagine.

With decent indignation, Smith objected to the anti-semitic tone of Anderson's remarks. Just how many lower-class Jews was Sir

Robert accusing of sheltering the murderer, he asked? Two dozen? Two hundred? Two thousand? It was a 'reckless accusation' against 'a class whose conduct contrasts most favourably with that of the Gentile population of the Metropolis.'

Sir Henry assumed that the Goulston Street graffitus had prompted Anderson's suspicions, and the Met's disrespect for his own authority over that chalked clue still rankled.

> The writing on the wall may have been written – and, I think probably *was* written – to throw the police off the scent, to divert suspicion from the Gentiles and throw it upon the Jews. It may have been written by the murderer, or it may not. To obliterate the words that might have given us a most valuable clue, especially after I had sent a man to stand over them till they were photographed, was not only indiscreet, but unwarrantable.

And in his peroration Smith employs some pretty sarcasms.

> Sir Robert says 'the Ripper could go and come and get rid of his blood-stains in secret.' The criminal, no doubt, was valeted by his co-religionists – warned not to run too great risks, to come home as soon as he could after business, and always to give notice when he meant to cut up another lady! On three occasions – the only three of which I can give reliable details – there was no need to provide the murderer with hot water and Sunlight soap. In Berner Street he did not mutilate the woman, and probably had very few blood-stains about him; in Mitre Square he used the woman's apron; and in Dorset Street he carefully washed his hands at the sink.

Sir Henry Smith's rhetoric is fun. His sense of personal involvement is engaging. And his hostility to anti-semitism is appealing. But I am afraid he is almost incapable of giving us a single reliable detail. What he does demonstrate is that, in spite of Dew's assertion that there was excellent co-operation between the Metropolitan and City Forces, this co-operation did not extend to the highest ranks.

13

Heading the Met:
Warren, Monro and Bradford

If Sir Henry Smith has enjoyed a good press for a century, Sir Charles Warren has been consistently vilified. The police failure to bring the Ripper to trial has been laid firmly at his door, and a most unflattering portrait has been repeated.

A dull Colonel Blimpish soldier, Warren (it is asserted) was called in to command the police during panic over a working class demonstration that got out of hand in February 1886. With military severity he organized the Met into a dragooned army to hold down the unemployed. The first instance of his authoritarian overkill came at Queen Victoria's Jubilee of 1887, when he used unnecessarily heavy policing to control traffic, and was unfeelingly impenitent when one of his men arrested an innocent sempstress and accused her of soliciting. Later in the same year he used Life Guards and Grenadiers to back up his brutal police in suppressing a demonstration in Trafalgar Square against unemployment. On this 'Bloody Sunday' one person was killed, and over a hundred were injured. Meanwhile he was quarrelling with the most efficient of his colleagues, the professional policeman James Monro, who had been drafted back from India to head the CID. The Commissioner's annual reports showed that he was more concerned with boots and saddles for his infantry and cavalry than with crime control. His insistence on draconian penalties for constables who drank on duty, and his unwillingness to press their grievances over pensions demoralized the force, and when he engineered Monro's resignation and replaced him with his pliable toady Dr Robert Anderson, the detectives almost refused to co-operate. It was little wonder that this shabby incompetence at the top led to confusion and uncertainty in the handling of the Ripper enquiry. Warren's personal contribution was to make a fool of himself by letting bloodhounds chase him through Regent's Park, and then losing them when they were actually wanted. He refused all advice that he should post a reward for information. There was general rejoicing when his manifest incompetence in the murder hunt forced his resignation and return to the army.

Now Warren had his faults. He had no tact and little patience. His professional character was formed by an experience of military authority which left him unprepared for politicking with the Home Office. He wore a walrus moustache and an elaborate gold-braided uniform. Queen's Regulations inflicted both on the officers of the late Victorian Empire.

But in all other respects, Warren was as much like Colonel Lawrence as Colonel Blimp. He was a very promising archaeologist, and it was in that capacity that he first went abroad to the Middle East. He retained a lifelong interest in archaeology and palaeontology.

When Warren joined the Royal Engineers he was posted to the Sudan. He made his name in Egypt by a notable piece of detective work. An archaeologist named Archibald Palmer had disappeared mysteriously. Warren proved that he had been murdered, found the remains of his body, and proceeded to track down the murderers. *Prima facie* no better general could have been found to head the police.

He was unfortunate in his sponsor. Hugh Childers was the kind of politician whose administrative skills win him numerous cabinet offices, yet who is forgotten by history since he never looks Prime Ministerial, never introduces epoch-making legislation, and avoids notorious scandals. As respectively First Lord of the Admiralty, Secretary of State for War, Chancellor of the Exchequer and Home Secretary, Childers was prominent in the eyes of his contemporaries. But the army reforms he introduced were overshadowed by Cardwell's and he is lost among Gladstone's other lieutenants.

In 1886 Gladstone formed a very short-lived administration with the support of the Irish Nationalists. His own espousal of Home Rule, however, split the Liberal Party and the government fell within a few months. During its time in office Home Secretary Childers faced anxiety about the Pall Mall riot which had developed from an inadequately policed Hyde Park demonstration in February. The Home Secretary gratefully accepted the Metropolitan Commissioner's offer of resignation and appointed Warren. Childers was a forceful administrator, and welcomed Warren's decisiveness.

The new Commissioner came in as an energetic reformer, and won instant support from the press. He made the surprising observation that there were too many Indians and not enough Chiefs in the force. The divisional Superintendents were being overwhelmed by the attempt to retain contact with the Commissioner's office and administer their own divisions. Warren invented the Metropolitan rank of Chief Constable (borrowing the title of his provincial and county opposite numbers) to liaise between them. He also intended to use the new rank to thaw the rigid class division of his force. While he expected most Chief Constables to be ex-army officers, there should also be room to include civilians among them, and outstanding Superintendents might be promoted to the grade. He increased the number of sergeants and inspectors. He reintroduced regular six-weekly square-bashing, so that drilled constables could be moved quickly and efficiently from one street to another for crowd control. And he put his newly disciplined force to the test in controlling the crowds and traffic at Queen Victoria's Jubilee in June 1887. It thoroughly satisfied the middle classes, and earned Warren his knighthood.

Unfortunately his triumph was marred by the arrest of Miss Cass that evening. The unhappy forewoman had been shopping in Regent Street, and her humiliation confirmed one of the suspicions that had dogged the police since their formation. The Victorians always feared that uniformed constables with the power to prohibit soliciting might harass or blackmail innocent women. Warren's response to the public outrage was blunt, tactless and contradictory. He defended the offending Constable Endicott volubly. He headed a small and incompetent Commission of Investigation after which Endicott was privately prosecuted for perjury. And Warren was unapologetic, both to the constable and Miss Cass, when the man was acquitted.

Bloody Sunday that November earned Warren brickbats from the radical press, and started an intense campaign against him in the *Star*. Since that lively evening paper gave very full coverage to the Ripper murders, and saw them as a godsend in its crusade against the police, the anti-Warren position has been thoroughly absorbed by subsequent writers on the Whitechapel murders. None has recognized the danger of accepting without question the views of a newspaper which cheerfully blamed the murders on 'such economic systems as that of unrestricted competition, backed by the devil's gospel of *laissez-faire*.' One or two have blithely assumed that the *Star*'s strenuous espousal of socialism and anarchism in addition to Irish Home Rule, Gladstonian Liberalism and general radicalism reflects a powerful popular revolutionary undercurrent. In fact, the *Star*, as it very well knew, was promulgating minority and extreme opinions.

But it was a lively and widely-read London daily, and as the Ripper murders wore on it persuaded other newspapers to accept its hostile view of Warren and his Home Secretary.

For by the time of the murders, Sir Charles lacked the firm support of the Gladstonian who had appointed him. Henry Matthews, Home Secretary in Salisbury's Conservative administration, was a Catholic Irish lawyer, and a vacillator. While his sharp legal mind led fellow lawyers to see him as the best Home Secretary since Peel, his light rhetorical manner displeased the House of Commons, and politicians accounted him a failure. Matthews was unnerved by popular protest against Bloody Sunday, and unwilling to back up his Metropolitan Commissioner.

Warren was already finding the Home Office difficult to handle. He had expected that command of the police would carry overall authority with direct responsibility to the Home Secretary. In the event, he found that all financial decisions were taken by the official Receiver for the Police, Richard Pennefather: 'a very able man, but disagreeable to deal with; he rubbed everybody up the wrong way,' according to Evelyn Ruggles-Brise of the Home Office.

When disputes arose between the Commissioner and the Receiver, it fell to the Under-Secretary of State, Godfrey Lushington, to sort them out. He made them worse, proving, in the words of Robert Anderson, 'a blister, not a plaister'. And, indeed, this crony of Major Smith and the Reverend Bill Rodgers was not the perfect intermediary with Scotland Yard. He was staunchly left-wing radical in his opinions, and the High Tories of the Metropolitan Police felt that he prated undesirable libertarianism.

Warren was also a devout evangelical Christian. (A 'maladroit martinet, embroiling himself with all and sundry . . . a Puritan Jingo', according to the *Star*.) He ended his life as an extremely active force in the Boy Scout movement. That combination of boyish adventurism in the fresh air as moral inoculation against tobacco, alcohol, swearing, and any recognition of sex, was quite typical of the militant Christianity with which officers like Sir Garnett Wolseley and General

Gordon replaced the eight-bottle fornicating aristocracy of Wellington's day. The Victorian evangelical would not enjoy the company of jolly vicars who contemplated licensing prostitution. Warren and Lushington could no more co-operate than Warren and Pennefather.

When Warren appealed over the civil servants' heads to Matthews, he obtained no satisfaction. In the words of Ruggles-Brise:

> **Matthews was an exceedingly able lawyer, but quite incapable of dealing with men; he was a regular Gallio in his attitude to Warren's complaints. Later on he quarrelled with Bradford, and if you couldn't get on with Bradford you could get on with nobody.**

(Gallio was the governor of Achaia who refused to adjudicate between St Paul and the Jews of Corinth, for 'Gallio cared for none of these things.')

Inside the force, Warren was involved in an important policy dispute which challenged his authority. It is always difficult to decide whether crime should be controlled by a large and highly visible uniformed force to deter offenders, or a large body of detectives in plain clothes to catch them. As a soldier, Warren favoured the former, and assumed he was empowered to place the emphasis where he chose. He reckoned without the strength and independence of the CID.

A regular detective force had existed since 1842, but fell into grave disrepute in the late 1870s when a brilliant confidence trickster named Benson succeeded in corrupting its senior officers. In the wake of that scandal the ambitious lawyer Edward Vincent took over its management and restored its morale, while giving it a fairly low profile for the next six years. He improved the filing system, and raised the strength of the CID to 800.

In 1884 Vincent left the police to enter the House of Commons. James Monro, Inspector-General of the Bengal Police, was called home to succeed him as Director of the CID with the new rank of Assistant Commissioner of the Metropolitan Police. Despite the title, Monro felt that he was and should be the head of an independent Bureau, unaccountable to the Commissioner. He also felt the CID needed expanding.

The great crime Monro faced was terrorism. Fenians were planting bombs in England, and even succeeded in exploding one in Scotland Yard. Monro was ably served by his senior officers, and co-operated closely with Dr Robert Anderson, whose official title of 'political adviser' to the Home Office concealed his undercover secret service activities against Irish Nationalist excesses. The two felt that they were succeeding in controlling the terrorist campaign, and were particularly self-congratulatory on having forestalled a plot to set off a bomb in Westminster Abbey during the Queen's Jubilee celebrations. But such secret service work demanded confidential access to the Home Secretary, and Monro stoutly resisted Warren's attempts to bring the CID under his own control. At the personal level, he differed from Warren on religious matters, and his milleniarist tendencies probably brought him very close to Anderson.

Warren seems to have disapproved of the political bias Monro gave the CID. He was himself originally a Gladstonian Liberal, though not one who wholeheartedly endorsed the Grand Old Man's conversion to Home Rule. Though the radical press focussed their hatred on the Commissioner, the *Echo* reported:

Sir Charles Warren has always objected to the transformation of the detective department into a political police, and was at loggerheads with Mr. Monro over the latter's espionage of Irish Members of Parliament and the further attempt to connect some of them with convicted dynamitards.

Opposed by civil servants without and his own Assistant Commissioner within, Warren threatened to resign in the summer of 1888. The crisis arose when Monro demanded the appointment of Melville Macnaghten as Assistant Chief Constable in his section. Since Macnaghten's character was unassailable, and Warren had always said that civilians might enter this grade, the Commissioner initially agreed. Then, for reasons he refused to make public, he suddenly withdrew his consent. His enemies noted that two out of three existing Chief Constables and both Assistant Chief Constables were ex-army officers. They assumed that Warren was determined to be surrounded by soldiers. Actually, Warren had suddenly learned that Macnaghten was once beaten up by rioters in Bengal, and felt this showed that he lacked the authority for a senior policeman. Monro insisted. Warren decided that either he or Monro would have to go. He accepted that a civilian could replace the latter, and suggested that Dr Anderson from the Home Office would be acceptable. Anderson had his own reasons for wishing to give up his 'political advisory' role. And it was Monro whose resignation was forced.

But Matthews performed one of those manoeuvres that made him seem so untrustworthy to his contemporaries. He slipped Monro into the Home Office with the meaningless title of Head of the Detective Service, and allowed him to go on liaising with the CID behind Warren's back.

Monro and Anderson were both reticent, even secretive, by nature and training, and a Home Office demand that the proposed repostings be kept confidential led to a fear among the detective force that Anderson was spying on Monro, or Warren was spying on Anderson when the two pairs had preparatory private meetings. In addition, it seems likely that Superintendent Williamson, the senior CID officer who had done most of the groundwork against the Fenians, objected to either rubber planters or Home Office bureaucrats being appointed over his head. At any rate, he threatened resignation or non-cooperation, and his bolshiness was promptly rewarded by a well-deserved promotion to Chief Constable in charge of CID.

Meanwhile the uniformed force had not really welcomed the appointment of a soldier as Commissioner, and began to blame him for resisting their claim for improved pensions (especially for men invalided out after being injured on duty), and for the severe loss of seniority imposed on men who were found drinking. Actually, both policies were enforced by the civil servants, and Warren was doing his utmost to meet the men's grievance over pensions. But he was quite incapable of conveying this to inferiors, and his well-known evan-gelicalism led to the erroneous suspicion that he approved of the punitive anti-drink regulations.

When the Ripper crisis occurred, the changeover of Anderson and Monro had just taken place. None of the three men attached great importance to the murders at first, and (unlike Major Smith) all were rather unwillingly prodded by public opinion into giving any priority to what they saw as a statistically infinitesimal number of squalid and abnormal crimes, affecting only a tiny and unimportant section of the populace.

But the double murder made an instant difference to Warren's position. It sparked five public meetings in the East End demanding his dismissal. And the immediate offer of a £500 reward for information in Sir James Fraser's name put the City Police in a comparatively good light. Poor Warren actually agreed with the Vigilance Committee that a reward should be offered. But he could not budge the Home Office, and he could not publish his dissent from its belief that rewards only promoted false witnesses and mischief-makers.

The Whitechapel Board of Works met on 2 October and lamented the adverse effect the panic was having on business. And noting a suggestion made by the popular East End preacher Daniel Greatorex, they complained of regulations that transferred police from districts with which they were familiar. They wrote to Sir Charles, demanding that he 'regulate and strengthen the police force in the neighbourhood.'

Sir Charles replied with a long and belligerent explosion. This shower of public criticism on top of his difficulties with the Home Office was exasperating to a police chief whose powers did not allow him to impose his own solutions. He opened with a barely polite rejection of their request.

> **I have to point out that the carrying out of your proposals as to regulating and strengthening the police force in your district cannot possibly do more than guard or take precaution against any repetition of such atrocities so long as the victims actually, but unwittingly, connive at their own destruction.**

His point was a fair one which the CID would reiterate. As long as prostitutes deliberately took strange men to secret places they could not be protected from an unpredictable murderer. But Warren may have intended to be offensive when he went on to suggest that as 'popular representatives' the Board might use their good offices to dissuade Whitechapel strumpets from going into dark, lonely places with strangers or acquaintances. And he certainly swung into a counter-attack when he asked them to improve their street-lighting.

So far Warren had been uncompromising, but relevant and responsive. Unfortunately his letter grumbled on prosily and weakened his case. London was the safest city in the world, but murder could never be prevented by strong policing. Secrecy was the hallmark of detective efficiency, so he wouldn't say what the CID was doing, beyond 'straining every nerve.' Extra men had been drafted to Whitechapel, but the remainder of the metropolis still had to be policed. Would the Board see to the distribution of 10,000 handbills requesting information? The Reverend Daniel Greatorex was wrong in saying police were shifted from familiar territory; Warren had personally reduced the need to transfer detective officers into new districts, though (guarding secrecy) he couldn't say how. One Board member said a thorough revision of police arrangements was necessary: would the Board care to say what they recommended? It would receive his attention.

This diffuse scattershot put him in a bad light by seeming at once intransigent and confused. The *Star* delightedly quoted much of it as an example of 'Warrenism'. The *Pall Mall Gazette* came more cautiously into action against the police. Stead, as a fellow-evangelical, genuinely approved of Warren the man and the soldier. But he could not approve of policing which seemed more intent on harassing Socialists and Home Rulers than fighting crime. And he had no time at all for Matthews.

In a brilliant series on The Police and Crime in the Metropolis, Stead took such representative London streets as Gray's Inn Road and Hackney Road, and showed in elegant schematized charts that each had recorded nearly two hundred unsolved crimes over the previous eighteen months. More in sorrow than in anger, the *Gazette* told Warren it just wouldn't do.

But Warren's next move was to let the most attractive aspect of his personality, the enthusiastic, outdoorsy, have-a-go, incipient Boy Scout Commissioner, lead him into a new course of action that accrued more bad publicity.

Among the public's proposals for electric street-lighting, rubber soled police boots, safe homes for reformed whores, and steel-armoured detectives disguised as women, came the suggestion that bloodhounds might be helpful. Sir Charles regarded them favourably: they might track more criminals than the Whitechapel murderer.

Bloodhound breeders and fanciers were wildly enthusiastic. Edwin Brough of Wynyate, near Scarborough, sent to *The Times* of 8 October a fulsome account of the merits of English bloodhounds, though he doubted whether the Whitechapel streets offered good tracking territory.

Sir Charles probably sighed with relief at the opportunity of a little healthy open air activity, and a detective suggestion which did not entail scouring the seamy lives of Whitechapel whores. He instantly sent for Brough, who brought two dogs named Barnaby and Burgho to London. On a frosty Monday morning early in October the dogs were given a trial in Regent's Park. The conditions were deemed unfavourable, but the dogs were completely successful in running free on the mile-long scent of a fugitive with a fifteen-minute start.

Next day the trials were repeated under better conditions in Hyde Park with the dogs on leashes. Sir Charles himself volunteered as fugitive for two of the tests: a jolly Victorian gentleman in curly-brimmed bowler and tweed suit racing away down the smooth walks in the crisp autumn air. Surprisingly the dogs performed far less well than they had done over frost, but Warren was still impressed, and was said to have bought them for the police.

This, of course, was beyond his powers. The odious Pennefather would have to approve the purchase first. And with matters looking so favourable for some positive action, objections started to pour in. The hounds would balk at following any scent tainted by blood. The trials had been held in the wrong place. Dogs would have to be trained exclusively for city work from puppyhood if they were to be any use.

On 19 October a glorious report appeared that Barnaby and Burgho had run away and got lost while exercising in Tooting. In fact, this was a canard which several papers corrected within a week. But the correction was not picked up for nearly ninety years (when Donald Rumbelow spotted it) and Barnaby and Burgho enjoyed a long innings as the comedy duo of the Ripper legend. In fact, Burgho had been sent to Brighton to be shown. Barnaby was back with Mr Brough, who had been shocked when he was taken to the scene of a Whitechapel burglary before the police had actually purchased him. Brough feared that his uninsured dog might be poisoned by vengeful criminals.

The outing to the burglary had proved the critics right. The hounds were useless on well-trodden city streets. According to his grandson, Sir Charles had always feared this might be the case. But giving them a fair trial had unfortunately served to make him a laughing-stock, especially as he had genially consented to act as 'fox'. A recent writer has even embellished the story by claiming that the dogs caught and bit him! It has been suggested that one of his Home Office enemies deliberately encouraged him to make a fool of himself.

Warren was still conciliatory on 18 October when he thanked all classes and creeds of Whitechapel residents for their support in the thorough house-to-house search of the murder territory. The *Star* had suggested that this search constituted selective harassment of Jews, so the Commissioner was no doubt anxious to back up the Central

News Agency report that it had been universal. The *Star* was fully apprised of the danger of anti-semitism in the East End, where the left stood together and even Diemschütz's tiny group was visited by no less an international activist than Prince Kropotkin. It had come grudgingly to Warren's support over the erasure of the 'Juwes' message. His overbearing manner might have been 'Warrenism', but his motive was good and sensible.

All the time Warren was seething at the endless criticism to which he and his force were subjected, and exasperated by the running unco-operativeness of the Home Office. Anderson's appointment had not disposed of Monro. Four years shared experience of clandestine policing, during which time Monro had instituted the Special Branch (as the Special Irish Branch) had led to mutual respect, and Anderson continued to consult Monro about the Ripper case. He took Swanson and Moore for private meetings in Monro's Whitehall office, and Sir Charles received only sketchy reports of their conclusions. Yet the Commissioner bore the public attacks for the fruitless murder hunt.

The readers of *Murray's Magazine* encountered his response when they opened the new issue at the beginning of November. In an article entitled 'The Police of the Metropolis', Warren unleashed his indignation. It was Warren at his worst. 'London has for many years been subject to the sinister influence of a mob,' he raged in the opening sentence, 'stirred up into spasmodic action by restless demagogues.' No doubt Hugh Childers had encouraged him to believe this on his appointment two years earlier. But high-minded intellectuals like Shaw and William Morris who had been in Trafalgar Square on Bloody Sunday were not quite the bloodthirsty revolutionaries this implied. Sir Charles was recklessly indulging the voice of Colonel Blimp.

In the classic manner of middle-aged conservatives, he acknowledged that there had once been justification for working-class unrest. But that time had passed with Chartism in 1848. Now 'reform after reform has put the Government into the hands of the people'. (Sir Charles's distaste is barely concealed.)

The general public should help the police rather than criticizing them. Indeed, the police were obviously doing their job well when they were attacked, whereas insurgency was being plotted under cover and unmolested whenever no public protest about police excesses could be heard.

A large portion of the article aired Warren's running grievance over the CID. Although names were not named, this was an outrageous public laundering of dirty linen. The Home Office mandarins would never forgive such a dissemination of boundary disputes within their empire.

Nor was Warren's appeal to the public well-judged. He abused them roundly for failing to trust and support the police. He asserted that the force could be reduced substantially if only it was given proper public support. Unimaginative suggestions were quite useless. As a parting shot, Warren demonstrated the total lack of liaison between his office and the police working on the ground.

> If the people of London ... will keep cool, and recognize the fact that the police are doing their duty in an admirable and exemplary manner, so far as is in the power of flesh and blood, among all the temptations to which citizens submit them, they will come forward and assist the police, as so many Vigilance Societies are doing at the present time, in suppressing crime.

That final suggestion might have been read in the Home Office as covert encouragement for Mr Lusk and Mr Backert in their demands for a large reward to be offered. And it would certainly have dismayed Walter Dew, who knew that pavement vigilantes impeded proper policing.

The subversive tendency of such a publication was instantly demonstrated by an anonymous policeman who printed a critique of Sir Charles's piece over the pseudonym 'A Pc'. He accused the Commissioner of demoralizing the CID to the point that able men refused to volunteer for it. He objected to square-drill, especially as it was enforced on all ranks below the 'gentlemanly' caste, which simple constables thought was an intolerable humiliation for Inspectors and Superintendents. He profoundly objected to Sir Charles's designation of the populace as a mob; resented having had to participate in Bloody Sunday, and thought the policing of the Jubilee had been extravagant. He also aired the familiar grievances about drink and pensions, though acknowledging that the latter was more the fault of the civil servants than the Commissioner.

The *Star* was overjoyed by Warren's gaffe, and printed long sections. It certainly proved their case that the Metropolitan Commissioner neither recognized nor understood the right of humble citizens to hold political opinions which lay outside the approved and established mainstream.

The civil servants took instant revenge. They drafted a stiff reprimand from the Home Secretary's office pointing out that the Commissioner was not at liberty to publish any observations on his duties unless they had been cleared by the mandarins first. Sir Charles found this intolerable, and he responded furiously on 8 November that if he could not answer any attacks made on his force without first having his replies vetted, he would have to resign. He disdained to notice the *Star*, but made it clear that the *Pall Mall Gazette*'s campaign had stung. On 10 November, the day Kelly died, his resignation was accepted. Two days later Sir Charles had emptied his office and abandoned police work for ever.

'Whitechapel has avenged us for Trafalgar Square,' crowed the *Star*, 'for coercion in Ireland and in London, for a score of things which are rather more culpable than the failure to take the Whitechapel murderer.' The journal was too modest. Its own campaign, stimulating the *Pall Mall Gazette* to join in, had provoked Warren to overstep the limits and publish the piece which enabled his enemies and rivals in Whitehall to bring him down. Had it simply been a contest between an unsuccessful Commissioner and a successful murderer, the establishment would have shouldered arms behind their own man.

But there was a postscript to his term as a policeman which has been generally disregarded. While the nation rejoiced, all the Superintendents in the Met, with the exception of one who was absent on leave and two who were sick, went round to Warren's house in a body. They expressed their unanimous regret at his resignation; stated that they were fully aware that he had left them a better, stronger and more disciplined force than he found; and acknowledged that he had suffered public attack for drink and pension grievances that were not of his making. They were proud to have served under him, and wanted this testimonial of their respect for him to be widely known. Alas, it has proved more amusing to suppress it.

The best epitaph on Warren is probably that left by a contemporary, whose views sound similar to Anderson's:

Warren was the finest man we had in Whitehall, but probably the worst appointment, because he must be independent,

and the Commissioner of Police is held in very tight bonds by
the Home Office.

Warren resigned in the middle of the Ripper investigation. The
whole case was distasteful to him, as well as professionally
embarrassing. He published no opinion as to the murderer's identity,
though his grandson believed he accepted the common Scotland
Yard belief at the time of his death in the 1930s that the Ripper was a
doctor, probably a Russian, who had committed suicide at the end of
1888. Obviously Warren was never in a position to know for certain,
and would have been most unlikely to go back and enquire.

His successor was James Monro, returned in triumph from his desk
at the Home Office. But his triumph was to be short-lived. The *Star*
had handled him sympathetically while his resignation was ammu-
nition against Warren. With Warren gone, it suggested that Monro
was rightly sacked because he devoted too much time to preparing a
notorious series of anti-Fenian articles for *The Times*. When Monro's
appointment was announced the *Star* solemnly attacked it:

> In the first place it is notorious that Mr Monro, while an
> Assistant Commissioner, was constantly intriguing against his
> chief, and it is highly undesirable that departmental dis-
> loyalty should be rewarded by promotion.

Poor Warren! If only he could have had such support when he
needed it!

The editorial went on to suggest that Monro had 'got up' the bomb
scares, and repeated the rumour that he was responsible for the
anti-Parnell series in *The Times*. They were near the mark; several of
the essays on 'Parnellism and Crime' emanated from very close to
Monro.

In 1889 came the great Dock Strike. This was not the sort of police
work to which Monro had become accustomed, and Warren's
confident bourgeois severity might have proved more satisfactory to
the middle classes. Moreover, the battle with the mandarins
continued. Monro had no more success than Warren in persuading
Pennefather and Lushington to improve the pension conditions. A
new Police Bill was being prepared for Parliament, and Monro fought
tooth and nail for the provisions he wanted. In the view of Anderson,
an experienced and diplomatic civil servant, he was recklessly
uncompromising.

He also pressed for a greatly enlarged CID. (Though he immediately learned that Warren's supposedly ludicrous obsession with boots was the responsible concern of an administrator whose force was literally suffering from flat feet because of cheap ill-made footwear.)

At the same time as the Police Bill struggle, he embarked on another trial of strength with the Home Secretary, a curious replay of his last battle with Warren. Macnaghten entered the police as soon as Monro took over, becoming Assistant Chief Constable in the late spring of 1889. In 1890, Assistant Commissioner Lieutenant-Colonel Pearson died unexpectedly. Monro wanted Chief Constable Howard promoted to replace him. It may or may not have been coincidental that Howard was another veteran of the Bengal Police. But Matthews wanted to bring the Met under close Whitehall control by putting a mandarin of mandarins into the slot. Evelyn Ruggles-Brise came from an established political and administrative family. He had been Permanent Secretary to a succession of Home Secretaries. He knew the department's wishes better than anyone else and would never rock the Tite Barnacles' boat. His presence in Scotland Yard would have made Matthews' life much easier.

Monro was understandably horrified. The reasons he gave for public consumption were excellent: Ruggles-Brise's appointment would demoralize a force which expected some top posts to be filled by promotion, and there could be no justification for bringing in a man without legal, military or police experience. It sounded much better than objecting to having a Home Office mandarin working in Scotland Yard, and would have been convincing from anyone but Macnaghten's patron.

After a stormy meeting with Matthews on the Police Bill and the Assistant Commissionership, Monro resigned. The Home Secretary was now subjected to universal criticism: he had fired two Metropolitan Commissioners in as many years. And his manoeuvre to explain Monro's going did him little credit. He changed the provisions of the Police Bill from those he had placed before Monro; he announced Howard's promotion and dropped Ruggles-Brise. And he pretended never to have understood that Monro thought these issues could not be negotiated. He took a well-deserved pasting from the House of Commons, but Salisbury stood placidly behind him, and he did not resign.

Monro went back to Calcutta where he ran a medical mission until his retirement in 1905. He had failed as an administrator, but left a very high reputation as a policeman. His obituary recorded that

> He had an exceptional share of most of the gifts needed for this department of the public service, especially in the detective branch, and became a regular terror to the criminal classes of Bengal and, later, London. His memory for facts and faces, names and details of cases was extraordinarily tenacious.

He was the least self-publicizing of the senior police engaged on the case. He published no memoirs and no record of any opinions about Jack the Ripper. So close a confidant of Dr Anderson was certainly fully informed of the CID's views, and he undoubtedly knew that although the file stayed open, the case was effectively closed by the time he left the police. In Anderson's temporary absence he headed the Alice McKenzie enquiry personally, and saw that it did not lead to any official revival of Ripper-mania, even though no charges were ever brought. What he knew about any named suspects cannot now be determined. He told his son that the case was 'a very hot potato', and did not even tell his wife whom he suspected. A man so deeply experienced in secret police work, both in Bengal and against the Fenians, would be most unlikely to have released any information or comment to others.

Frances Coles was still alive when Monro resigned, so yet a third Commissioner headed the Metropolitan Police before the Ripper scare in the East End was finally over. Sir Edward Ridley Colborne Bradford was to prove a great success in the office.

Like Major Smith, he was the son of a clergyman. After schooling at Marlborough he joined the Madras Cavalry, and served in Persia and at the Indian Mutiny. For this he was mentioned in despatches, and three years later he was given command of the First Central Indian Horse. This made him *ex officio* Political Assistant in Western Malawa, thus giving him his first experience of secret political work.

In 1867 he suffered an imperialist's misadventure. He was out on a tiger shoot, and had injured a beast with his first barrel, when a twig from the foliage in which he was taking cover fouled his second hammer. The infuriated tigress sprang on him and starting crunching up his left arm. Bradford's trusty native bearer, Dulla, came running to his aid, and the colonel spiritedly warned the loyal member of the subject race to make sure he shot the animal and not his master. Dulla succeeded in this, and the one-armed colonel quickly established a reputation for riding to pig-sticking with his reins in his mouth, so as to leave his lance arm free.

From 1874 to 1878 Bradford was drafted to priority work in law enforcement, and directed operations against highway robberies and murders by thugee and dacoits. At the end of that posting he became the Governor-General's Agent in Rajputana and Chief Commissioner in Ajmir. He was knighted in the course of this work, and in 1887 was recalled to England to head the Secret and Political Department at the India Office.

He had acquired a good deal of experience in administration, confidential investigation and police work. He had military authority. He was an outgoing man, and rode to hounds in England, while remaining notably discreet about his work. The decision to follow Monro with another soldier rather than another professional policeman brought Bradford to Scotland Yard, and his years there (together with Anderson's at the CID) played a large part in winning the British bobbies that affection and respect they were accorded by the middle classes and foreign visitors for much of the twentieth century.

Bradford's style was diplomatic. He policed big occasions, like the Queen's Diamond Jubilee and Mafeking Night, discreetly rather than heavily. He kept himself out of the public eye, except when official parades demanded a police contingent, on which occasions he made a fine one-armed figure in uniform on horseback, inspiring confidence without calling attention to his policies. He succeeded in reaching a compromise with the Home Office over police pensions. In all dealings he seems to have proffered so personable a manner that nobody thought of him as secretive until they recognized his discretion after the event.

We have no idea what he thought about Jack the Ripper. He was not the sort of policeman who was especially interested in 'Lives of the Great Criminals', and would certainly never have repeated or recorded the contents of a secret file if he had been.

The conclusion we must reach concerning all three Commissioners who oversaw parts of the Whitechapel crisis is that there is no mystery about their silence on the murderer's identity. Warren wouldn't have known it. Monro and Bradford, in their different ways, were so professionally formed by the experience of secret, undercover and political policing, that the habit of silence came naturally to them. And this would certainly have been supported by their Assistant Commissioner (CID), Dr Robert Anderson.

14

Memoranda from the Met:
Sir Melville Macnaghten

Sir Melville Macnaghten, Assistant Commissioner and Head of the CID at Scotland Yard after 1903, is the only senior policeman concerned with the Ripper investigation whom one can envisage buying this book. As a boy he had been fascinated by true crime, loved visiting Madame Tussaud's Chamber of Horrors, and avidly read 'penny dreadful' lives of the great murderers – Rush, Courvoisier, Palmer and the Mannings.

The interest was still apparent when he ended his career as London's chief detective. The waiting-room to his office was ornamented with photographs of detectives in disguise as well as past officials, and contained an album of scene-of-the-crime photos for the entertainment of visitors. In the office itself, Macnaghten mixed mug-shots of famous criminals with his portraits of personal friends, and retained (under lock and key) the grisly photographs of the Ripper's victims. Hargrave L. Adam, who appears to have made a single observant visit to this office to interview the Assistant Commissioner remarked that

> Sir Melville ... took an active and intimate interest in both crime and criminals. He was a familiar figure at the scene of any big murder case, which had special features of interest to the mind of a police official. ... He had a curious flippant way of talking about crime.

This 'flippancy' only means that Macnaghten (as can be seen in his memoirs) faced the problem of treating intensely morbid material by using the modern style of detached, sometimes ironic comment (perfected by William Roughead and Edmund Pearson) rather than employing that Victorian manner of explicit shock, horror and disapproval last used by Edgar Lustgarten.

Major Arthur Griffiths who, as former Governor of the Millbank Prison, knew Macnaghten rather better than Adam, confirmed his more-than-professional delight in crime.

> It is Mr Macnaghten's duty, no less than his earnest desire, to be first on the scene of any such sinister catastrophe. He is therefore more intimately acquainted, perhaps, with the details of the most recent celebrated crimes than anyone else at Scotland Yard.

Actually, Macnaghten's earnest desire outran his duty. Adam observed that his 'extensive knowledge of crime and criminals' equalled that of his predecessor Dr Anderson, and added: 'This does not, it should be borne in mind, apply to all those who have served as Commissioners and Assistant Commissioners at Scotland Yard.'

Monro, Macnaghten and Anderson possessed detective skills and criminological interest that were greatly admired by contemporaries. Wensley remembered Macnaghten with the utmost warmth as a

> tall, charming-mannered man [who] managed to win and keep the devotion of all kinds of men in all ranks of the service. With fine tact he said just the right things in just the right way to impress a young detective-officer.... He was a very great gentleman, and I owe much to him.

The implication that Macnaghten exploited Warren's creation of a socially mixed Chief Constabulary and fostered the promotion of his successor from the ranks is pleasing, for in that world of gentlemen and players, Macnaghten was the most strikingly gentlemanly of all the police chiefs.

The fifteenth child of a sometime Chairman of the East India Company, descended from one of the original 'Prentice Boys of Derry, he was educated at Eton. He loved his schooldays, participating enthusiastically in cricket and amateur theatricals, and leaving in 1872 without benefit of university to go and manage the family estates in Bengal.

Planter life gave him an authoritative sahib's manner and bearing that suggested a military background. In 1881 he was beaten up by rioters during land agitation, and came into contact with James Monro, then Inspector-General of the Bengal Police. Seven years later Macnaghten returned to England and may, like Major Smith, have been in need of a job. Monro extended the fraternity of the Old

India Hands chapter of the Old Boys Network and invited him to come to Scotland Yard, with the consequences we have seen. It was June of the following year before Macnaghten was actually inducted into the police, but from then on, despite his sponsor's resignation, his career was steady and satisfactory. He spent two years as Assistant Chief Constable, and on the ageing Williamson's retirement in 1891, stepped into his shoes as Chief Constable in charge of CID. When Dr Anderson's successor, Major Henry, was promoted to Commissioner in 1903, Macnaghten followed him as Assistant Commissioner.

All of which may seem a little late for an authoritative inside account of the Ripper enquiry. And indeed, Macnaghten acknowledged in his memoirs that the greatest regret of his life was never having played cricket in the Eton v. Harrow match. 'The second was that I became a detective officer six months after Jack the Ripper committed suicide, and never had a go at that fascinating individual.'

This is an honest and modest admission. Macnaghten had made on-the-spot enquiries into the Pinchin Street murder, at which time he heard direct evidence that the Ripper terror still held sway over the East End tarts. He had accompanied Anderson to inspect Frances Coles' body in Swallow Gardens. Leeson and White had made themselves into primary Ripper-hunters on less experience. Major Smith had cheerfully extended his prescient detective interest back into the summer of 1888. Macnaghten stoutly refused to enlarge his role, and must be acquitted of any tendency to exaggerate through vanity. Indeed, as becomes a gentleman, Macnaghten was neither a liar nor a boaster.

Sir Melville left at least three sets of notes on the Ripper case. He was prompted to draft what he knew for the information of posterity (or perhaps misguided junior detectives) by a series on the Ripper in the *Sun* of February 1894. A young man named Thomas Cutbush had been arrested in Kennington for a series of assaults on women in which he ripped their skirts from behind. The *Sun* confused him with another maniac named Colicutt, who had narrowly escaped prosecution for stabbing women in the bottom, but overlooked the embarrassing fact that Cutbush was the nephew of a former Superintendent (Executive) at Scotland Yard.

Macnaghten's first draft of his refutation lay in roughly jotted notes which passed to his grandson Gerald Melville Donner, and were seen by Philip Loftus in 1950. Donner died in 1968, and the notes have disappeared. All we know of them comes from Loftus' recollections. They apparently mentioned three people: a Polish tanner or cobbler; a man who went around stabbing young girls in the bottom, and one M. J. Druitt. The stabber was obviously Cutbush/Colicutt, who was being exonerated. M. J. Druitt we shall meet again. According to a letter from Loftus to Lady Aberconway, traced by Keith Skinner, the Pole was named Kosminski and said to be the original suspect, Leather Apron. He was also given more extensive treatment in the seven foolscap pages of folio Macnaghten deposited in the Ripper file at Scotland Yard.

This fair copy is such an important document that its central section had better be reproduced verbatim. After dismissing Cutbush as irrelevant, and disposing of the claim that his knife was either the Ripper's original weapon or a replica, Macnaghten asserts firmly that the Ripper had only the five victims – Nichols, Chapman, Stride, Eddowes and Kelly. He observes that the murderer was undoubtedly disturbed by 'some Jews [sic] who drove up to a Club (close to which the body of Elizabeth Stride was found)' and goes on to say

It will be noticed that the fury of the mutilations increased in each case, and seemingly the appetite only became sharpened by indulgence. It seems, then, highly improbable that the murderer would have suddenly stopped in November 1888, and been content to recommence operations by merely prodding a girl behind some two years and four months afterwards. A much more rational theory is that the murderer's brain gave way altogether after his awful glut in Miller's Court, and that he immediately committed suicide, or, as a possible alternative, was found to be so hopelessly mad by his relations that he was by them confined in some asylum.

No one ever saw the Whitechapel Murderer; many homicidal maniacs were suspected, but no shadow of proof could be thrown on any one. I may mention the cases of three men, any one of whom would have been more likely than Cutbush to have committed this series of murders:
(1) A Mr M. J. Druitt, said to be a doctor and of good family, who disappeared at the time of the Miller's Court murder, and whose body (which was said to have been upwards of a month

in the water) was found in the Thames on 31st Dec. or about seven weeks after that murder. He was sexually insane and from private info I have little doubt but that his own family believed him to have been the murderer.

(2) Kosminski, a Polish Jew and resident in Whitechapel. This man became insane owing to many years indulgence in solitary vices. He had a great hatred of women, especially of the prostitute class, and had strong homicidal tendencies; he was removed to a lunatic asylum about March 1889. There were many circs connected with this man which made him a strong 'suspect'.

(3) Michael Ostrog, a Russian doctor, and a convict, who was subsequently detained in a lunatic asylum as a homicidal maniac. This man's antecedents were of the worst possible type, and his whereabouts at the time of the murders could never be ascertained.

The notes go on to detail inaccuracies and erroneous conclusions in the *Sun* reports, and, for good measure, discount the theory of a left-handed or ambidextrous Ripper, and eliminate Tabram, McKenzie, Coles and the Pinchin Street torso.

Donald Rumbelow discovered them in the archives at Scotland Yard, and described them in his book *The Complete Jack the Ripper* in 1975. Stephen Knight examined them a year or so later, and reproduced them *in toto*, with a few insignificant variant readings from Rumbelow's quotations. The Ripper files are now in the Public Record Office, though Rose Mylett's file has been separated.

But the existence of Sir Melville Macnaghten's notes was familiar before the files were opened to the public. As early as 1950 Dan Farson discovered that Sir Melville's daugher, Lady Aberconway, had a typed copy of the notes, and he used them as the basis of a television documentary on the Ripper with Druitt's name reduced to the initials M.J.D. Tom Cullen had also seen Lady Aberconway's notes, and in 1956 he published the central section in full. They were slightly longer than those deposited in Scotland Yard, markedly more personal in expressing opinions, and made a more definite choice between the three named suspects.

Personally, and after much careful and deliberate consideration, I am inclined to exonerate the last two, but I have always held strong opinions regarding No. 1 and the more I think the matter over, the stronger do these opinions become. The truth, however, will never be known, and did, indeed, at one time lie at the bottom of the Thames, if my conjectures be correct.

In 1972 Farson produced his own book on Jack the Ripper, with some additional details about Melville Macnaghten and M. J. Druitt. As with Rumbelow and Knight's versions of the Scotland Yard notes, Cullen's and Farson's transcriptions of identical passages from Lady Aberconway's notes show some trivial variant readings. Farson's second edition altered the definitely erroneous '3 December' to '13' – which was still wrong. Sir Melville's frequent underlinings were obviously a tiresome handicap to exact transcription. But Farson found considerable uncertainty about the Polish Jew's name, transcribing it as 'Kosmanski' from the notes, and quoting Donald McCormick as offering the further variant 'Karminski' as well as the familiar 'Kosminski' used in the Scotland Yard version.

These, then, are the various all-important Macnaghten notes. Any sensible attempt to identify Jack the Ripper must rest heavily upon them. They are the only attempt to name the murderer made by anyone with access to the files before the 1970s. They are a summary of the conclusions reached by a protégé of Monro, and colleague of Anderson and Bradford, Swanson and Moore, Abberline, Godley and Dew. The names Macnaghten proposes are certainly names that were being bandied around Scotland Yard in the 1890s. According to Macnaghten's original sources of information, none of them was necessarily Jack the Ripper; any of them might have been. All three are far more probable (since their names emerged from police scrutiny of a great deal of evidence unavailable to the public) than any of the candidates proposed by armchair detectives or Edwardian gossip-mongers.

The status of the different sets of notes has been the subject of mild controversy. Stephen Knight suggests that Lady Aberconway's version is a preliminary draft of the Scotland Yard notes. Knight is obviously misled by his enthusiastic determination to give absolute priority to the notes he had himself inspected. And there is not the slightest reason to agree with him that Lady Aberconway would have added her own opinions in the guise of her father's.

But that additional material, with its pondered asides ('to my way of thinking', 'as a less likely alternative', 'after much careful and considerate deliberation') suggests that Lady Aberconway received her father's further thoughts on the matter he had deposited in Scotland Yard. Clearly he had discarded the loose observation that these three (apparently picked from a number of promising suspects) were more likely to be the Ripper than Cutbush and come to the definite suspicion that M. J. Druitt was Jack the Ripper. This in itself justified Farson and Cullen in unearthing the facts about Druitt, and suggesting that he was the most promising suspect hitherto named: the chosen suspect of a man with the opportunity to study written reports at first hand, and question detectives involved in the case. But their findings, as we shall see, disclosed critical error in Macnaghten's information.

We do not know how long a time elapsed between the Scotland Yard notes and the Lady Aberconway notes. If Loftus's memory was good, there had been a rapid accretion of information between the first rough draft for Scotland Yard (which could not have been made earlier than Colicutt or Cutbush emerged, stabbing women in the bottom early in 1894) and the final notes. The entirely new suspect Michael Ostrog came into the picture as soon as Macnaghten pushed his enquiries a little further.

The other differences between the three versions are:

1. M. J. *Druitt* is merely named in the rough draft (unless Loftus was unable to remember details). This in itself suggests that Macnaghten already saw him as a weighty suspect, and needed no further memoranda on a name which would figure largely in his fair copy.

    The Scotland Yard notes describe him (wrongly) as probably a doctor of good family; date his disappearance to 'the time of the Miller's Court murder' (inexactly), and give the correct date for the discovery of his body in the Thames.

    Lady Aberconway's notes add his age (wrongly); are definite (and still wrong) about his medical standing; gloss the good family as 'fairly good' (a nice touch from the gentlemanly Anglo-Irish Protestant Ascendant); add the highly plausible detail of a season ticket to Blackheath; and reduce his 'sexual insanity' to an allegation.

2. *Kosminski* is not described as Jewish in Loftus's recollection of the draft. But his name and Polish nationality identify him with the

later named suspect. And he is given the occupation of a tanner or cobbler, and apparently, identified as the early suspect 'Leather Apron.'

The Scotland Yard notes add the name and describe him as a Jew, omitting all mention of occupation. They generalize on his homicidal misogynistic maniac nature, link it with a hatred of prostitutes, and place him in an asylum in March 1889, observing that other circumstances made him a suspect.

Lady Aberconway's notes repeat the general material, eliminating the mention of prostitutes, and adding that he is probably still incarcerated at the time of writing. His residence is refined from 'Whitechapel' to 'the very heart of the district where the murders were committed'. And the mysterious figure of 'the City Pc near Mitre Square' who made a rough identification of Kosminski appears. No such Pc was called to the inquest or described in the press.

3. *Michael Ostrog* appears for the first time in the Scotland Yard notes as a Russian doctor, convict, homicidal maniac, and asylum inmate of deplorable antecedents whose whereabouts during the murders were never ascertained.

Lady Aberconway's notes are rather more informative about the 'mad Russian doctor'. Habitual cruelty to women, and a long practice of carrying surgical knives and instruments around with him are added to his characteristics. And he is definitely said to be alive at the time of writing.

It is interesting to compare the details on the suspects with Macnaghten's generalizations about the murderer. From the time of the Scotland Yard notes he thought it probable that the Ripper killed himself after the Miller's Court excesses, or became so obviously demented that his family had him incarcerated. The first supposition can only fit Druitt; the second might fit Kosminski, but not necessarily Ostrog. Each of these hypotheses allows for a slightly surprising delay: three weeks between overwhelming murder and frenzied suicide in Druitt's case (he was last seen alive on 3 December); four murderless months before Kosminski reached his asylum.

By the time of the Aberconway notes, Macnaghten's belief in the suicide had hardened, and accordingly Druitt became his prime suspect. What the evidence he conjectured once lay at the bottom of the Thames may be, we do not now know. We do know that he was quite wrong in many of the details he recorded about Druitt and Kosminski.

Twenty years after the *Sun* provoked him to compose the private memoranda, Sir Melville published his memoirs. In these he gave a blow-by-blow account of the Ripper murders, which contains several small inaccuracies, but compared with some supposedly historical accounts of later date is a model of precision. Sir Melville's resolute refusal to swank or embroider makes it well worth while to note carefully what he regards as absolutely ascertained fact by 1914, what he puts forward as doubtful, and what he describes simply as his personal opinion.

He is (as he had been in the notes) absolutely clear that 'the Whitechapel murderer committed five murders, and – to give the devil his due – no more.' Of Emma Smith he asserts that 'there is no doubt that her death was caused by some young hooligans who escaped arrest.' He states correctly that Martha Tabram's throat had not been cut, nor her belly mutilated, but acknowledges slight uncertainty as to why charges were not pressed against the men reported in her company:

> I think I am right in saying that the soldiers were detained, but that the available witnesses failed to identify them.

He had, in fact, forgotten the more precise information available to him when he wrote in the Scotland Yard notes:

> This woman had, with a fellow prostitute, been in company of two soldiers in the early part of the evening. These men were arrested but the second prostitute failed, or refused, to identify and the soldiers were accordingly discharged.

Without explaining why, he says that the two murders of 30 September were 'unquestionably by the same hand.' He elaborates on the Pc near Mitre Square who supposedly saw a man resembling Kosminski:

> On this occasion it is probable that the police officer on duty in the vicinity saw the murderer with his victim a few minutes before, but no satisfactory description was forthcoming.

Manifestly this officer was not Watkins who discovered the body, and had passed through the square about fourteen minutes previously without seeing anybody, nor Harvey who came to the edge of the square four minutes before the body was found. Nor does Swanson's final report to the Home Office detail any such witness, though it covers the Goulston Street finds, Lawende's sighting of Eddowes with a man, the medical evidence, and the kidney sent to Mr Lusk. In fact, Sir Melville was quite wrong in believing the witness in question to be a Pc. His error proves conclusively that he was not privy to information held by Anderson and Swanson.

Sir Melville did not mention the three suspects proposed in his earlier notes, and he did not claim any certainty about the final end of Jack the Ripper. But he made a tantalizing reference to posthumous evidence supporting his suicide theory:

> Although . . . the Whitechapel murderer, in all probability, put an end to himself soon after the Dorset Street affair in November 1888, certain facts, pointing to this conclusion, were not in possession of the police till some years after I became a detective officer.

And he now dated that suicide on or about 10 November.

What were these facts and when did they emerge? Before or after the notes of February 1894? Or between the composition of the Scotland Yard version and Lady Aberconway's version? Macnaghten gives us no hint. Whatever they were, he made no use of them to support the merely commonsensical explanation of his belief that the Ripper was a suicide.

> [T]he probability is that, after his awful glut [in Dorset Street] his brain gave way altogether, and he committed suicide; otherwise the murders would not have ceased.

It is interesting that he used the same phraseology in the memoirs as the notes ('his awful glut' and 'his brain gave way altogether'). But since there is no other trace of reference to the notes, and positive evidence that he did not refresh his memory of Tabram from them, this must be the result of repeatedly telling the story over twenty years until the form of words became fixed.

With the straightforward common sense of all the police seriously involved in the case, he said robustly: 'The man, of course, was a sexual maniac', and justifiably commented on the difficulty of arresting such men because of the lack of any motives to connect them with their victims. He also remarked: 'Not infrequently the maniac possesses a diseased body, and this was probably so in the case of the Whitechapel murderer.'

Finally, Sir Melville concluded his observations with two sentences which began by putting down some rumours which had been started by the alienist L. Forbes Winslow and ended by proving that he himself was unaware of material familiar to his superiors.

> I do not think that there was anything of religious mania about the real Simon Pure, nor do I believe that he had ever been detained in an asylum, nor lived in lodgings. I incline to the belief that the individual who held up London in terror resided with his own people; that he absented himself from home at certain times, and that he committed suicide on or about the 10th of November, 1888, after he had knocked out a Commissioner of Police and very nearly settled the hash of one of Her Majesty's principal Secretaries of State.

A word from Anderson, Monro, Bradford or the Home Office mandarins might have taught him that it was departmental disputes, culminating in the indiscretion of the essay in *Murray's Magazine* that knocked out the Commissioner. Sir Melville's belief in the popular rumour about Warren shows that either he did not consult them, or they did not confide in him. Moreover, he could not have read Sir Robert Anderson's memoirs (published in 1910) which untangled many of the causes of Warren's resignation and dismissed the coincidental Ripper crisis. Delicacy might have prevented Monro from letting young Macnaghten know that his own proposed appointment had been one major step toward Warren's downfall.

Sir Melville's notes do not tell us what the police decided about Jack the Ripper, and are not the views of the CID chief who investigated the crimes. They were, until 1987, the unique source for three suspects' names. One (Druitt) has been attached to a real man with a demonstrable life-history; a second (Ostrog) has never been verified, but seems, in conjunction with some of Macnaghten's beliefs about Druitt, to have been the basis for a later generation of casual police opinion; and the third (Kosminski) seemed impossible to verify, and its congruence with the stated views of Dr Anderson was resolutely overlooked.

15

The Man Who Knew Too Much: Sir Robert Anderson

On three separate occasions – in 1907, 1910, and in a Preface written for *The Police Encyclopaedia* which appeared in 1920 after his death – Sir Robert Anderson insisted categorically that the identity of the Whitechapel murderer was known. In his words, it was 'an ascertained fact'. He frequently referred to the case as an illustration of his favourite proposition, that the police were blamed for failing to solve cases where they actually had moral proof of the criminals' identities, but not the legal proof acceptable to courtroom lawyers. And he resented the persistent belief that his first major case remained an unsolved scandal.

His counterclaim has never been taken seriously. Richard Whittington-Egan accords it tentative respect:

> It may well be that, with modifications, the view expressed by Sir Robert Anderson back in 1910, that the criminal was one of the immigrant population – very likely Polish, possibly a Russian – comes nearest to the truth.

He offers no reason for his modifications, but he is at least polite. So is Robin Odell, who says: 'Sir Robert was obviously keen to uphold the prestige of the police, but his claim to have known who the Ripper was lacked substantiation.'

Donald Rumbelow accords Sir Robert the respect of a reasoned dissent, but bases it upon a misleading selective quotation.

Other writers have been content to point to Major Smith's excoriation of Anderson, and the discomfiture of Warren, whose creature they assume Anderson to have been. This is taken as evidence that Scotland Yard was at sixes and sevens. Stephen Knight goes further:

> None of the police of the day agreed with ... Anderson's

views, as is shown by the wealth of writing on the case penned by policemen of all ranks; none of his claims is supported by a single word in the files of Scotland Yard or the Home Office; none of the so-called 'facts' he claimed were 'definitely ascertained' were ever more than his own airy speculation. Either Anderson was inventing his stories to throw investigators off the scent of the Masons, or he was fantasizing to inflate his own ego. The puerile boast: 'I know who Jack the Ripper was, but I'm not telling!' has been surprisingly prevalent among supposedly mature men. Either way, Sir Robert Anderson, Freemason, one of the most high-ranking policemen connected with the Ripper case, dealt in fiction.

Who was this liar whose distortions and boasting stick in the throats of commentators who swallow Major Smith's swaggering without turning a hair? What misplaced departmental pride made him claim success where honesty would have confessed to total failure? What serpentine cunning enabled 'Warren's toady' to survive for so long after his master had fallen?

Dr Robert Anderson (he took his Doctor of Laws in 1875, and was only knighted after his retirement) was first and foremost a born-again Christian. He was converted at a crusade in Dublin when he was nineteen, and his religion was far and away the most important thing to him for the long remainder of his life. This is shown in the list of his books and publications: two titles on crime and penology, three on the Irish question, one volume of professional memoirs, and twenty four works of theology. It is further attested by the list of good causes and sectarian charities which lamented the loss of an active supporter when he died:

St Giles Christian Mission
The Bible League
Council of Dr Barnardo's Homes
Council of the Victoria Institute
Protestant Truth Society
Prophecy Investigation Society (Vice-President)
Protestant Evangelical Mission
Church Association
Women's Protestant Union
Police Institute

After his conversion to milleniarist evangelicalism (the belief that Christ's Second Coming and the Last Judgement were imminent), young Anderson spent a long time walking and talking with the preacher who had changed his life. It was his earnest wish to devote his professional future to Christ, and he would have loved to become a full-time minister of religion. But the most extraordinary scruples inhibited him from seeking ordination.

As an evangelical fundamentalist, he accepted without question that the Devil was the lord of this world. But as a hard-headed realist, he could not deny that organized churches formed institutions that were of this world. (They owned real estate and investment property, for example, and administered it to fund ministerial stipends.) These institutions, then, were actually and directly under the lordship of the Devil, and it followed that, sooner or later, would-be Christians who adhered to the churches would find themselves unwittingly lured into worshipping Satan. This had obviously happened long ago in the Church of Rome! But Anglicans were deplorably blind to the episcopalism which perverted the purity of their own religion.

The only safe Christian conduct, in Anderson's view, was rigorous study of the Bible and the steady practice of good works. This did not mean abandoning corporate worship. It was beneficial and indeed necessary for the children of God to assemble together and hear the Word and praise Him. But they should do so in the spontaneity of evangelical missions, rather than the potentially diabolical forms of sectarian liturgical worship. Anderson became an active and combative lay preacher, travelling around Ireland as a young man, and joining Barnardo in his mission to the East End when he came to London. (Barnardo was brought up in the Plymouth Brethren, a milleniarist sect.)

To such a man, his secular career was merely the way in which he earned his bread and butter and the physical energy to carry out the good works which were his first duty to his Maker. He referred wryly in his memoirs to the fact that he was 'a Peeler'. *Sub specie aeternitatis* it was a comically humble occupation. Moreover, it was morally inferior. While he was still only a criminal lawyer with a desk in the Home Office he wrote

Moral qualities are of greater worth than mere quick-wittedness, and no one who has much to do with criminals and crime can fail to suffer morally. We are told that the

primitive attitude of the human mind is trust; distrust is the
prevailing characteristic of anyone who sees much of the
shady side of human nature. He degenerates into a sort of
high-class detective.

Still, when he became the very highest-class detective, Anderson
did not permit his beliefs to detract from the conduct of his duties.
Heading the CID was the most demanding work his secular life had
ever put before him, and while his preaching and charitable activity
remained unremitting, his decade as Assistant Commissioner
marked the only break in his constant output of theological writing.

Now one thing is certain about the dedicated and scrupulous
Christian: he is not a vainglorious liar or boaster. It might be argued
that Anderson's fellow evangelical philanthropist, Barnardo, was
guilty of really silly lying backed by amateurish forgery to support his
premature claim to the title of 'Dr'. But Barnardo, though dedicated
and devoted, was never scrupulous. Until threatened with exposure
he cheerfully faked 'before' and 'after' photos of rescued waifs,
careless of the distress this caused their parents. And he quietly left
the Plymouth Brethren and joined the Church of England when this
was socially advantageous.

Anderson abandoned a very dear ambition in resisting the
temptation of ordination. Yet he scrupulously refrained from
opposing or encouraging the son who declared his own wish to
become a priest, and would never have lied about his professional
life to enhance either his own or his police force's reputation.

Not that he was as priggishly truthful as Washington with the
legendary cherry tree. As an ex-Secret Serviceman, he had occasion
to make his attitude to mendacity quite clear. He said in his memoirs
that he perceived an obvious Christian duty never to lie to one's
brothers; but he denied that murderous terrorists and subversives
were brothers, entitled to hear truth they would only misuse. Still, he
felt that one of his associates was wrong to have taken the Fenian
oath of loyalty without intending to keep it. And Hargrave Adam tells
a story which shows that he would tell half-truths to a suspected
murderer.

Hair-splitting? Of course. That is the nature of scrupulosity. But it
is quite incompatible with publishing lies in books for a wide
audience.

After his conversion Anderson went on to read law at Trinity

College, Dublin, and was called to the Irish Bar in 1863. His brother Samuel was a successful lawyer with government connections in Dublin Castle where he became solicitor-general, and under his aegis Robert practised as a barrister for a few years. One early duty he undertook was making a précis of the vice-regal government's secret information on the Fenian underground.

This led to his being called to London in 1867 to help the enquiries into the Clerkenwell Prison bombing, a Fenian outrage, which led to the last public execution in England.

Anderson never returned to Ireland. The Home Office made him the 'control' of various secret agents infiltrating the Irish Nationalist movement. The best known was the strange adventurer Thomas Miller Beach who, under the pseudonym Major Henri Le Caron, had penetrated the Fenian organization in America. Beach sent reports through the mails to Anderson, and held clandestine meetings with him whenever he passed through Britain. For twenty one years he had no other contact with the English authorities, and processing intelligence was Anderson's principal occupation.

The active young Irish lawyer needed other outlets for his energies. Of course, he was preaching regularly in the London slums. And believing that the Christian life demanded a healthy body, he took long walks and, when it became fashionable, played a good deal of lawn tennis with Godfrey Lushington, the Home Office civil servant whom he would later come to dislike. He also found time to have himself called to the English Bar, where he expected to practise ultimately, and took his Doctor of Laws degree.

The Home Office unofficially recognized him as a 'political crime advisor', but had also to find overt work to justify his presence. So he served on the Prison Commission and became Secretary to the Commissions on Railway Accidents and Loss of Life at Sea.

He had become a fixture in the battle against Irish terrorism by the time Charles Stewart Parnell was elected to Parliament in 1875, and the whole nature of the conflict changed. Hitherto the lawyer Isaac Butt had resolutely distanced the parliamentary Irish Nationalist Party from the militant activist successors of Young Ireland. But Parnell made a truce with the Fenians, formed the Irish Land League to press for the remission of peasant grievances, and encouraged the civil action of strikes and boycotts by which the Irish tenantry made the lives of English landlords and their agents miserable.

To Anderson (like Macnaghten, descended from a 'Prentice Boy of

Derry) the Protestant Parnell was a traitor to his class and religion. Worse still, Beach reported that the Nationalist leader, despite all disavowals, associated with notorious terrorists based in America and endorsed the murders they financed. These came to a head in the 1880s. Bomb outrages multiplied, and in Dublin Lord Frederick Cavendish and his secretary were shot in Phoenix Park. Parnell condemned the shootings out of hand, but Beach and Anderson believed that he secretly approved.

James Monro's appointment to the CID in 1884 was welcomed by Anderson. The new Director co-operated closely with him, and by setting up the Special Irish Branch to act on information channelled from Beach and the other agents, brought the bombings back under control.

Anderson's unhappiest time at this phase of his life came in that brief interlude of Liberal government which brought Childers to the Home Office and Warren to the Metropolitan Police. Childers accepted Gladstone's conversion to Irish Home Rule, and evidently had little time for a spy system set up to infiltrate the Fenians. To Anderson's great indignation, he found himself refused his expenses over a period of months, since he had no official appointment bar his Commission secretaryships. For ever after he would resent Civil Service and Treasury control of financing, and became noted as an enemy of red tape. He also regarded Childers as an unreasoning bigot. (Actually he was himself appallingly bigoted in his attitude to Irish Nationalism and Catholicism.) Far from being Warren's creature, he was a potentially hostile element who had been in place for nineteen years at the time of Warren's appointment by an enemy!

In 1887 Anderson lit a slow-fuse that ensured he would leave the Secret Service in a crisis. In March *The Times* published its first three numbered articles on 'Parnellism and Crime', seeking to prove that Fenian terrorism and Irish Nationalism were identical by comparing Irish MPs' speeches with articles in the American *Irish World*. *The Times* remarked that these sources were all public, but threatened to produce secret material later.

In April, unnumbered articles included the infamous facsimile of a letter, apparently signed by Parnell, apologizing for having denounced the Phoenix Park assassinations.

In May, three more numbered articles took readers 'Behind the Scenes in America', giving a picture of the rather absurd Fenian underground with its infantile code made by shifting each letter of the alphabet one place. (Ireland was 'Jsfmboe'.) This material, and the accounts of secret caucuses at national conventions, came directly from Beach's information.

All the articles were anonymous, and when pressed *The Times* would admit only that they were by several hands, and the principal author was a very young man. But the British Library catalogue today confidently ascribes a reprint of most of them all to Sir Robert Anderson!

The catalogue is only partly correct. The first three, marked by an idiosyncratic use of sarcastic quotation marks, were probably by the young man, Woulfe Flanagan, son of an Irish judge. Another, on the criminal consequences of boycotting, may well have been by Assistant Commissioner Monro, who was charged by the *Star* with responsibility for the whole series. But the pieces on America are Andersonian, publishing material which he had obtained as official secrets. He admitted as much in his memoirs.

The immediate response was merely vocal. Parnell furiously disclaimed the letter in Parliament, and the matter might have rested there had not some more forged letters been produced a year later in a libel action brought against *The Times* by F. H. O'Donnell. For a second time Parnell denied having written them, but the House of Commons decided that these allegations against the Irish party must be investigated, and appointed a Special Commission of Enquiry.

Beach was delighted. It offered a new forum in which the secret alliance between Parnellite Land Leaguers and violent revolutionary Fenians might be aired. He was giving up active spying and leaving America, and he tried hard to involve himself and Anderson with the Special Commission. But Anderson (though he hardly breathed a word about it) must have been horrified. Every description we have of the man, including Beach's, stresses his impassioned instinct for secrecy. According to Major Griffiths

> he was the most discreet, the most silent and reserved of public functionaries. Someone said he was a mystery even to himself. This, to him, inestimable quality of reticence is not unaided by a slight, but perhaps convenient, deafness. If he is asked an embarrassing question, he quickly puts up his hand and says the enquiry has been addressed to his deaf ear.

Hargrave Adam contrasted Anderson's secretive 'depth' with Warren's troubling intellectual profundities.

· Beach insisted that he owed his very survival to Anderson's utter discretion.

> I served under this gentleman in the Secret Service, and no greater honour can I pay him than to say that during all this time I was never discovered.... [H]e never wavered or grew lax in his care.... To him, and him alone, was I known as a Secret Service agent during the whole of the twenty one years of which I speak. If others less worthy of the trust had been charged with the knowledge of my identity, then I fear I should not be here today on English soil quietly penning these lines.

Anderson's lips were almost sealed on his days as a spymaster. Beach's memoirs appeared in 1892 (*Twenty Five Years in the Secret Service: The Recollections of a Spy* by Major Henri Le Caron) with fulsome praise of him. Anderson made no comment, and in his own memoirs eighteen years later confined himself to a few observations on Le Caron's usefulness and character. He did tell of the emotional handshake with which he and Monro expressed their relief at the end of Jubilee Day, when their exertions had ensured that the good Queen's devotions were not disturbed by the explosion of an infernal machine in the Abbey. (The Fenians, with a pleasant jocularity that horrified the police, had solicited subscriptions for a 'pyrotechnic display' in honour of the occasion!) But Anderson did not support his claim with any substantiating evidence or names. The old oyster enjoyed releasing the odd fragment of pearl from his store of mystery long after everyone had stopped looking.

Significantly, he himself imposed the original secrecy. While it would have been a great triumph to have made a number of spectacular arrests, Anderson had discovered that the Jubilee bomb plot had previously been revealed to his predecessor, Samuel Jenkinson. He felt that the authorities might be accused of acting as *agents provocateurs* if this became known, and he won approval for a silent campaign of watching and intimidating. Superintendent Williamson was despatched to France to warn the plot's leader that he would be arrested the instant he set foot on English soil. The man fled to America, and, as Anderson hoped, his subordinates in England panicked and abandoned the scheme. One was closely followed and could have been arrested at any time. A second died of natural causes while under observation. And a third, who had been nursing him, escaped without the police succeeding in identifying him. It may be of passing significance that the dead terrorist's identity was also unknown, and Anderson referred to him in official reports by the aliases 'Brown' or '*Cohen*'.

It is entirely characteristic of Anderson that he should not want this triumph to be shrouded in secrecy for all time. His papers on this (and other spying successes) were carefully preserved. And he finally told the public there had been a success, without revealing any details. Anderson managed to retain a public reputation for extraordinary discretion, despite a Home Office file grumbling about articles using official information which he published in 1891 and 1901. And the second of these contained his first major public pointer to the identity of Jack the Ripper.

But apart from acknowledging the three anonymous articles he had written for *The Times*, and insisting that nothing they said had ever been controverted, Anderson said very little about *Parnellism and Crime*.

He was sufficiently human not to make a parade of his failures. And his appearance in Beach's evidence was sufficiently inglorious.

On behalf of the government, he had tried to dissuade Beach from testifying; had creamed off the best of his previous correspondence to refresh the spy's memory when he insisted; and had sent these official secrets to a very sinister figure named Houston, who had been responsible for obtaining the notorious forged letter for *The Times*. Both Anderson and Houston had met Beach clandestinely in their private houses, evidently trying to distance the government from its spy. Fortunately for Anderson, he was not at the time a well enough known figure for his name to attract notice.

The Parliamentary Special Commission into *The Times'* allegations against Parnell was a fiasco for the government. Houston was shown to have bought the letters from a shabby Dublin journalist called Pigott, who had for years been trying to resolve his chronic lack of money by a mixture of begging, blackmailing and peddling dubious information. Pigott broke down under cross-examination, fled to Spain, confessed to having forged the Parnell letters personally, and shot himself. Although the Unionists and the government made what capital they could out of the Commission's finding that the Nationalists had recklessly encouraged boycotting, had endorsed demands for complete national independence (as opposed to constitutional Home Rule), and had accepted tainted money from terrorist-infiltrated organizations, these crimes were as nothing compared with using forgery to traduce Parnell's character. The Gladstonians and the Irish members had a field day when the Commission reported early in 1890.

The importance of this enquiry completely overshadowed the East End murders in the eyes of the ruling class during late 1888. Dr Anderson, the Home Office advisor on political crimes, would have had to answer some sticky questions had he still been in place, and it became known that he had personally contributed to the feature series which triggered the debâcle. Moreover, Anderson, the spy-master had known for years that Pigott was a notorious blackmailer who had worked shadily for both Unionists and Nationalists, and *The Times* was riding for a fall.

This would explain the mysterious 'overwork' for which Dr Gilbart Smith prescribed two months complete rest followed by another two months of sick leave just as Anderson took up his new post with the CID. As we have seen, Anderson's previous duties were not especially onerous. But he may well have been suffering from work-related stress in the light of the impending scandal which threatened to destroy his career. For Dr Anderson, the move to becoming a 'Peeler' was probably a welcome escape from an ominous departmental enquiry. And the Ripper murders were a heaven-sent distraction from the far worse professional danger he faced if attention focussed on his past activities rather than his present difficulties. For both him and Monro, the Parnell Commission was almost certainly the first preoccupation throughout the Ripper inquiry and for the next year.

Anderson's immense success in keeping his head down became apparent when the radical press turned on Scotland Yard that autumn. Stead, obviously preferring to avoid direct attacks on Warren for the time being, scrutinized the CID in October, and discovered to his surprise that it was commanded by 'a Dr Anderson, a millenarian and writer of religious books', with only the profes-sional support of Williamson, 'a kind of Melchizedec of Scotland Yard, [who] may probably claim with justice to be the grandfather of the force . . . superannuated.' Had the *Pall Mall Gazette* realized that Anderson was not merely on leave in Switzerland, but also part-author of 'Parnellism and Crime', they would have made hay with him, indeed!

The *Star*, as we have seen, ascribed the articles to Monro. It did not take in Anderson's existence until the end of November. 'Mr

Anderson,' it wrote, 'is to be brought from Dublin Castle, where he represents the worst type of Castle official, to control the Detective Service of London.' This confuses Robert with his brother Samuel. It shows bland unawareness that Anderson had been in London since 1867, and the CID since the end of September. It entirely lets him off the charge of failing to catch the Whitechapel murderer. Altogether it represents a triumph for Anderson's discretion under the threat of partisan investigative journalism.

He kept his head down, too, when his friend Monro was in trouble. At the time of the quarrel with Warren over Macnaghten's appointment, the discreet switch of posts suited both men admirably. Anderson was officially entitled to consult the Home Office Head of Detective Service, and definitely did so until Monro's return to Scotland Yard as Commissioner. Thereafter he continued to seek his guidance on difficult cases, and although Monro laughingly refused to do his job for him, Anderson makes it quite clear that whatever help he needed was in fact forthcoming. The gifted and experienced detective Monro, then, was directly managing the promising newcomer Anderson throughout the Ripper investigation.

When Monro's final quarrel with the Home Office began, Anderson stayed under cover. As a natural civil servant and empire builder he had been delighted that Monro still wanted an enlarged CID. But he had also been the colleague of the Home Office mandarins for most of his working life and knew their ways. He knew that Monro was approaching them badly, and he had no personal objection to Ruggles-Brise. At the same time, the pro-Monro (or rather, anti-Matthews) press was already hinting that his own appointment had injected a large enough Whitehall presence into Scotland Yard. Anderson shared the working civil servant's belief that most publicity is bad publicity. He said nothing, and didn't stir things.

As Detective Chief he was an outstanding success. He proved, surprisingly, no great bureaucrat. He did little for the filing system, and failed to introduce card-indexing and typewriting when other offices adopted these advances. But such reform would probably have seemed to him mere red tape. What counted was that throughout his decade in office the crime figures steadily declined.

Major Griffiths, in a quick resumé of the CID's history from the time of the Benson corruption scandal, completely ignores Monro, but is lavish in his tribute to Anderson.

Dr Anderson, who was chief of the Investigation Department until 1901, when he resigned, was an ideal detective officer, with a natural bias for the work, and endowed with gifts peculiarly useful in it. He is a man of the quickest apprehension, with the power of close, rapid reasoning from facts, suggestions, or even impressions. He could seize on the essential point almost by intuition, and was marvellously ready in finding the real clue or indicating the right trail.

Hargrave Adam was impressed by Anderson's old-fashioned air of authority and omniscience: he saw him as

a tall, vigorous-looking man, with a determined expression of countenance and a Victorian habit of dressing. He is emphatic in speech and prolific in delivery. His rugged face is enlivened by superabundant energy.... He has a keen, rather a grim sense of humour which, when he indulges it, is accompanied by a demure and self-satisfied grin....

What he did not know about crime was scarcely knowledge on the subject. He had decided opinions about crime and criminals generally, and his sympathies for the latter were by no means easy to enlist.

That generalized quality of knowledge and opinion is most important in considering Anderson's remarks on the Whitechapel murders. He was definitely not, in the Melville Macnaghten/Chamber of Horrors sense, a true-crime enthusiast. He knew the names of the great murderers. But he was not really interested in murder. The criminals who interested Anderson were habitual thieves, for he was aware that robbery and receiving are the mainstay of professional crime and the heart of criminal investigation. He told no anecdotes whatsoever about lovable old rogues (as Adam had noted, he didn't believe in them) or dastardly villains. His facts were statistical. His suggestions were penological.

His references to Jack the Ripper all occur as illustrative material for his general theories. His first claim that the murderer's identity was known and he was incarcerated slipped out as an aside: a fragment of pearl that, perhaps, provoked one of his demure, self-satisfied grins. He opened *Criminals and Crime* with a complaint that the public was sadly misinformed about crime and tended to overreact with silly recommendations. As one example he took 'the Whitechapel murders' of the autumn of 1888. At that time the sensation-mongers of the newspaper press fostered the belief that life in London was no longer safe, and that no women ought to venture abroad in the streets after nightfall. And one enterprising journalist went so far as to impersonate the cause of all this terror as 'Jack the Ripper', a name by which he will probably go down in history. But no amount of silly hysterics could alter the fact that these crimes were a cause of danger only to a particular section of a small and definite class of women, in a limited district of the East End; and that the inhabitants of the metropolis generally were just as secure during the weeks the fiend was on the prowl as they were before the mania seized him, or after he had been safely caged in an asylum.

In *The Lighter Side of My Official Life* he was again drawn into a discussion of Jack the Ripper by his irritation with public folly:

When the stolid English go in for a scare they take leave of all moderation and common sense. If nonsense were solid, the nonsense that was talked and written about those murders would sink a *Dreadnought*.

Anderson typified the senior policeman in his attitude to the Whitechapel tarts:

[T]he wretched victims belonged to a very small class of degraded women who frequent the East End Streets after midnight, in hope of inveigling belated drunkards, or men as degraded as themselves.

Anderson had a practical and scientific proposal to make which seemed to him merely sensible and to most other people quite inhumane.

Let the Police of the district, I urged, receive orders to arrest every known 'street woman' found on the prowl after midnight, or else let us warn them that the Police will not protect them. Though the former course would have been merciful to the very small class of women affected by it, it was deemed too drastic, and I fell back on the second.

However the fact may be explained, it is a fact that no other street murder occurred in the 'Jack-the-Ripper' series.

This qualified claim to have saved lives was Anderson's only personal vaunt in the Ripper case. Those colleagues who remembered the Miss Cass scandal of the previous year must have shuddered at his temerity in proposing indiscriminate arrests!

A footnote explained why he attributed five murders only to the Ripper:

> I am here assuming that the murder of Alice M'Kenzie on the 17th July, 1889, was by another hand. I was absent from London when it occurred, but the Chief Commissioner investigated the case on the spot and decided that it was an ordinary murder, and not the work of a sexual maniac. And the Poplar case of December, 1888, was a death from natural causes, and but for the 'Jack the Ripper' scare, no one would have thought of suggesting it was homicide.

This is interesting on two counts. Since it explains his assertion that no more Ripper murders followed his recommendation that prostitutes be offered no police protection, it discreetly dates that recommendation for us: after Kelly's death, quite possibly during the two-week hiatus before Monro took over from Warren, but certainly Anderson's first strong action after his return from the continent. And secondly, it proves that he trusted Dr Bond of Westminster, A Division's Police Surgeon, more than any other medic involved in the case, for the Scotland Yard files show clearly that Anderson was directly responsible for the flow of doctors to Poplar that so upset Wynne Baxter, being quite determined to have Bond's professional opinion on a body which he and the uniformed branch agreed was obviously a victim of natural death.

Carried away by his own flow of memory, and grudgingly acknowledging public interest, Anderson proceeds to give his own fullest account of the Ripper: the conclusions which outraged Major Smith and Stephen Knight.

> One did not need to be a Sherlock Holmes to discover that the criminal was a sexual maniac of a virulent type; that he was living in the immediate vicinity of the scenes of the murders; and that, if he was not living absolutely alone, his people knew of his guilt, and refused to give him up to justice. During my absence abroad the Police had made a house-to-house search for him, investigating the case of every man in the

district whose circumstances were such that he could go and come and get rid of his blood-stains in secret. And the conclusion we came to was that he and his people were certain low-class Polish Jews; for it is a remarkable fact that people of that class in the East End will not give up one of their number to justice.

And the result proved that our diagnosis was right on every point. For I may say at once that 'undiscovered murders' are rare in London and the 'Jack-the-Ripper' crimes are not within that category. . . . I will only add here that the 'Jack-the-Ripper' letter which is preserved in the Police Museum at New Scotland Yard is the creation of an enterprising London journalist.

Having regard to the interest attaching to the case, I am almost tempted to disclose the identity of the murderer and the pressman who wrote the letter above referred to. But no public benefit would result from such a course, and the traditions of my old department would suffer. I will merely add that the only person who ever saw the murderer unhesitatingly identified the suspect the instant he was confronted with him; but he refused to give evidence against him.

In saying that he was a Polish Jew I am merely stating a definitely ascertained fact. And my words are meant to specify race, not religion. For it would outrage all religious sentiment to talk of the religion of a loathsome creature whose utterly unmentionable vices reduced him to a lower level than that of a brute.

Every Ripper expert in the world, including myself, is at fault for failing until 1989 to check or comprehend one vital difference in Anderson's serialized version of his memoirs in *Blackwood's Magazine*, where he observed,

I will only add that when the individual whom we suspected was caged in an asylum, the only person who ever had a good view of the murderer at once identified him, but when he learned that the suspect was a fellow-Jew he declined to swear to him.

Anderson dropped these words when the hostile Major Smith

pointed out that he laid himself open to libel action by accusing any Whitechapel Jew of concealing a felony. Yet not only (as Alexander Kelly had remarked) did Anderson identify the witness as Jewish; crucially he stated that the identification took place in an asylum. According to him, the Ripper was incarcerated as a lunatic, and not held as a murder suspect.

The general pother over Anderson's claim is elevated by Donald Rumbelow's critical suggestion that Anderson's reference to a house-to-house search carried out while he was abroad proves him to have based his conclusions on an investigation which was completed before the second murder. This pointed to John Pizer, the suspect who was decisively cleared at Chapman's inquest. Like Tom Cullen, Rumbelow accuses Anderson of casting unwarrantable aspersions on the character of a man he had been unable to convict.

There are three objections to this proposal (despite Rumbelow's attractive indication of a witness who purported to identify Pizer, but broke down under examination). The first is that Pizer was not at any time 'caged in an asylum', as Anderson had said of the Ripper. The second is that Anderson's memory was defective in recalling that the house-to-house was completed by the time he returned from abroad: it continued for another two weeks, before coming to a conclusion very like that reached from the earlier questioning of Pearly Poll and the denizens of Crossingham's. And the third is that Anderson carefully differentiates between 'the conclusion we came to' on examining the house-to-house reports, and 'the result' which proved this 'diagnosis' to have been correct. Rumbelow overlooks the second sentence, and so does not recognize that Anderson is actually taking a pride in having made certain correct deductions from the original enquiries, which were proved right by subsequent evidence. Typically, Anderson does not tell us what this evidence was.

It is interesting that both *The Times* and Inspector Swanson indicate that the detailed house-to-house enquiry was confined to an area north of Whitechapel Road. Swanson's precise report to the Home Office on 19 October is particularly revealing:

> 80,000 pamphlets to occupiers were issued and a house to house enquiry made not only involving the result of enquiries from the occupiers but also a search by the police and with a few exceptions – but not such as to convey suspicion –

covered the area bounded by the City Police boundary on the one hand, Lamb St., Commercial St., Great Eastern Railway and Buxton St., then by Albert St., Dunk St., Chicksand St. and Great Garden St. to Whitechapel Road and then to the City boundary. Under this head also Common Lodging Houses were visited and over 2,000 lodgers were examined.

A detailed and thorough search of a very precise wedge-shaped area, indeed. Exactly the area of maximum Jewish settlement. Yet Stride's murder (on which Swanson is formally reporting) had taken place two main roads and a tangle of back streets away to the south! And Buck's Row is just excluded. The omissions that were deliberately made with precautions against their arousing suspicion show that this was not a random dragnet: a month after Pizer's release Swanson knew who or what he wanted to find, and he knew certain locations where he might find him or it. He wanted the men on the ground to bring back copious information, without scaring away some individual. Anderson is silent about this suggestive fact.

His final statement on Jack the Ripper was made in support of his pet theory about moral and legal proof. It contains no further data, merely another assertion that the murderer's identity was known.

So again with the 'Whitechapel Murders' of 1888. Despite the lucubrations of many an amateur 'Sherlock Holmes', there was no doubt whatever as to the identity of the criminal, and if our London 'detectives' possessed the powers, and might have recourse to the methods, of Foreign Police Forces, he would have been brought to justice. But the guilty sometimes escape through the working of a system designed to protect innocent persons wrongly accused of crime.

Notice that Anderson never said that 'the Police' knew who Jack the Ripper was (even though Hargrave Adam put that natural interpretation on his words). Nor does he say 'I' or even 'we' knew the murderer's name. He describes a police enquiry from which 'we' constructed a theoretical profile of the likely murderer. And thereafter he passes stiffly to impersonal statements:'The result proved that our diagnosis was right'; 'I am merely stating a definitely ascertained fact'; 'there was no doubt whatever as to the identity of the criminal'.

It is unthinkable that Anderson should not have told his

Commissioner when he believed the case was solved. He certainly told Swanson and may have told Moore that there was reason for the file to be closed. But clearly it was not shared widely. The men at the top – Anderson, Monro and Bradford – had all come to the police with a training in secret political work. They respected very tight 'need to know' restrictions. Police on the ground thought the Ripper was still at large. Abberline apparently thought he had been taken in 1902. Macnaghten himself, most obviously, was not told any reason why Sir Robert believed, beyond the shadow of a doubt, that someone akin to 'Kosminski' was the Ripper.

Anderson's words make it plain that he saw something more than 'many circumstances' making his Polish Jew a strong suspect. And, as we shall see, Macnaghten's description of Kosminski, barring the incarceration, might equally be a description of Pizer, who so closely resembled Anderson's unnamed suspect.

It is incomprehensible that no commentator has pounced on the identity between Anderson's Jew and Macnaghten's Kosminski. Anderson might, of course, have been wrong (he was always opinionated!). But he was the officer responsible for closing the file. Everything claimed for Macnaghten as the repository of CID conclusions applies far more truly to Anderson. And we have seen that his nature and experience would dispose him to hug the secret to himself for many years, finally releasing fragmentary conclusions without substantiation. He would be highly unlikely to confide in a junior like Macnaghten, whose interest in true crime was utterly remote from the chilly evangelical's scientific distaste for the theft industry, and may even have seemed to him immoral and gossipy. Indeed, Sir Melville's preservation of Kelly's picture under lock and key in his own office would almost certainly have disgusted Sir Robert, who saw the body *in situ*. In his memoirs, Anderson revealed that he once became so exasperated with a prominent subordinate who made a silly fuss over a threatening letter, that he threw the offending document in the fire, thereby culpably destroying evidence. And Swanson's private marginal note in his copy of the memoirs identifies the irritating policeman as Macnaghten.

He would be in a position to bind the Chief Inspectors involved to secrecy if he chose. But some information from the earlier enquiries inevitably floated around the department, and Sir Melville picked it up.

It goes without saying that Smith the worldling and Anderson the millenarianist were utterly antipathetical personalities. Neither can be imagined having any comfortable dealings with the other, or willingly exchanging confidences.

And it need only be added that the humdrum solution Anderson proposes – an ordinary working-class sex maniac living in the district – coupled with the apparent impossibility of identifying one out of the 12,000 or so Jews estimated to be living in Whitechapel at the time, has been enough to put off researchers. Even so, Macnaghten had given a promising lead, and his notes utterly refute Stephen Knight's assertion that 'none of the police of the day agreed with either of Anderson's views'. Between them the two successive Assistant Commissioners confirm that the strongest suspicion rested on a Polish Jew who lived in the heart of the district, and who was committed to an asylum before a legitimate case could be mounted against him. Macnaghten (often wrong on details) adds that he was called Kosminski and was a tanner or cobbler. Anderson adds that he could go and come and change his clothes easily, and that his people would not betray him to the police, because such were the habits of their race. Both propound the silly late-Victorian notion that masturbation ('unmentionable' or 'solitary' vices) led to his loathsome madness. Both agree that he was positively identified by a witness whom Macnaghten describes as a constable on duty near Mitre Square, and Anderson recalls as unwilling to testify in court.

Since neither Anderson nor Macnaghten was given to lying or boasting, their joint testimony ought long ago to have been given the highest priority.

PART IV
THE SUSPECTS

16

Sexual Serial Murderers

We are better placed than the public in 1888 to assess the merit of suggested identifications for Jack the Ripper. Although the press then vaguely identified previous serial murderers from Bavaria and Paris, little was known about them. Although senior policemen knew they were hunting a peculiarly nasty sex maniac, the public was unaware of these rare perverts, and commentators bent their energies to devising rational motives. This uncriminological approach has remained popular. It produces sensational celebrities and even royal candidates for the role of Jack the Ripper. We may eliminate most of the wilder suggestions by a brief examination of sexual serial murderers known to us today, looking for the common features we might expect to find recurring in the Ripper.

Not every male multiple murderer of women is a sexual serialist. George Joseph Smith, confidence trickster and bigamist, drowned three 'wives' in baths. Since his clear motive was avarice – the inheritance of their estates and insurance policies – he is not comparable with Jack the Ripper. Nor, despite Abberline, is the bigamist George Chapman (Severin Klosowski) who poisoned three 'wives', apparently because this seemed the easiest way of terminating the relationships. Rapists who kill their victims to avoid exposure also evince rational motives.

But Peter Sutcliffe, the 'Yorkshire Ripper', thoroughly earned his title, battering and killing women who were unknown to him and slashing their bodies; finding his victims in the first instance by picking up prostitutes from familiar beats; continuing his activities while they caused a highly publicized terror in Leeds and Bradford.

John Reginald Christie, Britain's second most familiar multiple murderer, differs in that he was (in the popular sense) a necrophile. He could only, or most satisfactorily, enjoy sex with the body of a dead partner. The Ripper was evidently not like Christie, whose motive for killing women was to acquire a body for sexual partnership. Bizarre as that may be, the Ripper was still more extraordinary in wanting a body in order to cut open its abdomen and slice its face.

Mr Wynne Baxter proposed the rational motive of acquiring an internal organ for sale. Correspondence in *The Lancet* canvassed the possibility of a thief killing witnesses or victims to ensure he was not identified. Experience today tells us that lewd mutilation is always performed to yield the murderer some kind of sexual release, though this may well take the form of an urgent and ecstatic gratification of the feeling of power rather than sensory erotic pleasure.

The earliest purely sexual mutilation known to me is that of Elizabeth Winterflood in 1807. Her genitals had been chopped away and the flesh thrown under some parked carts. The trial and acquittal of her ponce, Thomas Greenaway, was reported at the time, and included in a small volume of three contemporary south London murders. Essentially, however, it attracted no attention. The erotic feature which would have drawn immediate notice today was dismissed as a trivial side issue, and the whole case was completely forgotten for 170 years. Certainly we have paid ever greater attention to sexual murder since 1888; I doubt, however, whether it is peculiarly a crime of our time so much as an interest.

From the information generated by that interest, we can draw certain general observations.

To start with, we are dealing with a male criminal. Men have been heterosexual, homosexual and bi-sexual mass-murderers. The very rare women sexual mass-murderers have all been heterosexual, with the exception of Erszeveth Batory, whose conscious motive was magical: the preservation of her youth by bathing in virgins' blood.

Next, we are certainly looking for a lone sexual killer. The California 'Hillside Murders' are the only familiar sexual series carried out by two accomplices, and as we might expect with two men present, the victims were raped. The Ripper's were not.

The idea of a rationally motivated murderer carrying out a steady search for Marie Jeanette Kelly and killing her associates on the way is intrinsically specious. This 'whodunit' approach to multiple murder is useful to the detective novelist; it allows a steady accretion of bodies and a tangled motive reflecting the interwoven relationships of varying characters. Unfortunately, it doesn't happen in reality. Mysterious multiple murders may happen within a family (the Croydon mystery is a good example). Terrorists and gangsters may kill a series of suspected opponents. But nobody has ever set off to look for one known but obscure victim, and killed 'the witnesses' as he went.

It was once widely assumed that the sexual serial murderer had a personality rather like Christie's: middle-aged, unobtrusive, pedantic and pernickety, undersexed, outwardly prudish, henpecked or a bachelor, utterly unlikely as a lascivious monster. Albert De Salvo the Boston Strangler exploded the image. He was youngish, imaginative, reasonably personable, and wildly active sexually. His thirteen murders were the high-points of a total of 1,300 sex-crimes, in addition to which his wife complained that his sexual appetite was insatiable!

In fact, the sexual serialist is usually a young, quite attractive man with a sufficiently active normal sex life to allay suspicion. Ted Bundy, who killed at least twenty women in the northwestern states and another four in Florida, was good-looking, able, articulate, and generally attractive to women. Richard Speck, who killed eight nurses in one orgy of murder, and may have been responsible for another mass killing and several individual rape-murders, was too pock-marked to be really good-looking; but possessed a quiet, gentle personality whose attractiveness to women contrasted surprisingly with his inability to retain a steady girlfriend. Norman John Collins who killed and mutilated college students and high-school girls in Ypsilanti, Michigan was a good-looking motorbike rider who normally dated two or three times each week. Sutcliffe actively used the prostitutes from whose numbers he drew his first victims, and formed a satisfactory marriage while he continued his killing.

The internal chaos suffered by these men only revealed itself in small signs: Speck's tattoo 'Born to Raise Hell'; Collins' alleged highly sophisticated cheating in college exams; Bundy's sordid loner's pornography-filled home life; Sutcliffe's tendency to drink and occasional violence.

Some of their partners might have been able to reveal instances of sexual incompetence belying their attractive exteriors. Collins' inability to feel anything but rage and disgust with menstruating or unwilling women, for example. Speck's half-hour long anal and vaginal penetration of the only one of his victims he engaged in physical intercourse. And Paul Knowles, who killed at least twelve women and five men for a variety of reasons, including robbery, rape and mere pleasure, travelled for a time with an English journalist whom he picked up in a bar. She reported that he was good company, but disappointing in bed. His lean and predatory good looks had attracted her, but he proved impotent in normal coitus.

Their psychological inadequacies were not accompanied by any mental deficiency. Ted Bundy was exceptionally intelligent, and hugely impressed lawyers and judges with his skilful self-tutored handling of his own defence. Dennis Nilsen was highly intelligent, with a markedly romantic creative urge, and some talent for writing and drawing. Paul Knowles made an acceptable companion for a sophisticated and gifted metropolitan journalist. Norman Collins was a good-average student in a small State University. Speck and Sutcliffe, with intelligence around or little above average, look pretty dull in the company of their peers!

Except for Speck, all these mass-murderers found their victims in the places where they normally found their sexual partners. Sutcliffe's prostitutes and Collins' fellow-students are obvious examples. None appears to have had any difficulty in persuading women to accompany them, either on non-specific dates or for commercial sex.

Nor did their general demeanour arouse suspicion among their family, friends and acquaintances. Peter Kürten's fellow-workers were convinced there had been a mistake when he was arrested. Collins' uncle was a policeman who never dreamed that he brought a murder victim into the family laundry-room. Sandy Fawkes, who was travelling in Paul Knowles' company when he was arrested, was astonished to learn that he had murdered people at all, let alone during the time they were together. Sutcliffe's wife staunchly believed in his innocence. Even Ed Kremer, whose screaming rows with his mother led her to see him as murderous when he was only thirteen, did not at first persuade the police that he was really responsible for the co-ed murders.

All the sexual killers kept their murderous activities within easy topographical range of their normal daily lives. Collins moved about within the Ypsilanti area. Sutcliffe's first five murders fell so clearly in the northeast Leeds/northwest Bradford region that it was evident to anyone capable of looking at a map that he must be based there. Of course, the age of cars and motorways allowed him to spread his net further when the police put heavy preventive patrols into the red-light districts of Leeds and Bradford, and so Manchester and Halifax came within his orbit. His first years of murder may be compared with the unnamed 'Jack the Stripper' who killed prostitutes in West London, all picked up on familiar beats in the Bayswater/Westbourne Grove/Notting Hill district, and transported no farther than was convenient for the small van he drove.

The motor-car allowed Bundy to operate across Oregon, Utah and Washington. The footloose petty criminal Knowles left a trail of murder across America, but it followed his habitual rootless lifestyle. Peter Kürten killed within the Düsseldorf area for thirty years. Frederick Gordon Cummins, a young airman who killed and mutilated prostitutes in blacked-out wartime London, consistently picked them up in the neighbourhood of Piccadilly. There is no known case of a sexual serialist repeatedly travelling to an out-of-the-way district to find his victims.

More striking still, when we reflect on Macnaghten's plausible suggestion that the Ripper killed himself after the total breakdown revealed in Dorset Street, the only sexual serialist to commit suicide was 'Jack the Stripper'. And he only did so because the police were so hot on his trail that he feared capture and exposure. Some psychiatrists believe that these murderers actually preserve their precarious stability through the release of tension afforded by murder. They are almost consciously aware that if they don't give way to the urge to kill at regular intervals, something worse will happen to them, the 'something' being (though they may not recognize it) a complete and hopeless mental breakdown. Macnaghten's error is so convincing because it is the outcome of a normal man's imaginative introspection. If you or I suddenly found we had done anything so dreadful as Jack the Ripper did to Marie Kelly, we should be appalled, and might well kill ourselves (as thirty per cent of all murderers still attempt suicide). But of course nobody would suddenly set about slashing apart the external flesh and internal organs of a dead woman. The Ripper worked up to that horrible crime by stages of increasing savagery. The evidence of his successors is that he would have gone on perpetrating such crimes as long as he was alive and at liberty. (Significantly, the police at the time recognized this.) The instinct for survival which prompted his repeated escapes and inhibited him from giving himself up would also have prevented him from killing himself.

Kremer again tests the rule by his exceptional conduct. He turned himself in and confessed. But it was in the wake of his matricide (which left him without a means of support), and not his sexual murders.

We may summarize the suggestive pattern emerging from the various sex murderers thus: Jack the Ripper was in all probability a man in his twenties. He was of at least average intelligence, and may well have been distinctly superior. He enjoyed a normal sex life with the Whitechapel prostitutes, who found nothing threatening or unusual about his appearance when he accosted them as a client. He need not have been unattractive to the women he approached, and might have been married. But he probably performed indifferently when actually making love. He lived in or near Whitechapel, certainly not in closer proximity to any other red light neighbourhood within his means. If he lived alone, his private rooms may have been a squalid reflection of his inner confusion. If he lived with his family, there was probably nothing extraordinary about his home life and they would not have noticed anything suspicious about him. Nor would his workmates and friends have suspected him. His murders suddenly ceased either because he died by some means other than suicide, or because he left the district (in which case he probably started murdering again in his new surroundings), or because he was completely incapacitated through illness or hospitalization.

None of this pattern is necessarily true of the Ripper, but any gross deviations from it render a named suspect highly improbable.

We may immediately dismiss the 'Jill the Ripper' theory, which postulates a midwife-abortionist disposing of her 'failures'. We may dismiss the convict's devout wife who sought and found the woman who infected her husband and ruined her marriage. Like 'the doctor', or 'Dr Stanley', seeking out the woman who diseased his son and killing those who guided him to her, she is a figure of excellent narrative fiction with no analogue in fact.

Neill Cream, who gave streetwalkers poisoned capsules, and may have started a confession to being the Ripper as he stood on the scaffold, was a different kind of serial murderer, and in any case, was definitely in Joliot Prison at the time of the Ripper killings. Frederick Deeming, executed in Australia for murdering his family, is also alleged to have made a confession. He, too, was actually in jail at the relevant time. George Chapman, like Deeming, had the rational motive of escaping unwanted marital ties for his three murders; like Cream he used poison and showed no interest in evisceration.

Celebrities known to have associations with prostitutes are only plausible suspects if they can be shown to have centred those associations on the Whitechapel streetwalkers. So Gladstone, who tried to 'save' West End harlots, Swinburne, who employed St John's Wood whipping-mistresses, and George Gissing, who married a fallen Manchester woman, are all exonerated. Furthermore, like Dr Barnardo, who actually did work among the Whitechapel strumpets, trying to persuade them to let him open a shelter for their children during the scare, they all lived on in freedom after the murders had terminated.

This last point also exonerates the batty self-publicizing alienist Dr L. Forbes Winslow, who maintained that he had identified and frightened away the real Ripper (an insurance salesman named Smith, formerly lodging near Finsbury Square) and that the jealous police deliberately suppressed his triumph.

Winslow's obsessive sleuthing drew down temporary suspicion on himself. Subsequently the police investigated his claim and found it groundless. (Bloodstained boots proved mud-stained, for example, Smith's landlord did not confirm Winslow's tale of his and his wife's suspicions of the lodger.)

Winslow's self-advertisement makes him a persistent background figure in Ripper investigations. He was the first to suggest that the murderer was middle class, because he must have had a private house wherein to clean up and change after each event. In fact the limited bleeding resulting from strangulation followed by throat-cutting discounts the necessity. Winslow also urged the theory of an escaped lunatic, and propounded the suggestion (later taken up and used in his own defence by Sutcliffe) that the homicidal maniac would believe he had a divinely ordained mission to destroy prostitutes. Unfortunately, Winslow's own clinical experience also told him that such an hallucinating madman would make no attempt to conceal or escape from his crimes, as he would be unaware of any real objection to them. And clearly the Ripper (like Sutcliffe) did not stand around looking proudly over his holy handiwork.

Ripper students had one lucky escape. In 1886 Dr Winslow put his name forward in the East Middlesex coroner's election. As both a lawyer and a medic, not to mention the man who believed himself to be the ideal Court of Appeal to determine any given murderer's moral responsibility, he would have been a quite intolerable coroner. Fortunately he withdrew, and threw his interest behind the mildly kindred spirit of Wynne Baxter.

Compared with the educated derelict 'Roslyn D'Onston' Stephenson, however, Winslow is modesty itself. This self-alleged doctor, army officer, Garibaldian freedom fighter and black magician went to elaborate lengths to persuade a pair of rather silly ladies in the Aleister Crowley circle that they had accidentally found him to have been Jack the Ripper. But Stephenson (like Crowley himself) had lived on unmurderously for years after the Whitechapel murders had ceased.

Earlier, he claimed to have learned from W. T. Stead that medical evidence proved that the Ripper sodomized his victims while killing them, and alleged that he knew the London Hospital doctor who must have done this. Apart from the unlikelihood of the puritanical Stead passing on gossip that went beyond the sensational to the disgusting, Brown's full report on Eddowes proves this to be quite untrue.

Although the kind of data instanced above obviously eliminates Sir William Gull and brother Freemasons, or the Duke of Clarence and his circle, these candidates have proved so attractive that they must be given a full refutation before we pass on to the only likely suspects.

17

Royals and Masons

The Duke of Clarence, eldest son of the Prince of Wales, died prematurely of pneumonia in 1892, and never ruled England. Already in his lifetime one effort had been made to embroil the young prince in scandal. A superior male brothel in Cleveland Street was exposed in 1889 when the Post Office messengers employed as nancy-boys were caught and confessed. The proprietors tried to buy off prosecution by threatening to implicate prominent clients. Their blackmail forced Lord Arthur Somerset, equerry to the Prince of Wales, into premature retirement to Dieppe. And Home Office papers show that there was a veiled threat to implicate a Very Prominent Person Indeed, which the investigators hastily and discreetly quashed. This may well have been the Duke of Clarence, though the desperate efforts of blackmailers who see prison looming represent a suggestion and not a proof of his dabbling in the homosexual underworld. Of course, if Clarence *was* homosexual, he could not have been a heterosexual serial murderer.

The unsubstantiated story that Clarence was Jack the Ripper began circulating after his death (I myself first heard it in 1960 or thereabouts). It was given the clothing of an argument in Dr Thomas Stowell's article in *The Criminologist* in 1970. Stowell never named his suspect, but referred to him as 'S'. There were clues to 'S' 's identity, however, and they pointed unerringly to Clarence. The case against him supposedly derived from papers left by Sir William Gull, physician-in-ordinary to the Queen, who was named. These allegedly showed that 'S' had not died of pneumonia as was popularly supposed, but of tertiary syphilis. The disease had brought on the lunacy which led to the murders. His horrified family placed 'S' in an asylum, but he escaped and committed the Dorset Street murder.

This cautious essay, published in a journal with very limited circulation, captured immediate public attention. It did, apparently, link two of the national obsessions of the British: Jack the Ripper and the Royal Family. On television Stowell flatly denied that 'S' was the Duke of Clarence, without, however, naming an alternative or providing convincing responses to questions about the obvious points of comparison. In November of the same year he wrote to *The Times*, again denying that he intended to accuse Prince Eddie. And a week later he died. His family destroyed the papers which had produced so much unwelcome publicity, so their provenance cannot be tested. But Stowell's lamentable work was done: the notion of a royal prince had been implanted in the Ripper-curious public mind and the idea refuses to go away.

Michael Harrison's life of Clarence exploded the myth absolutely. He drew on court records to show that Prince Eddie was in Sandringham for his father's birthday when Kelly died, and in Scotland shooting grouse at the time of the double murder.

Regrettably, Harrison believed he had uncovered the actual Ripper in J. K. Stephen, the prince's tutor at Cambridge. Harrison's knowledge of the murders was slight. He claimed there were ten Ripper victims, including Farmer and Mylett. The map on his endpapers indicates that he believed Mylett to have been killed in Dorset Street, with Kelly shifted out to a court off Fashion Street to make room for her. He needed ten victims because he believed that Stephen modelled his murders on a rugby song in which ten whores were killed.

He also supplied unsubstantiated motives, claiming that Stephen's poems display an intense hatred of women. And he suggested that Stephen and Clarence enjoyed a brief homosexual liaison, and that Stephen hoped, by killing whores on allegedly significant dates to persuade his former lover to return to him.

Both motives are absurd, but happily for Harrison, Stephen had suffered a severe blow on the head which damaged his brain and incapacitated him mentally, so that his insanity could be argued. Moreover, his father's growing senility could be claimed as a breakdown caused by the stress of recognizing his son's murderous lunacy.

That is absolutely all the evidence Harrison puts forward. Having seen the wafer-thin case put forward against Clarence, Harrison was clearly unaware of the kind of data necessary to bring a successful case in the courts of law or history. J. K. Stephen was not Jack the Ripper.

Men who lie gratuitously to boost their self-importance have played no small part in confusing the trail of Jack the Ripper. Walter Sickert, the great painter, allegedly told two separate stories about his own involvement in the case. They differ so radically that one at least must have branded him as a liar; and with his veracity thus challenged, it is easily observed that neither story was true.

The first tale was a version of 'The Lodger', made famous in Mrs Belloc Lowndes' novel and the film starring Ivor Novello. Sickert had rooms in Mornington Crescent (a blue plaque now marks the house) and learned from the landlord that the previous occupant had been Jack the Ripper. He was a young veterinary student who took long walks at night, and whose fireplace contained burned remnants of clothes in the mornings after the murders. Eventually the young man's people took him away, and the murders stopped.

Sickert told this story to Osbert Sitwell and Max Beerbohm. It is not intrinsically impossible. But the distance of Mornington Crescent from Whitechapel, and the comparative proximity of St Pancras and Camden Town, where prostitutes picked up clients at the pubs of Chalton Street and Royal College Street (as Sickert very well knew), make it inherently improbable.

The detail of the 'veterinary student' gives away Sickert's (or, charitably stretching a point, his landlord's) belief that some surgical skills were involved. Since the Ripper tried and failed to behead Chapman, not only is there no need to postulate a skilled dis-memberer, there is the certainty that he had no surgical experience and did not know how to sever a joint!

'Lodger' theories depend on mysterious nocturnal absences, especially on the part of bachelors. Like the Brixton doctor arrested by Spicer, however, healthy young bachelors might have had perfectly simple reasons for furtiveness in their midnight absences from godly households which believed they could and should enjoy total celibacy. The same explanation probably covers the majority of the London families who have traditions that great-grandfather or Old Uncle Dick aroused suspicion by mysterious comings and goings during the terror.

The most elaborate and extravagant of all fantasies woven around the murders is the second supposedly deriving from the creative mind of Walter Sickert. In 1973 the BBC decided to mount a television feature in which the popular TV policemen Inspector Barlow and Sergeant Watt should survey the Ripper material, and see whether the application of their fictional plain honest coppering could shed any new light on it.

With heaven knows what intent, a Scotland Yard contact directed the producers to Mr Joseph 'Hobo' Sickert, son of Walter and his sometime ward Alice Margaret Crook. From Mr Sickert they learned the strange tale his father had given him concerning his parentage.

The Duke of Clarence, so Walter Sickert claimed, had been sent to him in the 1880s for social and artistic tutoring, and became accustomed to visiting his studio in Cleveland Street. Two doors away was a tobacconists' shop where a Catholic girl named Annie Elizabeth Crook worked. She and Clarence fell in love, and secretly married. A child, Alice Margaret, was born to them, and the Irish Catholic girl Marie Jeanette Kelly was employed as the nursemaid.

When the Palace and the Cabinet learned of this they took immediate steps to separate the pair. Secret agents disguised as layabouts staged a brawl at one end of Cleveland Street, under cover of which, plain clothes men seized Eddie and Annie and packed them into separate carriages. Annie was hurriedly certified and placed in an asylum, from which she began a slow trail through infirmaries and workhouses, in the course of which her reason genuinely did collapse, and she died an unknown pauper lunatic. Eddie was firmly restored to his family and told he would never see Annie again.

But the child, Alice Margaret, had escaped, together with Marie Kelly. Sickert himself saw to the placing of Alice with poor relatives. Subsequently she, too, spent some time in workhouses; and eventually she became Sickert's ward in Dieppe. When she grew up, she made an unhappy marriage, following which she became Sickert's mistress and Joseph Sickert's mother. She died in 1950.

Back in the 1880s, Kelly took to the East End where, with three of her cronies, she decided to exploit her secret knowledge by blackmailing the government. Lord Salisbury, fearing that the scandal might overthrow the monarchy, turned to the Freemasons for help, and selected Sir William Gull to mastermind the suppression of the blackmailers. Gull called in brother-Mason 'Sir' Robert Anderson and a coachman named John Netley. Together the three drove through Whitechapel inveigling the luckless whores into Netley's cab where Gull could disembowel them at leisure, leaving mutilations which would be recognized by Freemasons as the sign of an exposed oath-breaker or secret-revealer. Stride refused to come into the cab, so Netley had to kill her on the spot. Eddowes was killed by mistake, since she was using the name Kelly.

Although Anderson and Sir Charles Warren used their influence to protect Freemasonry from coming under suspicion, and saw to it that all investigations were fruitless, Salisbury and other leading Masons realized that Gull had gone too far. In fact his mind had become unhinged, and so a spurious funeral was enacted, and he was incarcerated under a pseudonym as a lunatic.

Netley, apparently hoping to ingratiate himself with his former employers, made further attempts to eliminate Alice Margaret, running her over in the Strand on one occasion, and making a second attempt later in Drury Lane. This time he outraged the crowd, and in his flight from them threw himself into the Thames at Westminster Bridge and drowned.

Not surprisingly, Barlow and Watt dubbed this the most unlikely story yet! It is the immediate response of everyone who hears it, and it is remarkable that the conscientious BBC checked it out far enough to establish that an Elizabeth Crook *had* lodged in the right shop at the right time, and that the mis-spelling 'Juwes' in Goulston Street coincided with a Masonic term for the mythical 'Jubela, Jubelo and Jubelum', three 'traitors' who killed the imaginary master-mason 'Hiram Abiff' at the building of Solomon's temple, according to the secret knowledge proffered to Masonic initiates.

The young reporter Stephen Knight shared the general disbelief when the *East London Advertiser* sent him to interview Joseph Sickert on this new view of East London's best known murders. But Knight was surprised to find the old gentleman transparently honest, and apparently convinced by his father's weird story. Knight set out to check its details, and gradually became convinced himself, as it seemed to him that more and more confirmatory evidence emerged.

Knight, however, strongly doubted whether Anderson could have been present at the murders as Sickert claimed. (He couldn't, of course, since he was abroad when Chapman, Eddowes and Stride were killed, though Knight omits this obvious point.) This led him to believe that Walter Sickert himself must have been the 'Third Man'; a conclusion Mr Joseph Sickert reluctantly accepted. Salisbury, it seemed, might have secretly paid off the painter by silently buying a picture at an inflated price.

Knight's book *Jack the Ripper: The Final Solution* has seemed very persuasive to people unfamiliar with either the murders or scholarly method. So we must examine how much of his story he established: how much he supported by guesswork, and how much is contradicted by facts.

It had already been established by the BBC that there was a real Annie Elizabeth Crook. Knight found that she had indeed woven a sad path through hospitals, asylums, workhouses and infirmaries until her death in the 1920s. With the help of researcher Karen de Groot, he also established that there really was a coachman named John Netley (born in Kennington, 1850; died in an accident to a horse-drawn van he was driving, 1903). And they proved that an unnamed child was knocked down in the Strand in a street accident in October 1888, and that a man whose name was given as 'Nickley' attempted suicide by drowning from Westminster Bridge in 1892.

Now that is absolutely all that Knight actually established. Nothing about Clarence. Nothing about a secret marriage. Nothing about the Freemasons. Nothing about Salisbury's involvement.

To implicate Gull, Knight went back to some early stories. The royal doctor's identification with Jack the Ripper was first hinted in an article in the Chicago *Sunday Times-Herald* in April 1895. This claimed that the Ripper was a distinguished society physician, living in the West End: a former student of Guy's, and a passionate advocate of vivisection. When his colleagues discovered that he was quite mad and a murderer they set up a secret Commission in Lunacy which certified him, and sent him to an asylum in Islington under the name of Thomas Mason. His disappearance was disguised by announcing his death and shamming a funeral. The whole story had supposedly come to light because a Dr Howard, had given away the secret during a drinking session in San Francisco.

Much of the data on the famous physician fitted Gull. He had lived in the West End, trained at Guy's and advocated vivisection. But he had died of his third stroke and been buried in his home village of Thorpe-le-Soken in 1890 – or so it had been given out.

The story was repeated in the London *People* in May, and eight months later it elicited an angry response from Dr Benjamin Howard, an American doctor who had been in practice in London in the late 1880s, and had just been shown the article on a return visit. As Dr Howard said:

In this publication my name is dishonourably associated with Jack the Ripper – and in such a way – as if true – renders me liable to shew cause to the British Medical Council why my name with three degrees attached should not be expunged from the Official Register.

Unfortunately for the Parties of the other part – there is not a single item of this startling statement concerning me which has the slightest foundation in fact.

Beyond what I may have read in the newspapers, I have never known anything about Jack the Ripper. I have never made any public statement about Jack the Ripper – and at the time of the alleged public statement by me I was thousands of miles distant from San Francisco where it is alleged that I made it.

Howard's letter is absolutely convincing. The breathless and un-grammatical punctuation by dashes, coupled with the furious leaps on and off high horses ('my name with three degrees attached' and 'the Parties of the other part') combine to reveal a man gasping with indignation at what he has just read and snatching up his pen, his dignity and the implicit threat of legal proceedings.

The editor soothed him down with a personal letter and the silly story, which has all the hallmarks of an instant legend, was forgotten until Knight discovered a thin peg of truth on which the Chicago journalist might have rested his wonderful fabrication: there actually was a pauper named Thomas Mason, born in the same year as Gull, who died in Islington in 1896. But Mason was not, as Knight speculated, a lunatic. I have examined all the lunacy returns of the Islington Board of Guardians in the early 1890s, and Mason's name does not appear.

Gull, however, could be identified, and his name passed into the rumour mill. And the Chicago newspaper had astutely picked up another story connecting Gull with Jack the Ripper. This again did not name the great doctor. But it was certainly circulating during the murder enquiries, for we have seen that one of the hoax letters referred to 'your Lees'.

Robert James Lees was a spiritualist medium and clairvoyant, working in Peckham at the time of the murders. One night he suffered from a strange precognition that another murder was going to take place. When it was reported in the press that there had indeed been a killing that night, he was distressed, and went to inform the police who dismissed his story.

Subsequently he was travelling from Notting Hill on an omnibus when he realized (clairvoyantly) that another passenger was Jack the Ripper. At Marble Arch the man got out, and Lees followed him halfway down Oxford Street. A police constable wisely refused to detain the man on Lees' request, and a rather confusingly described journey allowed him to escape. After Kelly's murder, Lees concentrated all his 'powers' on the problem, and persuaded a police inspector to accompany him to the Mayfair house he psychically detected. It belonged to a distinguished physician whose wife confessed that her husband was sometimes mysteriously absent on murder nights. And when the doctor himself entered, he admitted to confused and amnesiac periods during the previous year, after a couple of which he had found blood on his shirt and scratches on his face.

A coda to the story synopsizes that falsely ascribed to Howard: the doctor was secretly certified and incarcerated, while a public funeral masked his disappearance. And Stephen Knight's search of directories has revealed that Sir William Gull was the only distinguished physician with a town house in the right place at the right time.

Now Lees was unquestionably not a liar. A gentle, sweet-natured man, he was the kind of saintly crank who inspires credence in his particular 'alternative' beliefs by the transparent sincerity of his convictions and the utter benevolence of his intentions. Lees may have believed he had extra-sensorily identified Jack the Ripper on a London omnibus and followed up his precognition with a visit to a Mayfair house where he spoke to the owner and his wife. But the whole story was unfortunately so welcome to spiritualist propagandists that it underwent considerable expansion and embroidery in their hands.

There is, however, supportive evidence to the effect that a spiritualist medium did pester Sir William and Lady Gull at the time of the murders. Unhappily, it comes from a most unreliable source, whom we have already met propounding the Clarence theory: Dr Thomas Stowell. As the junior colleague of Dr Theodore Dyke Acland, Stowell was familiar with Gull's daughter Caroline who had become Mrs Acland. By Stowell's account she told a story exactly like Lees' in outline, even to the point of her father's acknowledging the bloody shirts.

Some commentators accept this entire farrago as true (including the validity of Lees' visions). Some accept it as probable up to Gull's own confrontation with the medium, but baulk at the great man's confessing to black-outs and blood. But Melvyn Harris has shown the probability that the entire story was cooked up by a dining-club of practical jokers who specialized in perpetrating outrageous hoaxes in the 1890s.

Why did such a gentle aesthete as Lees suffer from such a blood-curdling delusion? There are related preoccupations in his *Through the Mists: Or Leaves from the Autobiography of a Soul in Paradise*.

Lees (or 'the Soul') describes a Heaven of limp sub-Shelleyan beauty, filled with adorable angels who lead sinners through the patches of affectionless purgatory. The book demonstrates a strong interest in romantically jealous women as sinners who need the support of strong, calm masculine souls; and it is evident that the writer derives pronounced satisfaction from envisaging male spiritual forces purifying fallen women. Lees, we infer, had unconscious reasons for noticing news items which highlighted the depravity of the women of Whitechapel.

And there is further evidence that his gentle nature was distressed by the sufferings of the East End. In Blakeian vision, he sees hosts of destitute waifs who enjoy the bliss of paradise every time they fall asleep. And great is the rejoicing in heaven every time one of them is dying in agony from consumption, for then it will never have to leave its happiness for the daylight misery of the world again! Spiritualism, it seems, might prove the opiate of the middle classes.

Knight filled in further details with impressionistic evidence. Vague symbolic items from Sickert's paintings (a man eating grapes for breakfast; Sickert's smiling housekeeper, subtitled 'Blackmail') are alleged to be clues. A photograph of the adult Alice Margaret Crook is placed beside one of Queen Alexandra at the same age, with the suggestion that their similar appearance suggests blood relationship. But a picture of Annie Elizabeth on the same page makes it clear that Alice derived her broad mouth, widely spaced eyes and oval face from her commoner mother, and not from her supposed royal paternal grandmother.

Socialist and freethinking attacks on royalty are cited as evidence that the monarchy was in danger and a secret Catholic marriage might have brought it down. This (together with the monarchy's importance to Freemasonry) is put forward to explain Salisbury's complicity. But the major political concern of the period was the Irish question. The monarchy was far more secure than it had been when

Victoria and Albert rescued it from the dismal disrepute into which George IV's self-indulgence and William IV's inarticulacy had brought it. Salisbury was not a reds-under-the-bed conspiracy-monger.

Vague details of Masonic oaths and a completely irrelevant Hogarth engraving of an autopsy are summoned as evidence that the disembowellings were a Masonic ritual. Sir Robert Anderson is repeatedly stated to have been a Mason, and it is assumed as a corollary that no dishonesty or breach of his professional duty was too great when the brotherhood was at risk. Unaware of Anderson's standing as both Christian and detective, Knight describes him as a liar and an incompetent. Dr Phillips, it is asserted 'must have been a Mason' (Knight admits he had no evidence) when his testimony conflicts with Sickert's tale. Conversely, people whose best efforts went unrewarded, notably Wynne Baxter and Inspector Abberline, 'must have been' non-Masons.

Stride's grapes are claimed as evidence of Gull's complicity, since the great physician expressed a preference for grapes or raisins and water as refreshment in circumstances where others might have wanted a tot of brandy. This, despite the fact that Knight's own argument places Gull at a little distance, waiting in the empty carriage, while Netley and Sickert were supposedly killing Stride in Berner Street.

Of course, Knight believes the 'Juwes' message betrays the hand of a Mason, and of course he thinks this is why Freemason Warren had it erased. Though what the three Jumbos, risen from the dead, proclaiming their non-blameworthiness, and killing whores right, left and centre, might be expected to prove to anybody, Mason or non-Mason, Knight wisely does not try to explain. (I suppose he might have riposted that Gull was mad anyway.)

And Eddowes' apron, used as a cloth? We've all heard of Masonic aprons, haven't we!

The Masonic aspect of Knight's book becomes depressingly silly. But his acceptance of a conspiracy-theory of Masonry is positively alarming, especially when he (somewhat guiltily) cites that diabolical forged libel, *The Protocols of the Learned Elders of Zion*, beloved of Hitler and other dangerous racist fanatics.

It is a relief to return to his Whitechapel topography. Here Knight makes none of the gross errors of some of his predecessors, but he believes that he has proved something by showing that his blackmailing tarts (Nichols, Chapman, Stride and Kelly) all lived, at one time or another, in or within spitting distance of Dorset Street. He has nothing to say of the fact that this is equally true of Smith, Tabram, Pearly Poll, Eddowes, Farmer, Mylett, McKenzie and Coles. They all lived there, for this was the 'wicked quarter-mile' whose common lodging-houses attracted prostitutes and undesirables from all over the East End. The fact that all the Ripper victims lodged in Spitalfields goes no way to prove that four of them were intimates and fellow-conspirators. They were four among an estimated 1,200!

Sickert's story is completely disproved by the weight of testimony that all the Ripper victims were killed where they were found. Netley's carriage supplied secrecy that was never needed for Gull's surgical skill, which was positively contra-indicated. That carriage never rolled through the Whitechapel streets with its burden of dead women to be dumped silently where they were found.

Finally Joseph Sickert confessed. He had made up the whole story of Jack the Ripper, imaginatively grafting it on to the already weird story of his parentage he had heard from his father. 'It was a hoax,' he told *The Sunday Times*: 'a whopping fib'.

Yet until his premature death, Knight continued to believe that he had 'solved' the Ripper mystery, and his book was deservedly acclaimed. The liberal Home Secretaryship of Roy Jenkins gave him access to the Home Office and Scotland Yard files, and he made wonderful use of them. Abberline's report on Nichols; Swanson's report on Eddowes; White's report on his interviews with Packer; Hutchinson's full statement to the police: all these appeared in full for the first time in Knight's book. From him we learned that Warren personally took down Packer's statement. He gave the twentieth century its first intimation of Israel Schwartz and his tale of the man who threw Stride down on the pavement. His researches brought up treasure, although he failed to recognize its proper worth. And he holds an honoured place among historians of Jack the Ripper.

18

The Russian Doctor

Were it not that the Russian doctor occurs in Macnaghten's notes under the name of Michael Ostrog he would seem to be entirely shaped by the imaginations of sensational journalists. The name itself is not to be found in that form in the English death registers, though a family of Ostrorgs lived in the north of England, and a Scandinavian photographer named Ostrororg died of natural causes in London in the 1890s.

Two tenuous fragments suggest that the Russian doctor became the Yard's prime suspect thirty years after the murders. Warren's grandson thought that Sir Charles believed him to be the murderer, also believing that he had committed suicide at the end of the year. (Obviously this combines 'Ostrog' with Macnaghten's view of Druitt.) And according to Donald Rumbelow, Sir Basil Thomson shared this opinion. Donald McCormick further described a letter in which Sir Basil Thomson claimed that the French police had confirmed the existence of a Russian maniac known as Konovalov who had terrorized Paris before coming to London.

The first contemporary reference to a Russian as the Ripper is found in the Star on 17 November 1888 which reported a story circulating in Whitechapel concerning one Nicholas Wassili who had been placed in an asylum in Paris after murdering a number of prostitutes in 1872, and released in January 1888. But a check with M. Macé, former Chef de la Sûreté, proved that no such crimes were recorded in 1872. It was true that a foreigner (not a Russian) had threatened women in Paris in 1875. But he had not killed any.

On 28 November the Star produced a more circumstantial story, derived from the Russian journal Novosti. This described Nicolai Vasiliyeff, an Odessa University student, born at Triaspol in 1847. He was said to have become a fanatical anarchist and gone to Paris in the 1870s. Here he developed the delusion that prostitutes could only be redeemed by their murder. After a number of murders he was caught and placed in an asylum. Shortly before the Whitechapel outrages he was released and came to London, where he lived among low-class Russian immigrants. Since the first murder, he had not been seen.

This was the story picked up by American journalist R. K. Fox, who published a 'quickie' on the Whitechapel Murders in 1888, and added the sentimental embellishment that Nicolas Vassili began his murderous career by stabbing a lace-worker he loved named Madeleine who had jilted him instead of joining his campaign of regeneration for lost women.

Guy B. H. Logan simplified the story in 1928, making the religious maniac a Russian doctor with a good command of English, who had been incarcerated in Russia, and resided in England for three years. He also claimed that the Russian police had warned Scotland Yard about him. But Logan's work is quite remarkably inaccurate. For example, he revived Mary Malcolm's hopelessly discredited testimony with the claim that Stride used the alias Elizabeth Watts.

In 1923 the journalist and popular writer William Le Queux produced a new version with a new name and aliases. In *Things I Know* he claimed that a Russian newspaper stringer named Nideroest had learned from an old anarchist named Zverieff that an infamous mass-murderer named Dr Alexander Pedachenko had been the Ripper. He had been living in Walworth, and had carried out the murders with two confederates: a man called Levitski and a tailoress called Winberg. The three regularly crossed the river to Whitechapel where Levitski would keep a look-out, Miss Winberg would engage the unsuspecting streetwalkers in conversation, and Pedachenko would come upon them and rip them up.

In support of this unlikely story, Le Queux cited the *Ochrana Gazette*, the bulletin of the Czarist secret police. In 1909 this advised all officers that Vasilly Konovalov alias Alexey Pedachenko alias Luiskovo, thought to be responsible for the murder of one woman in Paris in 1886, five in the East End in 1888, and one in Petrograd in 1891, was now officially regarded as having died in an asylum. He was described as having a curly waxed moustache, and being occasionally transvestite. Here is some support for Sir Basil Thomson's alleged recollection.

Le Queux further claimed that papers found among Rasputin's possessions confirmed that the secret police had deliberately allowed this notorious homicidal maniac to proceed to London, where his outrages would discredit Scotland Yard whose tolerance of subversive anarchist immigrants distressed the Czarists. When his fell work was complete, it was alleged, the Tcheka (Czarist ancestor of the KGB) smuggled him out of the country.

None of this farrago was taken seriously at the time. Le Queux was hard up and unscrupulous when he wrote it and Nideroest was a notorious liar and probable supplier of disinformation between interested Bolshevik and anti-Bolshevik parties. Rasputin's legendary memory as an almost unkillable mad monk and *eminence grise* was then at its height and any story involving him was marketable. Actually Rasputin had no political power or close connections with the secret police, being no more than a quasi-faith healer who rose to petty influence-peddling because of the Czarina's total reliance on his ability to check her son's haemophilia.

Dr Thomas Dutton, the amateur criminologist of Bayswater, was impressed by Le Queux's yarn, however. He described himself as a friend of Inspector Abberline, and claimed that Abberline at first genuinely thought Severin Klosowski (the murderer 'George Chapman') was Jack the Ripper. According to Dutton, the inspector had heard Klosowski addressed as 'Ludwig' in a hairdressing basement at George Yard, while he was investigating a German hairdresser of that name who was under suspicion. Klosowski's name was supposedly so unpronounceable that his workmates called him Ludwig Schloski. Abberline allegedly found his movements very suspicious, and when he discovered that the Polish barber had received elementary surgical training in his national service, his suspicion hardened.

According to Dutton, Abberline changed his mind when he learned that Klosowski had a 'double' in London, and the two switched personae for nefarious jaunts through London at night. Abberline's suspicions now fell on the mysterious double. It was Dutton's own speculation that this might have been Dr Pedachenko.

All this was told to Donald McCormick and supported by Dutton's hand-written *Chronicles of Crime* in the 1920s. When McCormick came to put it together from his own notes and recollections for publication in the 1960s, he found fringe supporting evidence – for example the listed existence of a doctor in Walworth whose assistant had been Pedachenko, according to Dutton. He made no comment on the fact that apart from the identification of Pedachenko with

Klosowski's double and the assertion that Abberline heard Klosowski called 'Ludwig', all Dutton's supported evidence had appeared in print in some form before the short-lived appearance of the *Chronicles of Crime*. He found absolutely no firm independent evidence for the existence of a Dr Pedachenko, let alone one who swapped identities with Klosowski. He did not pick up Mrs Kennedy's story of seeing Marie Kelly with two people at 3.00 am or Schwartz's tale of the two men in Berner Street: the only late sightings of victims which remotely supported the preposterous story of an accomplice to keep watch and a woman to decoy them. For on that absurdity alone, completely refuted by Lawende's testimony of seeing Eddowes negotiating with a lone man at Church Passage, the story of Dr Pedachenko falls to the ground.

Le Queux's story probably originated in Soviet disinformation designed to discredit the Czarist regime. (The claim that Nideroest had himself been an agent of Rasputin's and so enjoyed special information is not, as has been alleged, supported by A. T. Vassilyev, former head of the Ochrana. He confirms Rasputin's remoteness from all police and underground activity.)

Dutton's embroideries seem to derive from his own ingenious speculation.

McCormick's background research is like Stephen Knight's investigation of Sickert's fantasy. It provides some evidence for the existence of non-essential characters in the story. But it leaves the central claims where it found them: resting exclusively on the unsupported assertions of a witness whose veracity must always be doubted.

So the gaudy Dr Pedachenko alias Konovalov alias Luiskovo disappears from the investigation. What about Nicholai Wassili/ Vasiliyeff, scourge and salvation of the Paris prostitutes? In his romantic version as the jilted lover, he too must disappear. Fox, writing an instant book about an ongoing investigation, had a duty to meet publication deadlines and sustain his public's interest that outweighed his responsibility to history.

The *Star*, on the other hand, treated Wassili extremely responsibly in its first report. He existed only as a Whitechapel rumour: the Paris police denied that such crimes had taken place or that the perpetrator of similar ones had been a Russian. That initial check with M. Macé, though clearly not exhaustive, must weigh heavily in undercutting repetitions of the story.

In its second bite at the cherry the *Star* allowed itself to report all the facts without query, having quite properly shoved responsibility for them onto *Novosti*. Presumably the Russian press, circulating among immigrants in Whitechapel, was the original source of the story which *Star* reporters unearthed in the East End. The Odessa student anarchist probably represents the purest and most un-embellished form of the story to have reached England: the foundation on which all later variants were built.

Unhappily it contains one instantly detectable falsehood. Vasiliyeff is said to have been incarcerated in an asylum for murders in Paris. Yet Macé had denied this, and no research uncovered any Parisian multiple murderer who might have been Jack the Ripper. Since the press in 1888 busied itself with hunting for precedent serial murderers, and found them in Bavaria, Texas and France, this obvious and recent case would surely have been brought to light had it happened.

On the other hand, McCormick's *Ochrana Gazette* account of a man who committed one murder in Paris and another in St Petersburg might easily be true. If immigrant gossip noted that a Russian lunatic who killed one prostitute in Paris (thus escaping Macé's refutation of mass murder) had been released shortly before the Ripper scare, it might easily have travelled back to Russia when the man was finally incarcerated for his second murder.

And two details link Vasiliyeff or Vassili Konovalov with Macnaghten's Ostrog. Macnaghten's doctor had been detained in an asylum (though frequently, rather than once). And his whereabouts during the murders could not be ascertained, just as Vasiliyeff disappeared from the *Star*'s ken after the 'first' murder.

Assuming that 'Michael Ostrog' existed, was he in fact a doctor? Various searches of the medical directories have not unearthed any practising medic bearing any of the Russian names ascribed to the Ripper. We have also seen that the murderer was certain not to have enjoyed any medical training, and the fact that Macnaghten ascribes surgical skill to two of his named suspects demonstrates that his conclusions were encouraged by uninformed theory as much as established fact.

The amount of error Macnaghten can be shown to have included in his accounts of Druitt and Kosminski makes Ostrog a very shadowy figure indeed. I should not be surprised to learn that an educated Russian, possibly called Vassily or Nicolai Vassilyich Konovalov or

Luiskovo attacked a woman in Paris before 1888 and another in Petrograd subsequently. The Russian police may have wondered if he was Jack the Ripper, though Paul Begg has actually carried his enquiries as far as Moscow and failed to unearth any known criminals with those names. Certain 20th century policemen who decided 'a Russian doctor who committed suicide' was Jack the Ripper, plainly confused him with their misconception of Druitt, and were wrong.

19

Montague John Druitt

As the preferred suspect of Sir Melville Macnaghten, M. J. Druitt has seemed the most likely Jack the Ripper for the last twenty five years. Once Lady Aberconway had released her copy of her father's notes, and Druitt's name was known, his existence was quickly verified, and research uncovered a good deal of information about his personal history.

Macnaghten's Scotland Yard notes were correct in stating that Druitt's body was found in the Thames on 31 December 1888, and that it had been immersed for some weeks. His death certificate and west London suburban papers confirmed this, but corrected Sir Melville's information in other respects.

Druitt was not a doctor, as Macnaghten understood, though he came from a medical family. Nor was he forty one years of age, though the *County of Middlesex Independent*'s initial estimate on his unidentified body placed it around forty.

Montague John Druitt was a briefless barrister of thirty one. Educated at Winchester and New College, Oxford, he ate dinners and entered chambers in the Inner Temple. His father's death left him without an allowance to support him through the difficult early years at the Bar, and he found employment in a small private school at Blackheath.

For reasons that were never disclosed, he was under notice of dismissal from his teaching post at the end of November 1888, and he left a letter to his headmaster hinting at suicide. He was last seen on 3 December.

When his body was recovered the pockets contained a cheque for £50, another for £16, some sovereigns and half-sovereigns, a railway season ticket to Blackheath and a return ticket from Charing Cross to Chiswick. They were also filled with stones, presumably to expedite his drowning. The inquest at Chiswick returned a verdict of 'suicide while of unsound mind'.

His mother had been confined to a mental hospital earlier in the year, and a note left in his chambers suggested that Druitt feared that he might have inherited mental disorder. Those who think he was Jack the Ripper naturally believe his fears were justified, and accept Macnaghten's interpretation of his death as the result of a brainstorm following his last murder.

Tom Cullen established that he was a fine cricketer who had captained the school First XI, and that as a schoolboy debater he had consistently espoused radical causes. Cullen noted a tongue-in-cheek letter Bernard Shaw wrote to the *Star* suggesting that the murderer had achieved more than socialist agitators to arouse public conscience over the poverty of Whitechapel. Cullen tentatively proposed that Druitt hoped to draw attention to the squalor of the slums – which, undoubtedly, the murderer did! The notion of a philanthropist adroitly turning his atrocious sexual deviation to the good cause of publicizing poverty is quite preposterous, and has not attracted much support.

Dan Farson was content to accept Druitt's motive as the obvious one of sexual disorder, and turned closer attention to the problem of his residence during the murders. Cullen had suggested that Druitt's chambers in King's Bench Walk were a bachelor flat little over a mile from the murder sites, and a suitable base from which he could come and go to Whitechapel. There are two objections to this: first, King's Bench Walk lies in the wrong direction from Mitre Square. We know that the murderer headed north-east to Goulston Street with Catherine Eddowes' piece of apron. King's Bench Walk lies to the south-west.

The other objection, which never seems to have been noted, is the certainty that Druitt never used 9 King's Bench Walk as anything but a business accommodation address. True, surplus chambers in the Inns of Court were and are let as private apartments. But the principal use of chambers is and was as lawyers' offices. And barristers must be accepted members of a master's chambers, with their names painted on his door and entered in the directories, in order to practice. The eight sets of chambers in 9 King's Bench Walk housed two Queen's Counsel, fourteen unsilked barristers, two firms of solicitors, and one lay tenant in 1888. We may confidently assume that Druitt was listed as a member of chambers wherein a clerk worked permanently, the more active barristers regularly, and the unbriefed like Druitt left their names on the doors in the hope that fortune (or a solicitor) would smile with employment at last. An impossible place for changing and hiding bloodstained clothing!

Farson discovered that Druitt's cousin Dr Lionel Druitt had served as locum for a Dr Thyne in the Minories in 1879. From this he hypothesized that Montague John might have visited or stayed with him there. He also picked up some slender hearsay evidence that a man named Druitt had rented a room at the bottom of the Minories during the murder period, and that the name M. J. Druitt had been seen on some old (and now lost) voters' registers for the Minories.

All this seemed to Farson a convincing location of Druitt *in situ deventratoris*. Yet he was not unaware that Goulston Street argued forcefully against the Minories as the Ripper's home. 'He doubled back...' becomes a useful phrase for those who want the Ripper living in the wrong direction. They never postulate the question: 'Why?' With twelve minutes between each of Pc Harvey's anticipated inspections of Duke Street, five of them used up in mutilating Eddowes, why on earth would the Ripper cross over the street in which he lived, and move away from it in the opposite direction from his home? This wasn't just a night when he wanted to run away from the police who must ultimately discover his recent murder: the whistles from Berner Street had already been heard in Aldgate, signalling the discovery of Stride's body and the questing activity of H Division. What could induce the murderer to hurry toward that hornet's nest when it would have been easier for him to slip into the safe lodgings where he is supposed to have changed and cleaned up on all other occasions?

Farson offered further evidence in the form of a letter from a man named Knowles who claimed to have seen a pamphlet written in Australia by Lionel Druitt entitled *The East End Murderer – I Knew Him*. Since Lionel Druitt definitely emigrated to Australia in 1887, and Montague's mother's death was witnessed by an Emily Knowles, Farson felt he had found strong evidence that, as Macnaghten claimed, Druitt's family suspected him. He was understandably disappointed that Mr Knowles died before he could respond to further queries. In a brilliant piece of research, Martin Howells and Keith Skinner established that the Australian 'evidence' had actually been two irrelevant documents: an alleged last confession by the murderer Deeming (who used the alias Drewen), and a local newspaper supplement reproducing an East End landlady's illusion that one of her lodgers had been Jack the Ripper.

Unfortunately, Howells and Skinner went on to build a mountainous superstructure of speculation to the effect that Druitt was an associate of a circle of Cambridge homosexuals who were friends of the Duke of Clarence; that he took to murdering prostitutes when his mother was found to be suffering from tertiary syphilis, innocently acquired from her husband's unsterilised hands; and that the Cambridge homosexuals themselves murdered Druitt to suppress possible scandal. Like Knight and McCormick, Howells and Skinner could offer tentative evidence for the framework of their story – (Prince Eddy was friendly with Cambridge men, some of whom might have been homosexual; Druitt's mother was hospitalized in Stoke Newington, so that *if* he abandoned his normal habit of travelling everywhere by train, Druitt *might* have walked through Whitechapel to visit her). They even discovered the only genuine link ever established between the unfortunate Prince Eddy and a known police Ripper suspect: as good class residents of Dorset, Druitt and his mother were once invited to a dinner in his honour. But no part of their central case is proven. Like Farson and Cullen, they rest centrally on Macnaghten's error-filled memoranda.

The commonsense explanation for Druitt's sudden dismissal from Blackheath with £16 wages in lieu of notice is that he was found interfering with little boys. This is accepted by Howells and Skinner (though their inference that his paederasty would mean that he was attracted to men of his own age does not necessarily follow). It also, surely, offers adequate explanation for his suicide.

In 1903 Abberline gave a succinct explanation of Druitt's standing as a suspect:

> Yes, I know all about that story. But what does it amount to? Simply this. Soon after the last murder in Whitechapel the body of a young doctor was found in the Thames, but there is absolutely nothing beyond the fact that he was found at that time to incriminate him. A report was made to the Home Office about the matter.

Where it was not preserved, so that we may never know whether Anderson, Monro and Swanson also believed that Druitt was a doctor. We may reasonably guess, however, that talkative Inspector Abberline was one of Macnaghten's sources of information, since he unquestioningly reproduces his central error. We may also guess that Anderson reached his final conclusion concerning Jack the Ripper's identity very shortly after Abberline's retirement in 1892 – ('some years after [Macnaghten] became a detective officer') – and thereupon closed the file for 100 years without telling either the curious young Chief Constable or the garrulous old ex-inspector who he now knew the murderer to be. Macnaghten's decent but probably mistaken commonsense suggested that the murderer must have killed himself: therefore, of the names he had heard from Abberline, innocent Druitt became the prime suspect.

20

Jack the Ripper

Every book on the Whitechapel murders since Tom Cullen's *Autumn of Terror* has left me with three questions. Why has no one seriously followed up the evident suspicion of some doctor, possibly local, expressed in different ways by the police on the ground? Why did John Pizer or 'Leather Apron', disappear from everybody's calculations the moment he had proved an alibi? And why has nobody noticed that Macnaghten's suspect 'Kosminski' was obviously Anderson's Polish Jew?

The first question answered itself as soon as I compared police memoirs with newspaper reports and inquest testimony. Except for Dew, the police on the ground were underinformed or unreliable. And Dew pointed out that an unfamiliar doctor (or 'toff' of any other description) would certainly have been spotted and questioned by local police during the panic. Spicer's arrest of the 'Brixton doctor' with Rosie supports this, (and there is an oral tradition that he was actually a London Hospital medical student).

A local bigwig could, indeed, have passed through the streets unquestioned by H Division men, but he would have lost his advantage when men from other Divisions were drafted in and flooded the district.

The inquest reports and police files, moreover, showed a heavy majority of doctors convinced that the injuries were totally unskilled. Dr Phillips – effectively the lone voice for a medico-murderer – testified to the failed attempt to cut off Annie Chapman's head. And even when indoors and unpressed by time, the murderer could not behead Marie Kelly.

On the other hand, of the much-maligned police chiefs, only the supposedly efficient Major Smith proved damningly inaccurate. Macnaghten (like Dew) produced a proportion of honest error – as one would expect of an old man remembering – and seemed to have reproduced a good deal of misinformation quite honestly. Abberline, the popular favourite of most writers, proved *not* to have been in charge of the case, and not to have been fully informed by his superiors. Anderson – and this was my complete surprise – proved by character, situation and reputation, far and away the strongest witness; the obvious (if maddeningly peek-a-boo) 'best source' of information. Unreliable Major Smith's diatribe could not shake the evidence of Anderson's probity and ability. So I was not looking for a doctor; I was looking for a poor Polish Jew in an asylum, with Macnaghten's probably part-erroneous data on Kosminski as clues.

This brought Pizer and 'Leather Apron' back into the foreground. For it was clear that Cullen and Rumbelow were right in thinking that evidence leading to Pizer's arrest also led to Anderson's deductions on his return from the continent (after Pizer had been decisively cleared). Without being Jack the Ripper, Pizer was in some ways very like him. And why, after positively testifying to Leather Apron's existence and threatening behaviour, had the streetwalkers, as Cullen observed, failed or refused to identify him?

The 'Leather Apron' scare began on 4 September and dominated the newspapers for a week. It was given climactic support by the discovery of a soaked leather apron in the yard of 29 Hanbury Street, near Annie Chapman's body, though this proved to be John Richardson's property, undergoing quite normal washing.

On 10 September John Pizer was arrested; the next day he was produced before the inquest, identified as Leather Apron, exonerated and released. As far as the police were concerned, the Leather Apron affair was over. Chief Inspector Swanson's reports to the Home Office months later still made occasional reference to 'John Pizer, known as Leather Apron' who had been an early suspect.

But the public was not satisfied. As late as 30 September, Best and Gardner jeered 'Leather Apron' at Long Liz's client. Only the more lurid nickname 'Jack the Ripper' dispelled the universal belief that a killer called Leather Apron was at large.

And, whatever they told Scotland Yard, H Division detectives did not believe they had found the man known as Leather Apron. On 20 September, a week after Pizer's exoneration, the *Echo* reported

> Inspector Reid, Detective Sergeant Enright, Sergeant Goadby [*sic* ?Godley] and other officers then worked upon a slight clue given them by 'Pearly Poll.' It was not thought much of at the time; but from what was gleaned from her and other

statements given by Elizabeth Allen and Eliza Cooper of 35 Dorset Street, Spitalfields, certain of the authorities have had cause to suspect a man actually living not far from Buck's Row. At present, however, there is only suspicion against him.

Now 35 Dorset Street was Crossingham's Lodging House where Annie Chapman stayed; and Eliza Cooper was her rival for Harry the Hawker's and Ted the Pensioner's affections. And Ted, Crossingham's deputy Donovan, and another lodger named West, were witnesses who confirmed at Chapman's inquest that they knew Leather Apron and had last seen him at Crossingham's wearing a deerstalker hat.

The sentence, 'At present . . . there is only suspicion against him,' is another strong pointer to Leather Apron. It was used repeatedly in police comments to the press during the second half of the great Leather Apron scare, especially on Pizer's arrest. And it is found in the first written mention of Pizer: Inspector Helson's confidential report to Scotland Yard on 7 September:

The inquiry has revealed the fact that a man named Jack Pizer, alias Leather Apron, has for some considerable period been in the habit of illusing prostitutes in this, and other parts of the Metropolis, and careful search has been and is continued to be made to find this man in order that his movements may be accounted for on the night in question, although, at present, there is no evidence whatever against him.

This report is in itself fascinating. It is extremely assured about Leather Apron and his conduct, and remarkably familiar with Pizer: every other written description calls him John.

Sergeant William Thick arrested him three days later with the words, 'You're just the man I want.' A very friendly report in the *Daily News* described the arrest thus:

Detective Sergeant Thicke, H Division, who has long done duty in the district, receiving information which led him to believe that the man known by the name of Leather Apron was to be found in a house in Plummer's [sic] Row, also called Mulberry Street, succeeded in apprehending the man, whom he lodged in Leman Street Police station. The man's name is Piser, a Jew, who certainly bears a remarkable resemblance to the published description of Leather Apron.

This was wrong. Mulberry Street was not Plumber's Row, but the road parallel to it. (It ran from today's Mulberry Street – then Sion Square – to Commercial Road.) Moreover, it was not, as some writers have suggested, an out-of-the-way hiding place. It had been Pizer's home since boyhood, and he still lived there with his stepmother and married brother. He had, indeed, stayed prudently indoors when the streets became unsafe for Jewish leather workers. But it was quite normal for him to spend long periods inside working at the slippers his family made for his brother's father-in-law's wholesale business.

But his arrest was not arbitrary. Earlier that year he had been charged (unsuccessfully) with indecent assault, and he was probably the man described as John Pozer who served a three-week sentence in 1887 for stabbing. Nevertheless, the police conduct with 'Leather Apron' in their hands was truly extraordinary. He was not identified by the streetwalkers because he was never shown to them. Nor was he paraded before Donovan, Stanley or West. Instead Pizer was shown to a vagrant Hungarian or Bulgarian of mulatto appearance called Emmanuel Violenia, who confirmed that he knew him as Leather Apron and asserted that he had seen him talking to Chapman before her death. Yet shown her body in the mortuary, he became doubtful about her identity. The police decided he was unreliable and had only come forward from a morbid wish to see the body. Yet, as Pizer told the press, Violenia was the *only* person brought to identify him, and although he believed Violenia to be a boot-finisher they were not well enough acquainted for him to know his name, or Violenia to know any nickname by which Pizer was known. The police were reduced to putting forward Sergeant Thick as the sole evidence that Pizer was Leather Apron.

The friendly *Daily News* reported that Thick's evidence convincingly proved that Pizer, though innocent of the murders, was the man known locally as Leather Apron.

The evidence of Pizer's innocence was definite. On the night of Polly Nichols' murder he had been in Holloway, where he saw the great glow in the sky caused by a fire in the spirit warehouses on South Quay, London Docks, and he asked a policeman in Seven Sisters Road what it was. The constable remembered the conversation, and so confirmed the testimony of the deputy of the Round House in Holloway Road that Pizer was miles from Buck's Row when Polly Nichols died.

But the only evidence that Pizer was Leather Apron was Thick's assertion that he had known Pizer for many years, and had always heard him so called. Although Pizer himself replied, 'Yes,' when the coroner asked him if he was Leather Apron, all he meant was that the identification was the only reason he had been arrested. In fact, he, his family and friends were all anxious to refute the identification. He had never been known as Leather Apron; he never wore his apron on the streets; no one had ever referred to him as Leather Apron until Sergeant Thick turned up at 22 Mulberry Street to arrest him. His neighbours gave him a hero's welcome home, and confirmed all this to the press. Yet it was not allowed to emerge at the inquest.

Mr Baxter accepted Thick's evidence without question, and hurried him out of the box. Pizer shouted furiously, 'Sergeant Thick who arrested me has known me for eighteen years!'

But Mr Baxter silenced him with a soothing, 'Well, well, I do not think it is necessary for you to say more.'

And all the time, Tim Donovan, who knew Leather Apron by sight, was in court to give his own evidence, and could have confirmed or denied the identification. He was never asked to do so. What on earth was going on?

This was the start of the so-called police 'cover-up'. Hitherto, Inspectors Abberline and Chandler and Sergeant Thick (at least) had talked freely to the press. From now on, they were forbidden to do so. In three weeks' time, Warren would erase the Goulston Street graffiti, and issue the misleading statement that 'Juwes' did not mean Jews in any known language. For this, as he told the Home Office, he was personally thanked by the Chief Rabbi, though it must have been as clear to Dr Adler as it was to the *Jewish Chronicle* and everybody else that Juwes meant Jews to the writer. Scotland Yard was determined to suppress any hint that the Whitechapel murderer was a Jew. For since the press had reported that they were looking for a Jewish 'Leather Apron', dangerous race-riots were threatening. The police needed an arrest and identification quickly, even if it entailed equally quick exoneration. Pizer was taken the day after John Richardson's sinister leather apron had turned up in Hanbury Street; the weekend of the first serious assaults on innocent Jews.

The police wanted a Jew with a leather apron living in or near Plummer's Row. (The *Daily News'* unnecessary and incorrect indentification of the street with Mulberry Street makes it clear that this was part of the testimony about Leather Apron going the rounds.) Helson's report shows that three days before the arrest they were working on information from someone who knew Pizer well enough to call him Jack. Someone who had known him eighteen years, perhaps?

Sergeant Thick's nickname was 'Johnny Upright'. His colleague Wensley loyally declared that this was a tribute to his carriage and personality. But Arthur Harding, a Bethnal Green villain of the next generation, believed that the name was a sarcastic tribute to his willingness to 'fit up' a suspect. Obviously Pizer was not fitted up. But he was arrested prematurely by someone who knew his forename and where to look for him, and who then became the only person to aver that he was known as Leather Apron. According to an unreliable French book published in 1935 with accounts of the enquiry purporting to emanate from the sole surviving detective on the original case, Thick had originally insisted that the CID must search for Leather Apron without suggesting that he actually knew who he was. It would have been humiliating for Thick to have those who really knew Leather Apron confront Pizer, and it would have left the press free to continue the 'Where is Leather Apron the Jew?' sensation until it provoked a pogrom.

Yet a week later, as the *Echo* showed, the police were still looking for the early suspect identified by Pearly Poll and the Crossingham's women, who lived near Buck's Row (which was itself far nearer Plumber's Row than Spitalfields.) They no longer named him, however, or said he was Jewish (just as they would later strike 'Jewish-looking' out of their published version of Hutchinson's description of Marie Kelly's client.)

The Leather Apron scare did not collapse at once, but the prime police aim was achieved; the anti-semitic component died down. Only *The Times*, of all papers, revived it in a new form after the night of the two murders. Which was also after its cautious but leaky anti-Parnellite correspondent, Dr Anderson, had come back from abroad.

Putting together the three sources of information, a picture of the major police suspect emerges. Anderson, the first and most reliable, declared that the murderer was definitely a low-class Polish Jew living in the district, positively identified in the asylum by a Jewish witness who then refused to testify.

Macnaghten's three drafts of his notes placed the suspect in the heart of the murder area; gave him the occupation of leather worker or tanner, and, indeed, may have asserted that he was the real Leather Apron; dated his incarceration as the spring of 1889;

identified the witness as a City policeman near Mitre Square; and named the suspect Kosminski. But comparison with Macnaghten's Druitt notes shows that he was likely to be wrong on details.

The original Leather Apron inquiry supported both Anderson and Macnaghten in identifying a Jewish leather worker, and placed his residence near Buck's Row and Plumber's Row. It also indicated that he threatened streetwalkers for some time before the murders began.

One other straw in the wind supports a name like Kosminski. Abberline's alleged remark to Godley, 'I see you've got Jack the Ripper,' when George Chapman was identified as Severin Klosowski might have been merely an ironic observation on the first serial murderer of women since Cream. But it is a remarkable coincidence that it related to a Pole named K-something-ski. I began my search quite confident that a scrutiny of asylum records should turn up a Jewish K-something-ski who would prove to be Jack the Ripper.

The snag was that asylum records seemed unobtainable. Local history libraries in East London did not think any private records had survived. And the public records were closed for 100 years. Since the murderer was definitely at large until November 1888, and according to Macnaghten was not incarcerated till 1880, there seemed little hope of tracing him for two or three years. But one thing Jack the Ripper had to do was die. I made a preliminary inspection of the Death Registers at St Catherine's House to find whether anyone named K-anything-ski had died in the Barnet area (where Middlesex Asylum at Colney Hatch took the preponderance of London lunatics), or Ewell, where Banstead took others. This drew a blank: only Nathan Karnsky, dying in Barnet in 1908 looked possible. But he seemed too young, as he would only have been 15 at the time of the murders.

An alternative approach was through workhouse infirmary records. Most poor lunatics would be referred through their parish Boards of Guardians, and their first treatment would be at their local infirmary. These records were not sealed, and I started with Whitechapel Workhouse Infirmary Admissions and Discharge Book for 1888.

No Kosminski appeared. But on Saturday 24 March at 5.30 pm, Nathan Kaminsky, an unmarried Polish Jewish bootmaker of 15 Black Lion Yard with no known next-of-kin was admitted. He had one year's residence in the parish. He was 23 years old, diagnosed syphilitic, and sent to Ward B.B. Six weeks later he was discharged as cured.

This was a major discovery. The man was the right age (for a sexual serial murderer); the right race (for Anderson's Jew); the right occupation (for Macnaghten's Kosminski or Leather Apron).

'Kaminsky' was almost precisely one of the variants Dan Farson had recorded in his account of Macnaghten's notes (though I knew it was *not* the form of the Scotland Yard fair copy, and Farson had courteously answered a letter of mine regretting that he no longer had all his own notes on the Ripper, and could not remember the exact sources of his variants. In fact, it is now clear that Farson's difficulties with this and other precise words arose from damage in a hand-written section of Lady Aberconway's notes, which Keith Skinner has obtained and copied.)

Infection with syphilis proved an active sex-life among the local prostitutes: its incubation period is short, and local Jewish girls were totally implausible carriers. The infection also supplied a conscious motive for the initial 'Leather Apron' aggression to streetwalkers, before mania and bloodlust set in. Some men believe themselves justified in venting their hatred on women from whom they have acquired diseases which are only shameful because they choose to believe that their own actions are shameful. Macnaghten and Major Griffiths both suggested that the Ripper was 'probably' diseased.

Furthermore, I had already noted the attack on Ada Wilson in a nearby quarter of Mile End as being highly suggestive of an early attempt by an inexperienced Ripper. When I discovered that this occurred four days after Kaminsky's treatment started, my only fear was that he was presumably exonerated if he spent the next six weeks on his back in hospital. A careful re-examination of the Infirmary records allayed this misapprehension. Ward B.B. treated patients with minor ailments that would not render them bedfast: the itch (repeatedly); cuts, bruises and sprains; headaches. There was one similar women's ward. Nearly all other wards were identified by a letter and a digit (as B2) and held more serious cases: fractures, fevers, undiagnosed internal pains, epidemic diseases when they occurred. Evidently B.B. patients were at worst 'walking wounded': at best they might have been 'out patients', though nobody could tell me whether such a status existed in Victorian infirmaries. Still, it seemed highly improbable that economical Poor Law Guardians would 'pauperise' poor hypochondriacs with free food and lodging. I had little doubt that Nathan Kaminsky was free to come and go and try to kill Ada Wilson on the appropriate date.

But it was when I found Black Lion Yard that I was sure I had found

Jack the Ripper. This ran between Old Montague Street and Whitechapel High Street (where the Whitechapel Technology Centre stands today). It was near Buck's Row and opposite Plumber's Row. It was almost exactly at the centre point of the five murders. From its Whitechapel Road end, Plumber's Row ran down to Commerical Road (uninterrupted in 1888). From the Commerical Road end of Plumber's Row, Berner Street ran south to Fairclough Street and Ellen Street. Nathan Kaminsky lived four minutes' walk in one unbroken direction from the apparently out-of-the-way site of Elizabeth Stride's murder. It was actually closer to him than 29 Hanbury Street or Essex Wharf, Buck's Row.

He also lived precisely where he would have escaped Pc Mizen's beat if he went straight home after the Buck's Row murder. Old Montague Street and Hanbury Street joined Baker's Row at the same point in these days. Mizen was met by Cross and Paul in Hanbury Street. A murderer who went directly home along Old Montague Street would have avoided him without any need for evasive action.

Goulston Street also lay exactly on the murderer's route from Mitre Square to Black Lion Yard. A murderer taking the most direct route possible would cross it diagonally from New Goulston Street, making for Wentworth Street which led in a direct line to Old Montague Street. The doorway where the Ripper threw his piece of apron would be the first open door he passed leaving Mitre Square.

I had to trust my own methodology. I had not taken a third party's 'identification' of Jack the Ripper, and tried to force the facts to fit. I shared the view of all serious researchers that only the police had sufficient information to discover the murderer's identity. I knew that the City's house-to-house had proved more efficacious than any amount of Sherlock Holmesian deduction, turning up Lawende and his positive sighting of Jack the Ripper. And I could see that the Met was far more efficient than a hostile press chose to admit. Even its uniformed patrol of the streets had proved effective: the gap between the first two murders was a week; between the second and the night of the double murder, two weeks; and between that night and the last, five and a half weeks. After which the murders stopped. Obviously the police made it increasingly difficult, and ultimately impossible for Jack to rip.

I had examined the surviving police evidence and assessed its relative weight, finding to my surprise that the Scotland Yard chiefs took priority. I had extrapolated a profile of the man they were looking for. And now, in finding a man who fitted their description, I had also found the first suspect ever named who matched all the topographical clues provided by the murders themselves. Thus far I had indulged in no speculation whatsoever. I never doubted that I should find Nathan Kaminsky proceeding through the lunacy records somewhere to his final incarceration – quite likely with his name spelled differently – and the case would be solved.

Alas for human presumption! Infirmary after infirmary; register of lunatics after register of lunatics; dockets upon dockets of quarterly returns of pauper lunatics in care; all drew blanks. After several months' work, I had examined all the plausible records from the City and the East End, collected long lists of names of poor Jewish lunatics, and found no trace of anyone remotely resembling Nathan Kaminsky, bootmaker of Black Lion Yard.

Worse still, over the same months I had failed to find any record of his death. Advertisements in the *Jewish Chronicle* and telephone calls to Kaminskys in the directory elicited friendly and helpful replies, but invariably, no connection. The death registers revealed that a Nathan Kaminsky of almost the right age had died in Dalston in the early 1920s. With great difficulty I traced his (charming) descendants. There was no connection. The family was Russian, and had not immigrated until 1905.

Between 1888 and 1960 (by which time a surviving Ripper would have been at least 100!) only one other Nathan Kaminsky died in England. He was seven years too old to have been the bootmaker of Black Lion Yard, and by advertising in the *Jewish Gazette* I established that he had always been a tailor in Leeds, and had never lived in Whitechapel.

There was one other source to be investigated. The notorious Scotland Yard files, supposedly closed until 1992 had, in fact, as Scotland Yard told me, been open in the Public Record Office for the last 10 years. Everyone who had seen them confirmed, however, that they contained nothing helpful. Stephen Knight even believed that they proved Warren and Anderson had prevented Abberline and Helson from carrying out the useful investigation they had started, since their detailed reports from the murder sites ceased after Annie Chapman's death. In fact, as I saw very quickly, the files were bureaucrats' records, not detective information. Abberline's and Helson's reports were the bases on which Swanson had compiled his reports to the Home Office. They were retained until Anderson's return, so that he should know why the man he had posted as 'the Commissioner's eyes and ears' on Polly Nichols' murder had written as he had. Such reports ceased from the night of the double murder because Anderson himself was on hand, and could approve Swanson's work in the drafting stage if he wished.

Likewise, suspects and witnesses who were discussed on Scotland Yard's files were those who did not appear in court to be recorded by magistrates' clerks and coroners. Issenschmidt, the mad pork butcher of Holloway, and Piggott, the blood-cuffed lunatic of Gravesend both feature in previous books on the Ripper solely because Scotland Yard had to keep a record of these men they had caused to be certified. But two far more serious suspects, familiar to me from contemporary newspaper reports, did not appear. Charles Ludwig, a German hairdresser who terrified prostitute Elizabeth Burns under the railway arch in the Minories, was on remand in police custody when Annie Chapman died, and having been charged with threatening behaviour, did not need details of his case filed separately in Scotland Yard. Joseph Isaacs, a Polish Jew arrested on 6 December after his landlady testified that he paced up and down his room off Dorset Street at nights during the week of Marie Kelly's murder, and absconded the day after she was killed; does not appear in the files, either. He was charged with theft from a pawnshop, and although Abberline's removal of him from Drury Lane to Leman Street in a closely guarded carriage showed that the police thought they really had picked up the Ripper this time, there was no need to keep separate details up to and including the time they realised that he was only a thief and not a murderer.

Anything that (say) MPs might ask questions about in the House of Commons is recorded: answers to the Home Secretary's queries about numbers of lodging-houses and prostitutes in Spitalfields; details of the extra police drafted to Whitechapel; Schwartz's statement about the man attacking Long Liz; the interrogations of Packer (who was being grandly featured in the newspapers) by Warren and Sergeant White. And in the latter, a description of the whereabouts of the vital data from the original house-to-house inquiry: 'Any information that I could obtain I noted in a Book supplied to me for that purpose.' Obviously it was these special notebooks that Anderson examined for a day and a half. The material on file in the Public Record Office would hardly take an afternoon to study. And these notebooks have been lost; almost certainly destroyed quite innocently as dead material.

Case reports were also sent over to the Home Office which kept a file recording attempts to find evidence on known suspects. This has been thoroughly purged, so that its shrivelled remains, as the cover admits, only document absurd possibilities. Such as a doctor in Kensington who was a late riser, affable to ladies, and bore a remarkable resemblance to a doctor's visitor as drawn in a comic magazine. Or Sergeant Thick himself, accused in deepest secrecy by Mr H. J. Haslewood of Tottenham! Anderson, Swanson, Monro and Lushington variously note 'Rubbish' in the margins of these offerings, or carefully explain the obvious fallacies in the 'cases' they promote.

The file cover indicates numbered paper after numbered paper 'Removed' or 'Destroyed'. This was no secret elimination of establishment suspects. Somewhere among these lost papers, there must once have lain some of the documents that pointed to the characters named by Macnaghten: 'Ostrog', Druitt and Kosminski.

Today, among all the various files from Scotland Yard and the Home Office, there is only one faint pointer toward Macnaghten's suspects. It is in the Home Office file of information from abroad. A letter, forwarded from the Foreign Office on 14 December, apparently from the consul in Dresden (since the writer, Mr G. Strachey, makes no preambular identification of himself) refers to a Polish Jew. A German American named Löwenstein told Strachey that he had met a Polish Jew called Wirtkofsky in a Christian household near Finsbury Square, shortly before 'the first murder' (by which Löwenstein would mean Emma Smith's). Wirtkofsky asked Löwenstein to tell him whether he had 'a special pathological condition', and on learning that he had, swore that he would kill the woman responsible and all the rest of her class.

Strachey noted the possibility that Löwenstein merely wanted a free trip to London, but argued against it, first, because Löwenstein never suggested it, and did no more than to leave a Poste Restante address in Nuremberg where he might collect any subsequent response. And, second, because Löwenstein definitely said he did not know where Wirtkofsky was to be found; he could do no more than identify him if he were arrested.

Thin stuff, and there are no marginalia suggesting that the Home Office acted on it. They had suffered two months earlier from Warren's expressing interest in a transparent confidence trickster who gulled the ambassador in Vienna into giving him 200 florins for a journey to England to identify Jack the Ripper. (Lushington, Monro and Anderson had all recorded their disgust at the time.) But there are two microscopic hints that Scotland Yard might have received this information direct from the Foreign Office, and taken action. Martin Howells and Keith Skinner, following up their mistaken conviction that Stephen White saw a suspect leaving Mitre Square, discovered a *Times* report saying,

> At about the time when the Mitre Square murder was being committed two of the extra men who had been put on duty were in Windsor Street, a thoroughfare about 300 yards off, engaged, pursuant to their instructions, in watching certain houses, it being thought possible that the premises might be resorted to at some time by the murderer.

The Times, was, as usual, hopelessly wrong in its East End topography. Windsor Street ran off the City Road, near Micawber Street, well over a mile away from Mitre Square. But Windsor Place (the only Windsor anywhere within striking distance of Whitechapel) ran off the Hoxton Road, and might be described (by *The Times*) as about 300 yards from . . . *Finsbury* Square. The Wirtkofsky paper is the only document anywhere suggesting a reason for detectives to watch houses in that area.

The second very faint straw in the wind also emerges from Howells and Skinner's investigation of White's story. They note that *The People's Journal* states that it was White's description that convinced Anderson 'that the murderer was a Jewish medical student'. But Anderson had no such conviction. He thought the murderer was a 'low-class' Polish Jew, and the witness upon whom he relied was certainly not Stephen White. There is garbling and misinformation here, involving a medical student. And the only quasi-Jewish medical student anywhere on the official records is Löwenstein the German-American who offered to identify a Polish Jewish syphilitic. We may reasonably wonder whether Anderson let some colleagues know that he would like to take this witness seriously, and underinformed juniors misinterpreted this into a suspicion.

But all this carried one no closer to a bootmaker called Nathan Kaminsky. The Bethnal Green Board of Guardians' records proved that I had been right to wonder about Nathan Karnsky. He had indeed died in Colney Hatch, where they had him incarcerated from 1899. Nor were they sure of his age; their estimate changed from year to year, and the optimum guess (for making him a murder suspect) would have made him 18 in 1888. Even his name was in doubt: he was admitted to the Infirmary as Nathan Karonsky. Later I discovered that his real name was Arginsky, yet the authorities at Colney Hatch disregarded the fact when they knew it, and buried him under the erroneous name Karnsky. Was he, then, the missing Nathan Kaminsky? And if so, where on earth had he been from 1888 to 1899?

By now, the staff of the Greater London Archives realized that I was becoming perplexed, and their helpfulness extended to pointing out that as an historian and not a genealogist, it was very likely that I might receive permission from regional health administrators to inspect asylum records before the 100-years ended. I wrote at once to the various addresses they gave me, and after various delays, the permissions arrived.

Several hospital archivists kindly read out names from their records over the telephone to me, and I confirmed that people I had noted in the East End records were exactly where those records had claimed, and equally certainly were not Jack the Ripper. The records of Colney Hatch, where the vast majority of London lunatics were treated, were in the Greater London Archives, and I was delighted to find myself studying the Male Patients' Day Book from 1887–1890. In the period Macnaghten identified as the time of the Ripper's incarceration, Hyam Hyams gave me pause. He was a Jew from Whitechapel. He was very violent; 'a crafty and dangerous maniac', according to one case note. In attacking his wife with a chopper he had seriously injured his mother. He attacked attendants in the hospital, and tried to cut the throat of one.

But he was discharged as cured before the year was out (only to be brought back permanently the following year). His violence was based on the delusion that his wife was unfaithful to him, and he was dangerous to her and any man he suddenly decided was cuckolding him, even though his victim might never have met Mrs Hyams. He never deliberately attacked any other women. He lived in the wrong part of Whitechapel to pass through Goulston Street from Mitre Square. As a cigar salesman he had no connection with leather or aprons. And his wife quite definitely identified him. He had to be abandoned. He didn't fit.

The patient who certainly did fit Anderson's identification, taken on its own, was David Cohen. He was a foreign Jew, aged 23, and with no known relatives (*exactly* like Kaminsky). His incarceration, *and his alone*, was precisely timed to explain the end of the murders. He had been brought by the police to Whitechapel Infirmary on 12 December after they said they 'found him wandering at large and unable to take care of himself'. This was official Lunacy Act wording, meaning only that he seemed mad and they had not taken him from friends or a known address. He proved extremely violent; dangerous to himself and others. He threatened fellow-patients, refused food and was noisy at night. His first action in the Infirmary was to tear down the wire grating at the window and an iron pipe. Unless kept under restraint, he shouted and danced around the place. On 21 December he was sent on to Colney Hatch.

Here his antisocial violence continued. He was kept under restraint; force-fed when he spat out food; put in a strait-jacket. He had to be kept apart from other patients, and he spoke little but German. He destroyed his clothes if he could get at them.

He was taken ill on 28 December, and after growing stronger during 1889, suffered a relapse in October. When he died on 20 October, 'Exhaustion of mania' was given as the primary cause, with pulmonary phthisis as the secondary.

As far as asylum records went, this was the only possible Jack the Ripper. But how did he relate to Nathan Kaminsky? His age and race were identical, but his name was quite different; his occupation was given as 'Tailor', and from the outset he was recorded as living at 86 Leman Street.

This last point had made me discount him when I first discovered his admission to the Infirmary. It was the wrong part of Whitechapel, almost next door to H Division Headquarters. But the Post Office Directory revealed an anomaly. 86 Leman Street housed the largest Protestant Boy's Club in the East End, and its affiliated 'Blue Riband' Shoeblacks' Refuge. No Jew would have lived there.

Next door, 84 Leman Street, on the other hand, was the Temporary Shelter for Poor Homeless Jews. It was certainly a place where 'Leather Apron' might seek anonymous retreat as his own immediate neighbourhood came under intense police surveillance. Alternatively, the police might have given it as an address for an unchargeable suspect they wanted brought back next door to them, should the medics decide that the maniac was cured. The address was no insurmountable barrier.

An article by Terence Robertson in *Reynolds News* for 29 October 1950, mentioned by Tom Cullen and traced by Keith Skinner, suggested that Scotland Year had long believed the Ripper to be a Polish sailor. One ambiguous phrase – 'the Yard's theory, which marked the closing of their file' – was interpreted by Cullen as suggesting that there once was a closure note so worded. And anyone familiar with transcription errors would not be at all surprised at a 't' being read as an 's'. Moreover, I knew from the House of Lords inquiry into Poor Immigrants in the summer of 1888 that bootmaking and tailoring were the two trades that completely unskilled immigrants were given by their fellow Jews to support themselves. If an unskilled immigrant bootmaking Leather Apron had to hide and change his job as the police hunt drew near, he would undoubtedly move into a tailoring sweatshop and probably lodge at 84 Leman Street.

The great stumbling block was the name Cohen. Nathan could easily be misheard as David, in a nasal nineteenth century East End Jewish accent. But could a rambling lunatic Kaminsky so deform language as to be misheard as 'Cohen'? I speculated that he could, and so went to press with the first edition of this book.

It was too weak a link for many sympathetic observers. As Richard Whittington-Egan wrote of the whole argument, 'I like it. I *want* to believe it. But I can't.' And although I was quite convinced by the records I had seen, I could understand his misgivings.

As soon as I published, an explanation was provided by Jewish and Gentile informants from London, New York, Vienna, even the Far East. Didn't I *know* that Cohen was the usual 'John Doe' name that petty officialdom gave to Jews whose names were unpronounceable, hard to spell, or generally uncertain? Alas, I didn't. But I do now, and it has led me to admit the possibility that 'Wirtkovsky' may have been 'Kaminsky', and that Leather Apron's real name was unknown because he used a number of aliases, one of which fell into the K-something-ski class, but none of which seemed sufficiently reliable to justify labelling him when the police sent him to the asylum.

There was one more shock to absorb before the first edition appeared. With the book in proof, the publishers told me there was room for an Appendix. I decided to use this for a verbatim reproduction of the single-line entry on Nathan Kaminsky, and everything I could find about 'David Cohen' in the uncatalogued Colney Hatch records. I particularly wanted to know whether visitors' books would confirm an identification of this lunatic by a

City Policeman as Macnaghten suggested (or, with hindsight, a Jew, as Anderson said).

No visitors' books for the men's section in the period survive, but I did see the Admissions and Discharge Book for the first time, and unlike the Day Book with case notes which ran to December 1890, this ran to 1892.

And there, staring me in the face, was Aaron Kozminski, Hebrew hairdresser, admitted 7 February 1891, suffering from mania for six years, caused by self-abuse. He was *exactly* the same age as Nathan Kaminsky and 'David Cohen' (and, come to that, Abberline's suspect Klosowski!). His bodily state was fair; his main symptom was incoherence; he was not believed to be dangerous to himself or others, and he was discharged to Leavesden Asylum in 1894.

Leavesden was the Asylum for Imbeciles, and, knowing that no sexual serialist had ever been an imbecile, I had not paid any attention to Aaron, dying there in the Watford registration district in 1919. Rather, I had asserted confidently (and accurately) that nobody called K-anything-ski was in any asylum between 1888 and 1890, and assumed that this ended the search for Kosminski. Now the name had emerged, but attached to a man who had been at liberty for two years after the murders stopped and who was listed as not dangerous.

I had under a week to send for Kozminski's case notes and re-write my final chapter to incorporate a summary of them, keeping it exactly to the length it had been (to avoid inordinately costly re-setting) and relegating my argument to an Appendix!

If Kozminski had been Jack the Ripper I should have had some very expensive and very fast re-writing to do. But the case-notes showed clearly that he was not. He suffered from the delusion that his 'instincts' told him what everybody in the world was thinking, and commanded him not to accept food from other people. Consequently, he picked up and ate pieces of bread from the gutter. He was seen doing this in Carter Lane in the City among other places. His instincts also told him never to take a bath. He was alleged to have attacked his sister with a knife once, but was otherwise quite harmless and neurotically idle. He lived with his brother Woolf at 'Lion Square, Commercial Road' – a definite mistake, as no such place existed. Keith Skinner has now established that it was a clerical error for Sion Square, which actually ran off Plumber's Row. Kozminski had been treated very briefly in Mile End Old Town

Workhouse Infirmary in July, 1890, and again in February 1891 before being transferred to Colney Hatch. His name was so mis-spelled in the Mile End Admissions and Discharge Book that both Charles Nevin of the *Daily Telegraph* and I failed to identify the entries, and only the lynx-eyed Keith Skinner picked them up, after he had discovered correct entries in the (then) uncatalogued Creed Book.

Kozminski's condition slowly deteriorated over the years, until his tendency to apathy and indolence completely overwhelmed him and he was transferred to Leavesden, where he died of gangrene 25 years later.

This was positively not Leather Apron. For 18 months after the last murder he was a visible East End and City figure, picking up food from the gutter. He could have been identified by Eliza Cooper or Ted Stanley at any time. As a hairdresser, albeit one who never worked, he would not have owned a Leather Apron.

Nor was he the Ripper. He would not have gone north to Goulston Street from Mitre Square on his way to Sion Square. And, above all, his case notes – the hardest evidence about him – revealed an apathetic imbecile encumbered with delusions, totally lacking the intelligence and presence of mind which enable sexual serial murderers to lead double lives and escape suspicion.

In 1988, Professor Luigi Cancrini of the University of Bologna, made a psychological study of the Ripper murders, concluding that they evinced an explosive crescendo of increasingly theatrical violence which would culminate in a complete breakdown. In conversation, he agreed that 'David Cohen's' mania fitted the pattern, and felt that it might well have been triggered by rage at a bout of syphilis six months earlier, as experienced by 'Nathan Kaminsky'. The form of mania, he identified as malignly mischievous: deliberately breaking rules and challenging authority. And the word 'Mischievous' stands on its own in 'Cohen's' case notes. Professor Cancrini would have expected death by suicide rather than exhaustion and phthisis, however. And 'Cohen's' case notes show that he was, indeed, believed to have attempted it, and was guarded against it while under care. Kozminski's two years of inactivity, on the other hand, seem to Professor Cancrini completely incompatible with the personality perpetrating the Whitechapel murders.

Yet Macnaghten had obviously heard of the real Kozminski. His illness was attributed to 'self-abuse' by Colney Hatch and 'many years indulgence in solitary vices' by Macnaghten. He was, indeed, alive and still in the asylum when Macnaghten wrote (unlike 'David Cohen'). And, certainly, if Macnaghten knew of his symptoms, he would have concluded that Kozminski was innocent, no matter what 'circs' had once made him a strong suspect.

The confusion of Kozminski and Cohen, however, happened at a higher level of information than Macnaghten's. After I had published the apparently over-subtle claim that a lunatic registered as 'Cohen' had committed the Whitechapel murders and had thereafter been confused with an innocent lunatic of the same age and race named Kozminski, proof emerged that I was absolutely correct. Chief Inspector Swanson's grandson read in the *Daily Telegraph* that several new books on Jack the Ripper still proffered several different solutions. Mr Swanson had in his possession his grandfather's solution. He had also the inter-office memorandum in which Anderson appointed Swanson to head the inquiry into Polly Nichols' murder, and rightly thought this guaranteed the Chief Inspector's knowledgeability. (With typical confidence Anderson, shortly to take sick leave, regretted that he could not spare a few days to solve the murder quickly himself!)

Chief Inspector Swanson's observations on the Ripper were pencilled in the margins and on the endpaper of his copy of Anderson's *The Lighter Side of My Official Life*. His old chief's discreet indiscretions tickled his fancy, and he underlined the words 'the traditions of my old department would suffer.' Then, after Anderson's statement, 'the only person who ever saw the murderer unhesitatingly identified the suspect the instant he was confronted with him; but he refused to give evidence against him,' Swanson continued under the text

> because the suspect was also a Jew and also because his evidence would convict the suspect, and witness would be the means of murderer being hanged which he did not wish to be left on his mind. D.S.S.

In the margin, he went on

> And after this identification which suspect knew, no other murder of this kind took place in London.

And on the endpaper appeared

> After the suspect had been identified at the Seaside Home

where he had been sent by us with difficulty in order to subject him to identification and he knew he was identified.

On suspect's return to his brother's house in Whitechapel he was watched by police (City CID) by day and night. In a very short time the suspect with his hands tied behind his back he was sent to Stepney Workhouse and then to Colney Hatch and died shortly afterwards – Kosminski was the suspect –

D.S.S.

The *Daily Telegraph* showed this to Donald Rumbelow and me, hoping it would be able to print a simple story that Jack the Ripper was now found and identified as the Polish Jew Kosminski. Of course, it was more complicated than that. Swanson's notes were not one hundred per cent accurate: there was no such place as 'Stepney Workhouse', though the term was sometimes used colloquially for St George's-in-the-East in the 1880s. But both Whitechapel Workhouse (where Cohen was taken) and Mile End Old Town Workhouse (where Kozminski was treated) came to be administered by Stepney Board of Guardians in 1925, and many Londoners vaguely have regarded all the nearer land east of Aldgate Pump as 'Stepney'.

And the Colney Hatch records proved that Swanson was describing two men as one. 'David Cohen' did not live at his brother's house in Whitechapel. Aaron Kozminski did. Aaron Kozminski did not go to the workhouse 'in a very short time' after the murders; and far from dying in Colney Hatch, he was still alive when Swanson wrote his observations. That part of Swanson's description fits 'David Cohen' *and no other Colney Hatch inmate or East End pauper lunatic*. Furthermore, it is carefully recorded that the violent 'Cohen' was brought in to the asylum under restraint. It was most unlikely that harmless Aaron Kozminski would have been handcuffed.

My main conclusion was right. Anderson referred to 'David Cohen', and somehow he had been mixed up with innocent Aaron Kozminski. But how did this occur?

Macnaghten was little help. He was shown to be wrong about the date of the suspect's incarceration and wrong about the witness, who, as a Jew with conscientious objections to giving evidence against a fellow Jew, must have been Lawende. Why were the City CID following a man on Metropolitan territory? And why (as Donald Rumbelow pertinently asked) should there be any 'difficulty' in taking a suspect for identification in a major murder inquiry?

Where did this identification take place? Anderson said in the asylum, where both Cohen and Kozminski had been placed with no difficulty at all. Now Swanson pointed to a Seaside Home. What was it? The Police Convalescent Home in Brighton was usually so described by officers, but it did not open until 1890. On the other hand, the Convalescent Home Fund had been the most popular police charity since 1887, and throughout 1888 officers were being sent to a Seaside Home in Bexhill for rest and recuperation. But why should any identification take place there?

It was not till I had slept on this new evidence, and the professional impressions gleaned from Donald Rumbelow, that I saw the probable explanation of the whole mystery. Swanson and Macnaghten both made unusual references to the City Police. Unknown to each other, *the City and the Met investigated different men*, and each poached on the other's ground to do so. The Met hi-jacked the City's witness, Lawende, without informing Major Smith, only to find that he refused to stand by his identification if it would convict a fellow-Jew. This, somehow, lay behind the professional oddities Swanson described, and possibly misremembered. 'Cohen' probably could not have been charged in any case if, as Anderson said, he had already been certified and incarcerated on the Met's initiative.

The City Police, meanwhile, had staked out a watch on the 'known lunatic' (in Macnaghten's words) who ate out of their gutters. This took them to Sion Square, Whitechapel, where they should have arranged for the Met to do the watching. They found, of course, that their man was innocent, and was simply committed by his brother when his madness became intolerable.

As I had already shown, relations between the two forces were far from cordial at the top. And when, after Kozminski's incarceration, the investigators found that they had each been following 'a 23-year-old Polish Jew from Whitechapel who went into Colney Hatch,' they assumed they had been after the same man. I know of no other pair of patients with the same age, gender, minority race and religion, going from the same parish into the same asylum in the space of two years.

The City (as Swanson stressed) had found their man's home and sane brother, so their discovery of his name was accepted by the Met. They assumed it *was* the name of the man they had incarcerated as 'David Cohen'. And they never let on that they had been responsible for incarcerating him (as they thought) under a pseudonym. They didn't, after all, think he *was* a lunatic. They thought he was a sex maniac; someone quite fit to plead in court and be hanged. It was a second-best and rather underhand business to have him certified. Rumbelow instantly spotted professional oddities about the identification and incarceration. Every policeman I have talked to agrees, however, that in a case like this, they would still 'Get him under the Mental Health Act' to protect the public if they had a positive suspect but knew they would have difficulty in bringing the case to court.

And until Anderson, characteristically, spilled half a bean, nobody below the rank of Swanson (and maybe Moore) was to be told. It would open up the antisemitic reaction again, and it might lead to awkward questions about the certification. We simply don't know whether Anderson shared Swanson's misconception that 'Cohen' was really called Kozminski and lived with his brother. I am inclined to doubt it, though.

Anderson remains alone among the Scotland Yard chiefs in asserting definitely that 'the Polish Jew' was Jack the Ripper. Macnaghten's informants evidently told him that he was a strong – perhaps the strongest – suspect. Swanson only called him 'suspect', and clearly saw the cessation of the murders after the positive identification as the second strongest reason for suspecting him. Abberline actually said there was 'nothing in it'. Anderson had no doubts or reservations, and rested his case on the identification and (we may infer) whatever previous suspicions had led the witness to be taken to the asylum for the identification. My own guess is that those initial suspicions were the statements made by the prostitutes about Leather Apron. I think that, suspecting they had Leather Apron under lock and key at last in December, the Met surreptitiously took Lawende out to Colney Hatch. That single positive identification was all the admissible evidence they had against him, and their key witness would have been hostile if forced into court. Worse still, the suspect was apparently unfit to plead. It was a dilemma which on all counts prohibited any triumphant public announcement of the end of the case.

Indeed, I doubt whether the majority of the Scotland Yard chiefs decided that the identification was unquestionably reliable until Macnaghten had been (as he said) 'several years in the force'. In 1892, in fact, given that the file was originally closed until 1992. Around the time of Abberline's retirement from the force. Three years after 'Cohen's' death. But two years before Kozminski's transfer to

Leavesden, making it most improbable, as Paul Begg suggests, that Swanson simply assumed that Kozminski's disappearance from Colney Hatch in 1894 meant that he had died. Abberline's 1903 interviews, together with an 1895 *Pall Mall Gazette* piece hinting at Swanson's opinion, indicate that both the Inspector and the Chief Inspector believed the lunatic suspect died in the asylum.

Then, in 1892, I suspect, Anderson, Swanson, Bradford perhaps, Moore maybe, fetched out the old case papers from the Home Office file and went over them to decide which of their final suspects had really been the man. In September 1889 Monro still wasn't sure he had been stopped. Macnaghten, who wrongly imagined that 'the Polish Jew' went into the asylum around March 1889, would assume that he was not the Ripper once he learned that the murderer was finally believed to have been inactive from November 1888. He was never told that this was a deduction based on a new recension of the old facts rather than a new discovery. A deduction made positive since it was now clear that neither Clay Pipe Alice nor Frances Coles had been victims of a resurgent Ripper, let alone Rose Mylett, whom Anderson still mentioned specifically in his memoirs. And *after* that recension and deduction, somebody in Scotland Yard heard from a City police source that 'the 23-year-old Whitechapel Polish Jew who went to Colney Hatch' was 'really' called Kosminski, passing the information on so that it reached Macnaghten and Swanson. The latter may have accepted it the more willingly if he had once been supervising a search for Nathan *Kaminsky*. That name may have stirred echoes in Abberline's mind when he heard of one Klosowski.

And Major Smith, who never heard of 'David Cohen', was understandably furious when he found Anderson saying that Jack the Ripper was a Polish Jew. A 'reckless accusation' indeed, if, as Smith assumed, Anderson meant Aaron Kozminski. Of course, Anderson really meant 'David Cohen'. The man who was unhesitatingly, but secretly, identified by Smith's witness, Mr Joseph Lawende, who had seen him at Church Passage with Catherine Eddowes. And the times at which City Pcs Watkins and Harvey passed Mitre Square proved, without question, that he was the man who murdered her. Jack the Ripper has been found.

Sources

GENERAL
Throughout, the dedicatees' books are accepted as the basis of modern received opinion and familiar speculation. These are:

Donald McCormick, *The Identity of Jack the Ripper*, Jarrolds, 1959
Tom Cullen, *Autumn of Terror*, Bodley Head, 1965
Robin Odell, *Jack the Ripper in Fact and Fiction*, Harrap, 1965
Dan Farson, *Jack the Ripper*, Michael Joseph, 1972
Donald Rumbelow, *The Complete Jack the Ripper*, W. H. Allen, 1975
Richard Whittington-Egan, *A Casebook on Jack the Ripper*, Wiley, 1975
Stephen Knight, *Jack the Ripper: The Final Solution*, Harrap, 1976

The Times reports of the crimes and enquiries make a convenient basis for press opinion, as they are indexed. Other newspapers, therefore, tend only to be cited when they provide essential additional or variant opinion, although the *East London Observer's* accounts of the inquests are extremely full and colourful, and in some respects *The Daily Telegraph*, the *Morning Post*, and the evening papers give better coverage.

Sworn testimony at the inquests outweighs other forms of evidence, where it survives, and the coroners' notes available reveal lacunae and errors in press reporting. Quotations of direct speech are usually taken from inquest testimony; occasionally from press interviews or memoirs.

The precise topographical data and the detailed maps are derived from a careful comparison of the 1875 and 1893–4 5ft-to-the-mile ordnance survey maps with witnesses' statements and Kelly's Post Office London Directories for the period, as well as repeated walking through the district.

WHITECHAPEL MURDERS
Evening News, 11 Sep 1888
Walter Besant, *East London*, Chatto & Windus, 1903
Charles Booth et al, *Life and Labour of the London Poor*, Macmillan, 1902
G. R. Sims, *My Life*, Nash, 1917

SOURCES

The Mysteries of Modern London, Arthur Pearson, 1906
Robert Sinclair, *East London*, Robert Hale, 1950

The Times, 22 Oct 1888
Public Record Office (Kew), Home Office Papers MEPO 3/142

PRELUDE
The Daily Telegraph, 11 Sep 1888
East London Advertiser, 14 Apr, 7 Sep 1888
East London Observer, 31 Mar 1888
Illustrated Police News, 14 Apr 1888
Pall Mall Gazette, 10 Nov 1888
Reynolds Newspaper, 19 Aug 1888
The Times, 8, 10, 24 Aug 1888
L. Forbes Winslow, *Recollections of Forty Years*, Ouseley, 1910

The name 'Fairy Fay' is cited from 'the press' by Cullen, but I have found no contemporary instance of its use. Her non-existence is established by scrutiny of the Death Registers in St Catherine's House.

POLLY NICHOLS
The Daily Telegraph, 24 Sep 1888
East London Advertiser, 8 Sep 1888
Pall Mall Gazette, 1 Sep 1888
Reynolds Newspaper, 2, 9 Sep 1888
The Star, 1, 3, 5 Sep 1888
The Times, 1, 3, 4, 7, 18, 24, 26 Sep 1888
Walter Dew, *I Caught Crippen*, Blackie, 1938

ANNIE CHAPMAN
British Medical Journal, 6 Oct 1888
Daily News, 10 Sep 1888
The Daily Telegraph, 12, 13, 14, 15, 29 Sep 1888
East London Observer, 15 Sep 1888
Evening News, 14 Sep 1888
Illustrated Police News, 15, 29 Sep 1888
The Lancet, 22, 29 Sep 1888
Reynolds Newspaper, 16 Sep 1888
The Star, 8, 10, 12, 15 Sep 1888
The Times, 10, 11, 12, 13, 14, 15, 19, 20, 26, 27, 28 Sep 1888

THE NIGHT OF THE DOUBLE MURDER

Daily News, 1 Oct 1888

East London Advertiser, 6, 13 Oct 1888, 19 Jan, 23 Mar, 6, 13 Apr 1889

The Echo, 24 Sep 1888

Illustrated Police News, 13 Oct 1888

The Times, 1, 2, 12 Oct 1888; 19 Mar, 26 Apr 1889

Dew, *I Caught Crippen*

Martin Fido, *Murder Guide to London,* Weidenfeld & Nicolson, 1986

William J. Fishman, *East End Jewish Radicals,* Duckworth, 1975.

Lt-Col Sir Henry Smith, *From Constable to Commissioner,* Chatto & Windus, 1910

Corporation of London Records, Coroner's Inquests (London), 1888, no. 135

Public Records Office, Home Office Papers MEPO 3/140, HO 144/A49301 c

ELIZABETH STRIDE

East London Advertiser, 15, 22 Sep, 3, 6 Oct 1888

East London Observer, 15 Sep 1888

The Echo, 24 Sep, 15 Nov 1888

Evening News, 1, 4, 10, 17, 31 Oct 1888

Illustrated Police News, 13 Oct 1888

Jewish Chronicle, 14 Sep, 5, 12 Oct 1888

Morning Post, 1, 6 Oct 1888

Pall Mall Gazette 6, 8 Oct 1888

Reynolds Newspaper, 7 Oct 1888

The Times, 1, 2, 3, 4, 6, 15, 16, 18, 19, 24, 25 Oct 1888

Dew, *I Caught Crippen*

Corporation of London Records Office, Police Box 3, 13–18 (534c)

Greater London Archives, Whitechapel Workhouse Infirmary Creeds, Book 1888–9

Public Records Office, Home Office Papers, MEPO 3/141

Thames Magistrates' Court Attendance Register, 1887–8

CATHERINE EDDOWES

City Press, 7 Nov 1888

East London Advertiser, 13 Oct 1888

The Echo, 19 Oct 1888

Evening News, 10, 17, 20 Oct 1888

Pall Mall Gazette, 8 Oct 1888

Reynolds Newspaper, 14 Oct 1888

The Star, 5, 11, 12, 13 Oct 1888
The Times, 1, 2, 4, 5, 6, 8, 9, 11, 12, 18, 19, 22, 25 Oct 1888
Dew, *I Caught Crippen*
Smith, *From Constable to Commissioner*
Corporation of London Records Office, Coroner's Papers (London), 1888, no. 135

MARIE JEANETTE KELLY
East London Advertiser, 6 Dec 1888
Evening News, 12 Nov 1888
Morning Post, 12 Nov 1888
Reynolds Newspaper, 11, 18 Nov 1888
The Star, 9, 10, 12, 14 Nov 1888
The Times, 10, 12, 13, 14 Nov 1888
Greater London Archives, Coroner's Papers, MJ/SPC/NE/Box 3 no. 19

FALSE ALARMS
East London Advertiser, 29 Dec 1888, 20 July 1889
Illustrated Police News, 1 Dec 1888, 17 Feb 1891
The Star, 21 Nov, 22, 24 Dec 1888, 3, 10 Jan, 17, 18, 19 Jul, 15 Aug 1889, 14, 16, 17 Feb 1891
Ben Leeson, *Lost London*, Stanley Paul, 1934
Sir Melville Macnaghten, *Days of My Years*, Edward Arnold, 1914

THE CITY AND THE MET
H. L. Adam, *The Police Encyclopaedia*, vol 1, Waverley, 1920
Dew, *I Caught Crippen*
J. F. Moylan, *Scotland Yard and the Metropolitan Police*, Putnam, 1929
Sir Basil Thomson, *The Story of Scotland Yard*, Grayson & Grayson, 1935
Swanson Papers. Private Information, Jim Swanson.

THE COPPERS ON THE GROUND
Pall Mall Gazette, 24, 31 Mar, 3 Apr 1903
Dew, *I Caught Crippen*
Martin Howells and Keith Skinner, *The Ripper Legacy*, Sidgwick and Jackson, 1987
Leeson, *Lost London*
Macnaghten, *Days of My Years*
F. P. Wensley, *Detective Days*, Cassell, 1931

HEADING THE CITY FORCE
The Times, 13 Nov 1888, 15 Apr 1892

Smith, *From Constable to Commissioner*

HEADING THE MET
The Echo, 6 Sep 1888
Murray's Magazine, Nov 1888
Pall Mall Gazette, 8 Sep, 8 Oct 1888
The Star, 1, 11 Sep, 6, 13, 25 Oct, 12, 13, 19, 28, 29 Nov 1888
The Times, 8, 10, 13, 15 Oct, 12, 13, 16 Nov 1888, 15 May 1911, 30 Jan 1920
H. L. Adam, C.I.D.: *Behind the Scenes at Scotland Yard,* Sampson Low, 1931
Sir Robert Anderson, *The Lighter Side of My Official Life,* Hodder & Stoughton, 1910
Dictionary of National Biography
George Dilnot, *Scotland Yard: Its History and Organisation,* Geoffrey Bles, 1929
Howells & Skinner *The Ripper Legacy*
Moylan, *Scotland Yard and the Metropolitan Police*
A PC, *The Metropolitan Police and Its Management,* E. Dyke, 1888
Bernard Porter, *Origins of the Vigilant State,* Weidenfeld & Nicolson, 1987
Thomson, *The Story of Scotland Yard*
Watkin M. Williams, *The Life of Sir Charles Warren,* Blackwell, 1941

MEMORANDA FROM THE MET
H. L. Adam, *Police Work from Within,* Holden & Hardingham, 1914
    C.I.D.: *Behind the Scenes at Scotland Yard*
Major Arthur Griffiths, *Mysteries of Police and Crime,* vol 1, Cassell, 1901
Macnaghten, *Days of My Years*
Thomson, *The Story of Scotland Yard*
Wensley, *Detective Days*
Public Record Office, Home Office Papers, MEPO 3/141

THE MAN WHO KNEW TOO MUCH
Pall Mall Gazette, 8 Oct 1888
The Star, 12 Dec 1888
The Times, 7, 10, 12, 19, 29, 21 Mar, 18, 20 Apr, 2, 13, 20 May, 17 Jun 1887, 5 Mar 1889, 18 Nov 1918
Adam, C.I.D.: *Behind the Scenes at Scotland Yard*
(Sir) Robert Anderson, *The Lighter Side of My Official Life*
    A Doubter's Doubts About Science and Religion, Kegan Paul, 1889

Criminals and Crime: Some Facts and Suggestions, Nisbet, 1907

Griffiths, *Mysteries of Police and Crime*, vol 1

Howells & Skinner, *The Ripper Legacy*

Henri Le Caron, *Twenty-five Years in the Secret Service*, Heinemann, 1892

A. P. Moore-Anderson, *Sir Robert Anderson*, Morgan & Scott, 1919

The Parliamentary Select Commission (24 vols), *The Times*, 1890

Gillian Wagner, *Barnardo*, Weidenfeld & Nicolson, 1979

PRO, Home Office Papers, HO 144/1537/1:2

SEXUAL SERIAL MURDERERS

East London Advertiser, 23 Feb 1889

Evening News, 2 Oct 1888

The Star, 16 Nov 1888

Anon, *The Trial of Weeping Billy for the Wilful Murder of Ann Webb, etc*, London, 1807

Gordon Burr, '. . . *somebody's husband, somebody's son* . . .', Heinemann, 1984

Fido, *Murder Guide to London*

J. H. H. Gaute & Robin Odell, *The Murderers' Who's Who*, Harrap, 1979

Ludovic Kennedy, *10 Rillington Place*, Gollancz, 1961

Edward Keyes, *The Michigan Murders*, New English Library, 1977

Leonard Matters, *The Mystery of Jack the Ripper*, Hutchinson, 1929

Brian Masters, *Killing for Company*, Cape, 1985

William Stewart, *Jack the Ripper: A New Theory*, Quality Press, 1939

L. Forbes Winslow, *Recollections of Forty Years*, Ouseley, 1910

Mad Humanity, Pearson, 1898

Insanity of Passion and Crime, Ouseley, 1912

Colin Wilson & Pat Pitman, *Encyclopaedia of Murder*, Arthur Barker, 1961

Colin Wilson & Donald Seaman, *Encyclopaedia of Modern Murder*, Arthur Barker, 1983

ROYALS AND MASONS

The Sunday Times, 18 Jun 1978

Fred Archer, *Ghost Detectives*, W. H. Allen, 1970

Melvyn Harris, *Jack the Ripper: The Bloody Truth*, David & Charles, 1987

Michael Harrison, *Clarence*, W. H. Allen, 1972

Robert James Lees, *Through the Mists*, George Redway, 1898

Greater London Archives, Islington Board of Guardians' Returns of Lunatics In Care, 1888–95

SOURCES

MONTAGUE JOHN DRUITT

No sources used outside the books listed under General, except
   Howells & Skinner, *The Ripper Legacy*, and Paul Begg, *Jack the Ripper,
   the Uncensored Facts*, Robson, 1988.

THE RUSSIAN DOCTOR

The Echo, 17 Nov 1888

Alex de Jonge, *The Life and Times of Grigorii Rasputin*, Collins, 1982

Guy B. H. Logan, *Masters of Crime: Studies of Multiple Murder*, Stanley
   Paul, 1928

A. T. Vassilyev, *The Ochrana*, Harrap, 1930

JACK THE RIPPER

Daily News, 10, 11 Sep 1888

The Daily Telegraph, 12, 13 Sep 1888, 19, 23 Oct 1987

East London Advertiser, 15 Sep 1888

The Echo, 18, 20, 28 Sep 1888

Evening News, 10 Sep, 17 Oct, 8 Dec 1888

Pall Mall Gazette, 8, 12 Sep 1888

The Star, 4, 5, 6, 21, 22 Sep, 4, 10, 17 Oct 1888

Paul Begg: *Jack the Ripper: The Uncensored Facts*

Corporation of London Records Office, Returns of Lunatics in Care
   and Register of Pauper Lunatics, City of London 1888–95

Greater London Archives: Pauper Lunatic Registers and Quarterly
   Returns, Workhouse Infirmary Creed Books, and Admissions and
   Discharge Books for Bethnal Green, Mile End, Poplar, Stepney,
   Whitechapel, as variously available 1888–1900. Colney Hatch
   Hospital Male Patients' Admissions and Day-Book 1887–9,
   Thames Magistrates' Court Attendance Book 1887–8

Metropolitan Police History Museum, Minutes of Committee on the
   Police Convalescent Home, 1888–9

St Catherine's House Registers of Deaths in England, 1888–1960

Public Record Office (Chancery Lane) Register of Naturalisations,
   1880–1920

Public Record Office, (Kew), HO 144/A49301, A49301/C, D, I

Swanson Papers

Private Information from sources mentioned in Acknowledgements